STREETS, BEDROOMS, AND PATIOS

University of Texas Press
Austin

Streets, Bedrooms, & Patios

The Ordinariness of Diversity in Urban Oaxaca

Ethnographic

Portraits of

the Urban Poor,

Transvestites,

Discapacitados,

and Other

Popular Cultures

**MICHAEL JAMES HIGGINS
AND TANYA L. COEN**

With the Editorial Assistance of
Marsha Moore-Jazayeri

First edition, 2000

Requests for permission to reproduce material from this work should be sent to Permissions, University of Texas Press, Box 7819, Austin, TX 78713-7819.

∞ The paper used in this book meets the minimum requirements of ANSI/NISO z39.48-1992 (R1997) (Permanence of Paper).

Higgins, Michael James.
    Streets, bedrooms, and patios : the ordinariness of diversity in urban Oaxaca : ethnographic portraits of street kids, urban poor, transvestites, discapacitados, and other popular cultures / Michael James Higgins and Tanya L. Coen ; with the editorial assistance of Marsha Moore-Jazayeri.
        p.   cm.
    Includes bibliographical references and index.
    ISBN 0-292-73133-7 (cl.: acid-free paper) — ISBN 0-292-73134-5 (pbk. : acid-free paper)
    1. Oaxaca de Juárez (Mexico)—Social conditions. 2. Social groups—Mexico—Oaxaca de Juárez. 3. Poor—Mexico—Oaxaca de Juárez. 4. Gays—Mexico—Oaxaca de Juárez. I. Coen, Tanya L. (Tanya Leigh) II. Title.

HN120.018 H53 2000
306'.0972'74—dc21   99-056420

We would like to dedicate this book
to the memories of:

DOÑA MARÍA ELENA DE SOSA

GUADALUPE MUSALEM

MARTIN DISKIN

—Three very strong spirits in the diversity of urban Oaxaca.

Presente!

CONTENTS

ACKNOWLEDGMENTS

Throughout the development of this project and the bringing of it to fruition in this publication we have been graced with the aid and support of many people in both the city of Oaxaca and the United States. We would like to thank all the people in Oaxaca who are in the book, who gave their time to produce this work and became our friends in the process. For various forms of direct and indirect help we thank the directors of the Welte Anthropological Library, particularly Gudrun Dohrmann, Art Murphy, and Martha Rees. Also for suggestions and encouragement we thank Alicia Barabas, Julia Barco, Miguel Bartolomé, Margarita Dalton, Pedro Lewin, Salomón Nahmad, and Rafael Reyes. And a special acknowledgment goes to the legendary staff of the Bar Jardin and to Miquel and María at Playa Zipolite.

We would like to make a very special acknowledgment to the Research and Publication Board of the University of Northern Colorado, which provided most of the funding for this project. We thank Marsha Moore-Jazayeri for her wonderful help in copyediting, Ted Scheffler for his help in developing the proposal for this book, and David Loftis and Mark Trimble for their computer assistance. We also thank the following people for reading and critiquing sections of the book: John Brentlinger, David Caldwell, James Charlton, Samuel Colón, Sasha Cousineau, Marcus Embry, Linda Hunt, Roger Lancaster, Cheleen Mahar, Jean Rahier, Tracy Sedinger, Alex Stepick, and Kerri Ward. For their aid with translations we thank Ethel Jorge and Joseph Wachsmann. For their help with the photography and video work we thank James Haug, Jason Holland, Michele Kelly, Shea Kelly, James Kimberling, Joni Kubana, Julia Knop, and Jonna Liebasch.

We would like to express our appreciation to Jayne Howell at California

State University at Long Beach for the use of her work on the "knitting" prostitutes of Oaxaca and to Bruce Trono, a graduate student in anthropology at York University in Toronto, for the use of his work on the urban gay community of Oaxaca.

We thank the members of the Department of Anthropology at the University of Northern Colorado, who have been patient and helpful over the years that we have been working on this book: Robert Brunswig, Sally McBeth, and James Wanner. Our thanks also go to all the students in anthropology classes for their patience in listening to different sections of this work. We thank Paul Driskill and the Greeley Gay, Lesbian, Bisexual, and Transgendered Alliance for putting on a drag queen show for the benefit of Renacimiento.

We would like to thank Theresa May and the friendly folks at the University of Texas Press for all their help. Further, we thank the many others who helped us over these years whose names are not mentioned here.

We offer a special thanks to the Sosa family and send our heartfelt sympathy to them for the loss of their mother, Doña María Elena de Sosa.

As always, the final quality and strength of this work lies with us.

Readers should note that I, Michael J. Higgins, have been doing ethnographic research in Oaxaca since the 1960s. During the 1960s and 1970s, I did collaborative work with Cheleen Mahar. I, Tanya L. Coen, have been doing ethnographic research in Oaxaca since the mid-1980s in collaboration with Michael J. Higgins.

CHAPTER ONE

Streets,
Bedrooms,
and Patios

The Ordinariness of Diversity
in Urban Oaxaca

■ ■ ■ ■ ■

Women are just lazy! They do not like to spend the time fixing their hair or doing their makeup right. It takes a lot of time, and you have to work very hard at it. It's all part of how you develop your look.

—*Debra Blanca and Iracema Gura, male transvestite homosexual prostitutes in their twenties, talking about their views on women while standing on their street corner waiting for clients*

DEBRA BLANCA AND IRACEMA GURA are both young male transvestite homosexuals who work the streets of Oaxaca as prostitutes. Debra is from the coastal city of Pochutla. She has been living in the city of Oaxaca for about five years and has been working the streets for nearly that long. Iracema is from the other side of the state, near the city of Tuxtepec. She has been in the military and has studied nursing. About three years ago she moved to Oaxaca and began living as a transvestite and working the streets.

Both Debra and Iracema are proud of their sexuality, of their socially constructed gender, and of the work they do. They are part of a collective of fifteen transvestite male prostitutes in the city. They are hip, literate, and politically concerned about sexual rights and the problem of AIDS. They seek a level of respect and tolerance that they know is not yet present in the city of Oaxaca.

■ ■ ■ ■ ■

I did not do much in my youth. In fact, I spent most of the time in bed. I did not go to primary school until I was about sixteen.

—*Rocío Matos, a twenty-four-year-old woman who has had polio since infancy, sitting in front of her bedroom at her parents' house and talking about her life*

WHEN ROCÍO was an infant afflicted with polio, her parents were attempting to make a living farming in the coastal regions of Chiapas. The special needs brought on by her illness caused the family to move back to the valley of Oaxaca. Her mother is from one of the Zapotec communities on the Mitla end of the Oaxacan valley. They lived in her mother's village for a while. During this time her father and older brothers worked in the United States, and through their earnings, the family was able to build a house in the city of Oaxaca. Rocío, her older sister, and her mother maintain a store and have various small-scale vending enterprises, such as selling tamales. Rocío stayed home until she was about sixteen years old; then, through her own motivation, she started primary school. At that time she either had to be carried or had to use a wheelchair to get around. She heard on the radio that there was a new program at the Civil Hospital that could give people with polio an operation that would allow them to walk. Thus began for Rocío a six-year odyssey of operations, rehabilitation programs, more operations, and constant struggles to learn how to walk. Now, with the aid of braces and crutches, she walks and has become an autonomous young adult attempting to make her own life. She is active in sports and has been taking classes in dressmaking and computers, hoping to have her own business someday. She recently ended a relationship with a young man who was "normal." She felt that no matter what he said, at some point he would abandon her for someone who was also "normal."

■ ■ ■ ■ ■

I do not give a fuck what anyone thinks because I am cursed with the behavior of always telling people frankly what I think. I guess you can say that I have a lot of balls.

—*María Elena de Sosa, a woman in her early sixties, sitting at a table
on her patio in Colonia Linda Vista and explaining her views on life*

MARÍA ELENA DE SOSA is an urban poor woman who has lived in the city of Oaxaca most of her adult life. She met her husband in her early teens when he was working on a construction project out on the coast of Oaxaca, near the city of Pochutla. They returned to Oaxaca and were among the first squatters in Colonia Linda Vista. They had eight children, six of whom survived to adulthood. Her husband died about twenty years ago, and through various forms of small-scale commercial enterprises, she has maintained her family. She is extremely proud of the fact that she was always able to work at home and thus watch over her children, for she knew better than anyone else that they could be *hijos de la chingada*. A passionate believer in the Virgen de Juquila (the patron virgin of Oaxaca), María Elena de Sosa holds that the Virgen has been her protector and guide throughout her difficult life. Politically, she expresses typical contradictions of the urban poor of Oaxaca: The government only "wants to fuck the poor people." Yet when she votes in elections, she casts her vote for the long-empowered Partido Revolucionario Institucional (Party of the Institutionalized Revolution), or PRI, the dominant political party in Mexico. Equipped with a strong personality to match her strong language, María Elena feels that our contemporary world suffers the wrath of God because we have lost the willingness to be kind and respectful to each other.

■ ■ ■ ■ ■

Only the spoon knows how empty the pot is.

—*Guadalupe Castilla, a female prostitute in her mid-forties, standing in front of her one-room apartment (basically just a bedroom) and expressing one of her many* dichos, *or insights, about the lives of the poor*

GUADALUPE CASTILLA has worked as a prostitute since her late teens. She grew up in the northern part of the state of Oaxaca near the community of Huajuapan de León. In her early teens she moved to the city of Oaxaca after the death of her mother. Her work as a prostitute has taken her from the northern borders of Mexico to the resort areas of Cancún. In her youth she worked in the cabarets, but now she works the streets of Oaxaca in the afternoons for less than two dollars a client. She has saved her money and is now in the process of building a very modest house (or rancho, as she calls it) in a colonia some fifteen miles outside the city of Oaxaca. She is a wonderfully caring person who feels she took the best option open to working-class women like herself. She hopes she can soon quit and live on her little rancho. Unlike Debra and Iracema, she is not comfortable talking about either her sexuality or her profession.

■ ■ ■ ■ ■

I think that my landlord wanted to throw us out. Last night I brought home a woman who was in the last stages of AIDS. I put her up in my bedroom, for her family did not want to take care of her and she had no money. Tragically, she died in the night, and we had to go through a lot of hassle to get her into a funeral home, again for lack of money. The landlord was furious because I let a person with AIDS die in his house.

—*José Antonio Peña, a thirty-plus gay male who is the chair of Renacimiento ("rebirth"), an AIDS care group in the city of Oaxaca, sitting in his bedroom and talking about his current conflicts with his landlord*

JOSÉ ANTONIO faces death every day. He is the chairperson of a local group called Renacimiento that directly helps people with AIDS. His group members openly express their gayness and thus have found themselves on the margins of the city's organizations. They have limited access to funding and receive little respect. José comes from a large working-class family in the city of Oaxaca. He has been actively gay since his early teens but has been "out" for only the last five years. The AIDS crisis and what it has done to his friends and lovers motivated José to become an activist. He was a primary school teacher for many years but now devotes himself to full-time support work. José is very open about his concerns and his belief that the organizational world should respond to the reality of gay lifestyles in Oaxaca. This position has placed him and his group in conflict with the other organizations in the city.

INTRODUCTION

From the summer of 1994 until now, we have come to know the people introduced above as friends, collaborators, and allies in the various concerns with which they and we were dealing. We knew María Elena de Sosa for more than thirty years through our ethnographic work in Colonia Linda Vista; others, like Debra and Iracema, we met during 1994, when we were anthropologists returning to the city of Oaxaca to relearn the social and political dynamics taking place among the popular cultures there. Throughout the year, we encountered these folks in the context of their personal lives and in the context of the social networks that framed their fluid identities and affinities. We spent a great deal of time with them in the streets, in their bedrooms (which were often the only rooms in their homes), and on their patios, hearing about what streets, bedrooms, and patios meant to them in their personal or professional lives.

What all these people have in common is their attempt to compose their own *ondas*—that is, their own ordinary, everyday lifestyles in the context of rapid urban growth in the city of Oaxaca, Mexico. We refer to this as the ordinariness of diversity within a rapidly changing urban space. The social actors that we are dealing with represent not groups of exotic people but real people living in the actual material conditions of a Oaxaca that is being integrated into the postmodern world of consumer capitalism. This process over the last thirty years has transformed Oaxaca from a sleepy provincial

1. One of the main streets in the center of the City of Oaxaca. Photo by Tanya Coen.

town with a population of eighty thousand into a sprawling urban center of more than half a million (see photo 1).

Though the economy is still anchored in the tourist industry, Oaxaca has all the dynamics of rapid urban growth: housing shortages, congested traffic, pollution, unemployment and underemployment, contesting political movements, and the dollarization of the local economy through the twin forces of free trade and migration. The majority of the city residents who try to make some kind of sense out of these various forces can be referred to as members of the popular classes or cultures of the city.

The discourse on popular classes or cultures in Mexico and other parts of Latin America has been developed as a means of discussing the diversity of the social actors who make up the populations found in rural areas and, predominantly, in urban regions. This discourse attempts to combine Marxist insights about capital accumulation with a contextual understanding of class composition derived from the history of political struggles in Latin America (Mariateguí 1979), in an effort to account for the fragmented social space that actors have occupied in this world of developing consumer capitalism (Bonfil Batalla 1988; García Canclini 1989; González Casanova 1986; Lowe 1995; Rowe and Schelling 1991).

What we hope to do with this book is to expand the view of these popular cultures of the city by presenting the *ondas,* or lifestyles, of groups most often described by anthropologists—the urban poor and ethnic migrants—along with groups that are not often viewed or talked about in this discourse—transvestites, *"discapacitados,"* bohemians, and gays and lesbians—who also compose parts of the popular sectors of the city of Oaxaca. We will present their understandings of such issues as racism, sexism, sexuality, spirituality, class struggle, and the dynamics of popular culture in the context of their own everyday lives. We will juxtapose their understanding of these issues with our own in order to seek a synthesis through the use of what we term "ethnographic praxis," and thus we will engender a richer appreciation of how to act within the context of the politics of our everyday lives.

The question of how one is to do ethnographic writing continues to be problematic at the end of this century. The discourse of the knowing subject or the distanced observer has been effectively decentered by what Foucault has called "subjugated knowledges" (Foucault 1979). In Latin America these would be the knowledges expressed within popular cultures and classes. Such knowledges have been broad alliances crossing ethnic, social, sexual, and gender boundaries (Cabezas 1988; García Canclini 1989). In North America, these knowledges are more fragmented and are often expressed in the discourses of identity politics centered around issues of race, gender, sexuality, class, or ethnicity and in the intellectual prose of postmodernism (Calderón 1996; Nicholson and Seidman 1995). As we read "through" these discourses, we are struck by their expressed hope that located, situated, or positioned points of view can offer greater insights into everyday life and politics than can grand theories or master narratives. Specification or contextualization is required of both those who analyze and those who are being analyzed. A crossing of the hegemonic terrains of race, sex, gender, class, ethnicity, age, location, and occupation is needed in order to weave a critical narrative of everyday life (Karim 1996). As ethnographers, we can operate within these discursive domains by developing textured ethnographic portraits of how social actors compose and are composed by these currents in their everyday lives. This involves a collaborative research style that includes the actors in the process of composing these portraits. For us, this is another part of ethnographic praxis.

Such an approach allows us to work within these discursive fields in a manner that is respectful to these newly emerging critical forms of knowing. It also allows us to meet the sentiments of the actors we have worked with critically in order to present a portrait that they have collaborated in developing. The difficult and often confusing debates generated through the decentering of the knowing observer are not academic issues to us. These are daily struggles with our own self-constructions regarding how to do anthropology and how to be critical and reflective of our own situated positions, particularly as middle-income Anglo actors (female and male) from the United States working with different popular sectors in the urban context of Oaxaca. From such a style of collaborative research, we hope to gain insights into how to use the context of everyday life as a site for resistance to the oppressive realities existing in consumer capitalism.

In terms of these goals, we wish to make this book readable and accessible to a general audience. It will have a collage-like structure. We will present a series of ethnographic portraits, using different styles and voices throughout the text and presenting much of the material in the direct voices of the people who collaborated with us. This will involve the presentation of life-history material or narrative accounts of events and activities of these actors. We will present essays, poems, and recipes written by the people themselves. The sections will vary in length and in style. Some will be longer and in the voice of the person; others will be shorter, paraphrasing what people told us. Other sections will be our interpretive writing about what we understand the situations to be (see Map A).

QUE ONDA MEXICO Y OAXACA?

Here we offer briefly some of the *ondas*[1] (happenings) of Mexico in an international and national context as well as in the regional context of the state and city of Oaxaca. In Mexico the people are experiencing another period of complex social changes. Because of external forces, both those who are governing Mexico and those who are being governed are attempting to understand the country's position in the global economy of neoliberalism and free trade and how the political and social worlds of Mexico are being reconfigured in terms of worldwide telecommunications transformations. In terms of internal dynamics, the people of Mexico are attempting to find out why Mexico's location in this global economy means worse everyday living conditions for the majority of Mexicans; whether there is any difference between the ruling elite and the *narcotraficantes* (drug lords); and

Map A: Mexico, showing the state of Oaxaca. Map by Purpura Disño of Oaxaca.

why, as the end of this century approaches, conflictive regionalism is raging throughout the country. Whether from the columnists in *La Jornada*—a progressive daily newspaper in Mexico City—or the surveys from the World Bank, there is a consistent awareness that from the middle class on down, living conditions have not been so bad in decades. In terms of cost of living, disposable income, and wages and work, the quality of life for the majority of Mexicans is not good—no matter that it is often stated that the crisis is over. Regional conflicts and differences in Mexico range from the armed struggle of the Internet-friendly Zapatistas of Chiapas, to the less-than-cuddly Ejército Popular Revolucionario (EPR—Popular Revolutionary Army) of Oaxaca and Guerrero, to the middle-class *norteños* who feel that they live in another country, to the "over the river" Mexicans trying to reside in the United States, which is involved in a frenzy of anti-Mexican and immigrant *ondas*. These dynamic areas of Mexico's current *ondas* are in need of critical analysis and interpretation; for the narratives that we will present about the urban popular sectors of Oaxaca, however, the patterns mentioned here will act as broad guidelines, for several reasons. First, a thorough analysis is far beyond the scope of what we can attempt to do in this presentation.

Second, given that styles of argumentation have been reconfigured in the postmodern world, the value of such grand narrating is problematic at best. Further, many fine Mexican and international writers are boldly attempting to confront these problematic issues, and we will draw upon their work throughout our own presentation (Arizpe 1988; Barta 1987; Bartolomé 1997; García Canclini 1991; Poniatowska 1993). Thus, we request that our readers and critics trust that we understand the "bigger" picture as we present our local portraits of folks in Oaxaca. Now, having stated the preceding concerns, we will briefly address our understanding of these *ondas*.

The current traveler in Mexico can encounter the international globalization of the economy at its most absurd in the arrival of Burger King and the dominance of northern Mexican styles in Mexican consumer culture, in which, for example, the *norteño* rock band Los Broncos draws fifteen thousand young Oaxacans to its concerts. Mexicans have just completed a national highway system that was partly financed by the private sector and now links the whole nation with a series of highways that are superior to those in the United States. When you drive on them, however, you feel as if you are in a different Mexico because almost no one uses these roads. The tolls on the highways are too high for most Mexicans; only the truck drivers bearing the fruit of NAFTA seem to be able to pay the fare.

Various writers in *La Jornada* have estimated that during 1995 more than six political protests were staged each day in Mexico City. Close to the same number took place in the *zócalo* of the city of Oaxaca. The political climate of Mexico can be both dramatic and irrelevant at the same time. After Salinas's six years of mirage governing, it is now apparent that some of the elite sectors of the PRI (the party that has ruled Mexico since the 1920s) and the *narcotraficantes* (drug lords) are shamelessly interrelated; however, such revelations seem to aid the more conservative political alternatives in Mexico, such as the PAN (El Partido Acción Nacional, or Party of National Action—a party assumed to be the conservative party), whereas the national left has been able to respond poetically to a localized Zapatista movement (Krauze 1997). There has, however, been no corresponding national mobilization of the popular classes in Mexico (Rabasa 1997). The closest approximation to a national movement is the middle-class movement referred to as *el barzon* (the yoke of the oxen), which was formed to protest the destruction of credit to the middle class. From the Zapatistas to the PRD (Partido de la Revolución Democrática, or Party of the Democratic Revolution), the leftist opposition party formed in 1988, there are calls for a progressive political discourse that can search for a way to compose what they refer to as a new civil society as the means to attain needed political transformations. Sadly, this primarily means only recomposing the structures of institutional democracy so that there might be some space for economic democracy. The people we will present in this study find the crisis of the political economy more relevant than a call for a new civil society.

In Mexico and Oaxaca various popular discourses are being composed that seek new locations for social action. Many of these *ondas* appear in new places or attempt to repair old spaces. The Zapatista movement reflects the struggles of indigenous peoples throughout the Americas, and in Mexico particularly it has engendered a reexamination of how racism and colorism still frame social and political issues (Marcos 1995; Nash 1997). For the last decade in Oaxaca, indigenous anthropologists like Jaime Martínez Luna and Victor De la Cruz have expressed a discourse of ethno-resistance/autonomy and development, where the focus of social action is on community or regional issues over either state or national issues (De la Cruz 1983; Luna 1994). The work of these researchers parallels the work of various international anthropologists, such as Stefano Varese (1988), Alicia Barabas and Miguel Bartolomé (1986), Martin Disken (1983), Salomón Nahmad (1990), and many others, who have worked with the concept of ethno-development, which searches for a means toward (post)modernity that will be framed and attained within the logic and hopes of the indigenous communities themselves. For us, one of the more dramatic examples of these developments has been the projects coordinated by Jaime M. Luna in Guelatao, Oaxaca. Guelatao, a beautiful sierra town in the heart of the Zapotec region, is the birthplace of Benito Juárez, Mexico's heroic president of the mid-1800s. Jaime M. Luna is an anthropologist who has envisioned a way to combine critical anthropology with community development and advocacy for his own community. About fifteen years ago, he returned to this community to work on his vision. That vision now includes a cooperative linking of eight sierra Zapotec communities for the recapturing of their lands, forests, and cultural history. The core of this project is the cultural center in Guelatao, which began as a small recording studio and now has a radio, television, and recording studio, with production in both Spanish and Zapotec (Luna 1994).

The various Mexican discourses on gender and sexuality have a long genealogy in the social history of Mexico. We contend that the gender roles of the idealized patriarchal male and the willingly submissive female have never been as normative in Mexico as people have assumed (Franco 1989 and 1994). The people we present in this study certainly do not fit nicely into such assumptions. In the post–World War II social context of Mexico, it seems that each generation rediscovers a historical person to challenge these stereotypes; in the 1970s and 1980s it was Frida Kahlo, closely followed by Sor Juana, with Sub-Comandante Marcos engendering new gender images for the late nineties (*La Jornada* 1997b). An acceptance of postmodernist assumptions about the fluidity of gender and sexual roles and identities in opposition to the claims of fixed or given identities also has to apply to the past along with the present. For example, in the area of sexuality, particularly male sexuality, we know that Latin males have moved and continue to move in a much more flexible social space than their North American counterparts. The passive/active separation within Mexican male sexuality creates a social space in which the passive male is stigmatized not for having sex per se with another man but for his assumed passive role in that dynamic (Cornwall 1994; Kulick 1997; Lancaster 1992). Currently many passive gay men in Mexico use this difference to compose new social spaces for themselves while attacking the inscription of stigma to their sexual preferences. These gender and sexual contestations take place not only in Mexico City but also are actively and creatively dealt with in the provinces. In Oaxaca, gender and sexual domains have been and continue to be fluid discursive spaces where the configuration of roles and behaviors is contested and recomposed, from feminist collectives to drag queen prostitute unions.

In Latin America popular culture and class discourses were composed as a means to enrich Marxist understandings of social dynamics by contextualizing these discourses in the historical and social realities of Latin America. The recontextualization of these discourses is a continuous process. The social groups who are moving into such social spaces are focused not only on class struggle but also on issues of personal liberty (Laclau and Mouffe 1985; Melucci 1989). Those who pursue issues of personal liberty could be loosely referred to as participants in new urban social movements—such as environmentalists, *discapacitados* (people with disabilities), punks, rockers, *cholos,* sexually diverse people (drag queens, male prostitutes, and female prostitutes), and street anarchists (Beltran 1989; Gomez-Martínez 1990; Landi 1992; Valenzuela 1988). Though these groups are addressing issues that clearly focus on the political economy, their concerns are also about how one can express more personal liberty in one's daily life. That is, in the social domains of race, gender, class, sexuality, and ethnicity, these newly recognized popular sectors are confronting such issues not just in terms of national policies but as a process of composing new social spaces for their social and personal actions (García Canclini 1991). Again, this is not just something happening in the large urban areas of Mexico; it is also happening out in the provinces. For example, there continues to be a national gay pride march held in Mexico City every year, representing that segment of the urban population. For the last decade, however, there has been a Ms. Gay Oaxaca contest in the city of Oaxaca that has been used to support a local AIDS activist group in the city. Though the problems of *discapacitados* have been discussed at the national level, the most dramatic movements in this area are coming from the local actions of *discapacitados* like the Acceso Libre group in Oaxaca. Historically, various youth political groups have been active at both national and regional levels, but they have tended to be the youth sections of existing political parties. Now radical youth political groups are emerging, with a focus more on cultural issues and confrontations than on the civil issues sought by many in the progressive movements. For these youth, the quest for personal liberties is part of class and generational struggles. These young people define themselves as punks, rockers, street anarchists, and others; they have thoughts and hopes about how to compose this new democratic civil society and they want to be heard (Valenzuela 1988). In Oaxaca the youth group called Los del Sótano (Those from Below) works within such a context.

These various groups are recognized as part of the popular sectors that García Canclini calls hybrid cultures (García Canclini 1989). These groups do not attempt to celebrate some kind of authentic cultural past; instead, they celebrate the diversity of the social spaces that they are engendering. For García Canclini, these urban popular sectors are involved in repositioning and recomposing themselves in the shifting and contested sites of social action. Those who find Haraway's claims about cyborg realities to be too much in the realm of science fiction (Haraway 1991) may find the appearance of these various hybrid examples of cultural action and creativity useful (García Canclini 1989). For us, these *ondas,* in Mexico generally and Oaxaca specifically, involve the way in which various social actors navigate through the newer hegemonic terrains of existing consumer capitalism. What intrigues us about the navigations of these groups is that what seem to be abstract concepts about social action and identity formation in academia are for them actual lived experiences. What we attempt to account for in our theme of the ordinariness of diversity is exactly how they manage this navigation.[2]

THE ORDINARINESS OF DIVERSITY

The discursive spaces of postmodern argumentation have been filled with discussions of the meanings, importance, and validity of differences among social groups (Moraga 1993; Minh-Ha 1989). Various voices have proclaimed that differences are the surface expressions of historical conflicts that hide some kind of common human core. This idea is often expressed as "We are all just people, and if we could get beyond these historical conflicts, we could begin to accept our common humanity" (Clinton 1996; Sen and Grown 1987). Countering these claims have been the voices of various subordinated groups—ethnic, sexual, or gender communities—suggesting that such a quest for commonality works to erase the histories of racism, homophobia, or sexism that have been part of the specific historical context for the formation of these groups (James and Farmer 1993). For these groups, failing to recognize differences means that the uniqueness of their creative responses to systems of domination and regulation are to be glossed over to reach a common ground, which often tends to be heterosexual, white, and male. Still other voices continue to stress that the resolution of such concerns is neither possible nor understandable in the context of existing consumer capitalism in which the diversity of consumption acts to subvert historical difference into various purchasable lifestyles (Lowe 1995). We offer a postmodern apology to all these various authors, whose serious positions we have so briefly summarized, but our purpose in this study is not to prove our skill at resolving theoretical and political disputes but to suggest another story.

We think all three positions are useful, though we tend to be more supportive of the positions advocated by those voices concerned with the reality of subordination. As anthropologists, we accept that as Homo sapiens, we are all the same in terms of genetic structure and cognitive potentiality; that's the history of human evolution (Boyd and Silk 1997). Beyond that, we do not think that as humans we have anything in common but our differences; there is no general human nature to be found, nor will the deconstructing of social or cultural practices reveal some kind of common human core (Yanagisako and Delaney 1995). We also feel that the neo-Marxist concerns about how consumer capitalism subverts differences into lifestyles as commodities clearly illustrate one of the regulative hegemonic patterns of existing consumer capitalism, but capitalism has not and probably cannot reduce all differences to consumer options, for to do that it would have to be able to resolve the dynamics of racism, classism, and sexism within the system.[3]

We are suggesting that we do not have to see difference or diversity as a problem to be solved or avoided (Eller 1997). We choose to view it as the "ordinary" reality of the postmodern condition. That is, diversity is the given reality of human social action—it does not have to be found; it is already there. We do not need programs of inclusion per se to increase diversity; we need to understand that diversity is already present in our existing social contexts. We are not arguing for any kind of radical individualism. In fact, if anything, we are arguing for a much more radical use of the discourse on the social construction of reality. Haraway and many others have developed the argument about situated knowledges as the context for understanding the dynamics of diversity (Haraway 1991 and 1997; Nicholson 1990). The domains of gender, ethnicity, race, class, sexuality, age, and ableness are contested sites of social composition and recomposition. An understanding of such composing activities would require a historical contextualization of the process of composing in terms of existing modes of production, political economy, hegemonic terrains of power and authority, and ecological practices (Sheperd 1987). Metaphorically, the dialectic relationship between the social composition of situated knowledges and their historical contexts would be what anthropology has called cultural systems (Escobar 1995). That is, any cultural system is structured in terms of its diversity, not its commonality; diversity is the ordinary reality of cultural systems. For us, this is true for such different cultural systems as Australian Aborigines (Bell 1983), North African Bedouins (Abu-Lughod 1993), and the popular cultures of urban Oaxaca (Murphy and Stepick 1991).

People act within the context of their cultural systems in ways that express their own personal agency, and often such expressions constitute transgressive behavior within those cultural systems (Battaglia 1997; Durrenberger and Erem 1997). We suggest that actors within any cultural context play with their context, and in that process they both reproduce and alter the system. Clearly, in terms of the current material conditions of postmodernity, these play activities take place in the social spaces where personal agency and transgression can engender expressions of cultural behavior in the hybrid styles that many writers are now exploring (Bal and Boer 1994; Lancaster 1997a). What we suggest is a framework within which these cultural dynamics take place. Our personal preferences are for expressions of personal agency and transgressive behaviors that work against the horrors of existing consumer capitalist realities, but we recognize that these are our preferences and we do not assume that such sentiments are hidden in the actions of the people that we present here. We do, however, think that their actions offer valuable insights about how one navigates the hegemonic terrains of existing consumer capitalism (Coen and Higgins 1994).

For us, the politics of pleasure can also express how personal agency and transgressive behaviors are part of the dynamics of the ordinariness of diversity. Paraphrasing from Viegener's argument on queer theory (Viegener 1993), we share the feeling that the politics of pleasure calls for entirely different critical and cultural practices, informed by the strategies of punk and camp and far removed from intellectual assumptions, either traditional or organic. For Viegener, it no longer suffices for the Western homosexual to be identified with poverty and victimization. To build one's politics from the position of the victim is a doomed endeavor, for it misconstructs utopian desires for the location of being class victims. If we continue to build our cultural practices around only the theme of oppression and alienation, Viegener contends, we will never learn to speak with the radical accent of the popular language of our times, which is "the language of pleasure, adventure, liberation, gratification and novelty" (Viegener 1993).

We did not expect the appearance of this "radical accent" among the different urban groups that we encountered in Oaxaca. That is, not only do these social actors talk about their realities of oppression, but they speak with a voice of "utopian desires" that seeks to share the abundance and pleasure that exist in their current social worlds. Many of the actors who will be presented here have clearly composed their stories with quite assertive attitudes and styles. This is evident in the stories of the drag queens and the *discapacitados* and also in the voices of María Elena de Sosa and Guadalupe Castilla, in the way they recompose their meanings of tradition. One of the most surprising elements for us in their stories was the absence of the voice of the victim. They do give stories that tell about the realities of the struggles they have faced, but they do not often see themselves as victims in these stories, for they speak with pride of what they have accomplished in the face of all the shit that they have to deal with.

ETHNOGRAPHIC PRAXIS

Like many other anthropologists, we have been looking for effective ways to link our ethnographic research to our personal politics and to the concerns of the communities that we have worked with (Higgins 1997; Higgins and Coen 1992). We have wanted to push applied anthropology into more direct political concerns while still doing basic ethnographic research (Coen and Higgins 1994). We have come to call this approach ethnographic praxis: it involves a process of negotiation and collaboration with the people with whom we are working to develop the type of research that is to be carried out, how to produce the results, and what the use of the research will be for the people themselves.

Through various informal approaches, we encountered the various actors who will be telling their stories in this book. When we first started telling people we were doing an ethnographic project on the urban poor, *discapacitados,* transvestites, and other popular urban sectors in Oaxaca, many wondered why we wanted to work with such marginalized groups, and they thought that such work must be very depressing for us. We were surprised by these reactions; we did not see these groups as marginal or as depressing. We saw them as part of the urban panorama of Oaxaca. To us they seemed quite lively, witty, and insightful about their own and other people's *ondas* in the urban context of Oaxaca. Some friends suggested that what these different groups had in common was that they were all stigmatized in various ways by the mainstream population of Oaxaca. That, however, was not what we wanted to present about these groups—that is, how they were stigmatized—nor was it what they themselves talked about in terms of their own concerns. Most of these folks were well aware that many others in Oaxaca saw their *ondas* in a negative light that could be labeled as a stigma. However, what we encountered from them was a quest for creating social spaces and attitudes in Oaxaca that would allow them space for their own pleasure and hopes and that would also engender new expressions of civility and tolerance for everyone's *ondas.* This was true of the drag queens, who sought tolerance for their lifestyles, and for the *discapacitados*, who were seeking new life opportunities. Further, their expressions of agency and transgression were geared to the very specific details of their everyday lives, like most Oaxacans and Mexicans. They wanted people to know how ordinary they were, at least in their own context.

This is the point at which we saw a way to link the ordinariness of diversity to ethnographic praxis. Could we convey the ordinariness of these people's everyday lives to others, and could their stories convey what we are trying to capture with the idea of the ordinariness of diversity? If we could convey the ordinariness of our new and old friends' *ondas* to a broad public, we would be moving in the direction of their concern for more tolerant and civil social spaces for themselves and others in Oaxaca.

THE POLITICS OF REPRESENTATION AND RESPONSIBILITY

We are clearly aware of the problematic status of what we are attempting to do with the presentation of ethnographic portraits of these different urban popular sectors of the city of Oaxaca (Bonfil Batalla 1988). In urban Oaxaca, these various social actors and their particular social spaces do represent highly contested social roles and sites that deal with the realities of race, gender, sexuality, class, ethnicity, and ableness. Further, we are aware that for at least the last decade, North American and European anthropologists have been questioning the logic and rationale of what has been referred to as ethnographic realism (Clifford 1988). These and numerous other important issues can be referred to as the conflictive questions that compose the discursive areas of the theories and politics of representation, and we would add questions about the theories and politics of responsibility (Brentlinger 1996; Chomsky 1987).

We are not attempting to speak for, or in place of, any of the actors presented in this project. The narratives that follow this introduction are a collage of styles: some materials are presented directly in the voices or writings (recipes and poems) of the actors themselves, some materials are presented in descriptive styles so as to be able to tell stories about the activities of these folks and activities that we have shared with them; in other sections we have paraphrased comments by them and juxtaposed those comments with our own observations and interpretations. We also include some short essays by other anthropologists offering their views of some of these urban actors. We acknowledge that we have acted as mediators or translators for concerns of the various actors (Bauman 1987), as well as seeking some means to ground our work and writing in a form of praxis (Bauman 1973).

We also recognize that, in our activities of editing the various materials that we have gathered, we have been in control of the overall composition of this volume, and that means that we have been involved in a form of speaking for these actors (Abu-Lughod 1993; Behar 1993; Bell 1983; Embry 1996). We hold that this is true for any form of narrative account, and we admit that we have no better solutions to these contradictions than any of the other numerous authors who have been grappling with these issues (Fanon 1963; González 1996; hooks 1990; Irigaray 1985; Jennaway 1989; Lancaster 1992; Reid 1996; Said 1978; Schutte 1993). Also, like many others, we have chosen to work collaboratively with the folks who participated in this project and to share with them questions about the style of writing to be used in this book (El Guindi and Hernandez 1986; McBeth 1993; McBeth and Horne 1993 and 1998). None of the above efforts exempt us from the reality of the politics of representation: we clearly stand in a more privileged position in the production of knowledge in the postmodern context than do these various actors whom you are about to meet (Anzaldua 1987; Radcliffe and Westword 1993). However, it is also, for us, an important step for a politics of responsibility to recognize this context and our location within these dynamics (Calderón 1995; di Leonardo 1992; Marchand 1995; Marchand and Parpart 1995; Moraga 1993).

ETHNOGRAPHIC PRAXIS AND THE POLITICS OF RESPONSIBILITY

The diversity and complexity of the hybrid social spaces that we have been talking about are processes engendered by the productive dynamics of existing consumer capitalism (Lowe 1995). How to read and act within these hybrid social spaces is of paramount importance in composing any kind of ethics and politics in the postmodern world.[4] We feel that in this postmodern world the classic bipolar models of control and regulation (whether they be class, race, gender, sex, or ethnicity) are of limited use for our politics of everyday life. In fact, such bipolar opposition may have only historical value now (Haraway 1997). We are not saying that racism, sexism, and classism have been transformed—*far from it!* We, like so many other writers, are only stating that since these sites of subordination and domination in existing consumer capitalism do not operate in terms of bipolar oppositions, our forms of resistance also have to be composed beyond the bipolarity of such confrontations. As the existing system becomes more pernicious in its regulatory power, we have to become more creative and flexible in the styles and modes of our resistance. To ethnographically capture this social world of fluid, crossing, and merging hybrid identities and social spaces, we need narrative accounts that are reasonable presentations of how these dynamics are expressed in people's everyday lives, accounts that can be a means for rethinking how we can creatively respond politically to changing conditions.[5]

We are not claiming that everything in the areas of social justice (such as racism or sexism) has been settled, only that the sites where one can fight for social justice have changed along with who will do the fighting (Coen and Higgins 1994). If we accept the demise of grand narratives in the postmodern world, then in the fights for social justice there will be no working-class heroes, feminist warriors, or indigenous leaders who can unite us through a call to our common humanity. For us, the material and social context of our humanity is not our assumed commonality but our lived experiences of diversity. Admittedly, the various narratives and interpretations that we present here are political. We have attempted to tell the stories of these people in the current material and social conditions of urban Oaxaca. How these actors navigate the various terrains expresses for us what we refer to as the ordinariness of diversity. Conveying these *ondas* in a critical and supportive style is for us an expression of ethnographic praxis and the politics of responsibility.

CHAPTER TWO

Better to Arrive Than to Be Invited

The Urban Poor of the City of Oaxaca

INTRODUCTION

Who are the urban poor of the city of Oaxaca? We have been exploring this question from various ethnographic and thematic perspectives for more than thirty years. Partial answers to this question can be found in material that I (MJH) have published over those years, ranging from *Somos gente humilde* (Higgins 1974) to this current work. One of the more systematic treatments of the question can be found in Murphy and Stepick's book on the history of inequality in the region of Oaxaca (Murphy and Stepick 1991) and in a fair number of articles and monographs by various Mexican and international anthropologists and social scientists who have worked in Oaxaca (Welte Institute for Oaxacan Studies 1996).

To understand the urban poor of the city of Oaxaca, one needs a brief overview of the state of Oaxaca, which is located in the southwestern region of Mexico. It is a small state in terms of territorial size and population. The current population is estimated to be more than three and a half million. The overall political economy of Oaxaca is a regional variation of national patterns with some differences (Clarke 1992 and 1996). Since the mid-1700s, Oaxaca has been economically marginal to overall capitalist development in Mexico. There never was a large hacienda system in Oaxaca (Chance 1978 and 1989), nor was there adequate infrastructure in terms of roads and transportation to encourage economic growth. During the 1800s, the only economic growth in the valley of Oaxaca was in the area of mercantile concerns, with no significant attempts at industrialization. In the late 1940s the international highway was finished into Oaxaca, and with that came the beginning of a more general integration of at least the valley of Oaxaca into the national economy. In that process, the mercantile interests of the city became the dominant economic players in the southwestern region of Mexico. Later, in the 1970s, when national government agencies began the programs of decentralization, Oaxaca also emerged as the government service center for this region (Murphy and Stepick 1991).[1]

Economically, the state can be divided into four areas: (1) the city and valley of Oaxaca, (2) the sierra regions of both the Zapotecos and the Mixtecos, (3) the Pacific coastal areas, and (4) the eastern lowlands that border on the state of Veracruz. The growth areas in the state are the city and valley; the Isthmus, with the development of the Pemex oil refinery (the national petroleum industry), has become a viable economic region; the eastern border area of Tuxtepec has been developing industries around paper production; and the northern region of Oaxaca is growing enough to turn Huajuapan de León into a city of some size. The sierra and coastal regions are the least developed, except for the tourist industry in the areas of Puerto Escondido and Huatulco.

The economy of the city is still centered around mercantile enterprises, tourism, and small-scale "artisan" production. The class structure of Oaxaca includes a very small upper-class elite, a large and diverse middle class (ranging from local merchants to the professional classes, who are primarily in the areas of academics, the arts, government agencies, and medicine), and the popular classes. The diversity among this last group is the theme of this book (Clarke 1992; Murphy and Stepick 1991).

SOCIAL HISTORY OF COLONIA LINDA VISTA

In the early 1960s, the city of Oaxaca was on the cusp of rapid urban growth. The population then was around eighty thousand, and on the northern end of the city, new urban *colonias* (or squatter settlements) were appearing, an expression of urban developments all over Latin America. That is, people were moving onto land they did not have title to, building communities, and then seeking legal title to the lands they had taken (Alonso 1980).[2] Colonia Linda Vista was formed within these types of social contradictions. In the early 1960s, a local schoolteacher, Sr. Narvisa, began planning to develop a new *colonia* on the Cerros del Fortín, which is in the northern foothills of the city, along the highway that goes toward Mexico City. New *colonias* were already being formed on this hillside, some of them by squatters. People in other *colonias* were claiming to hold title to their lands. It seems that Sr. Narvisa thought he had bought several hundred square meters of land that began at the highway and went up the hillside about a hundred meters. He invited people to join his new community, and he began to divide the land into sections to sell. More than thirty families, in what they thought was good faith, bought lots from Sr. Narvisa, moved onto them, and started building their homes. Some others checked out the boundaries of land that Narvisa was selling, went outside of these boundaries, and squatted on that land. One of the original settlers was Humberto San Miguel, who had purchased several large tracts of land in the community for his various businesses. In the process of attempting to get access to municipal services for his businesses, San Miguel discovered that Sr. Narvisa's land claims were invalid—that is, he did not have legal title to the land he was selling. San Miguel called a public meeting, at which he denounced Sr. Narvisa as a fraud and declared the *colonia* to be a squatter settlement because no one had legal title to the land. Further, San Miguel invited more people to move into the *colonia* and take land. San Miguel's claims turned out to be true: Sr. Narvisa's land titles were not legal. He was jailed for a short time, gave up the fight, and became a vague memory in the social history of the *colonia* (see photos 2 and 3).

Out of these land conflicts two opposing factions emerged within the *colonia*. The original settlers claimed that even if Sr. Narvisa's claims were not legal, their claims were legal because they had bought the land in good faith. The other faction claimed that no land claims were legal and that the community needed to organize itself to gain legal recognition from the city and state governments. Each faction formed political groups—*mesas directivas*—and each group actively competed with the other over who actually could represent the *colonia* to outside political structures of the city and state. From this political competition, the residents of the *colonia* were very successful in getting access to basic city services. The method of attaining city services involved the *mesa directiva* (of either group) lobbying for services (like getting water into the *colonia*) by offering to provide *tequios* (volunteer laborers) for projects if the government would provide the materials.

By the end of the 1960s, the San Miguel group was the dominant faction in the *colonia* in terms of numbers. All the new squatters who had moved to the *colonia* were affiliated with his group, and it became clear to many residents that Sr. Migüel had more *palanca* (leverage) than the leaders of the older but smaller group. The smaller group held on to the belief that their land titles were valid. This form of dueling *mesas directivas* lasted throughout most of the 1970s. Gradually, the groups merged—not because they had resolved their differences but because of the indifference of the new residents, who were not interested in past conflicts. Also, after several land crises in which the residents thought that they might all be evicted, they were able to get the city to recognize Colonia Linda Vista as a legitimate community, and they began a land regularization process. The city did not grant the community legal title to all the land in the *colonia* but allowed each household to apply for the legalization of its particular lots through already existing laws for this process. During this time San Miguel no longer lived in the *colonia;* he was now devoting his economic and political *palanca* to his other

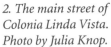

2. *The main street of Colonia Linda Vista. Photo by Julia Knop.*

3. *Colonias on the Cerros del Fortín of the city of Oaxaca. Photo by Tanya Coen.*

interests. The residents of the *colonia* found themselves on their own, with little reason to maintain their old factions and conflicts. The two groups merged into one, which continues to act as the *mesa directiva* for the *colonia*.

Other social dynamics also operated during this time. When the residents had common needs, they would work together. For example, everyone in the *colonia* needed or wanted access to electricity and water. However, when these residents addressed such projects as laying sewer pipes or paving the

Center of the City.		Colonia Lindavista / Cerro del Fortín	
Metropolitan area.		Colonia Hidalgo / Monte Albán	

Map B: The Colonias. Map by Purpura Diseño of Oaxaca.

roads in the *colonia*, not all households were in agreement. If they did not have the funds to build a bathroom, why would they want to give money or labor to build a sewer line that they could not use? If they did not have a car, why would paving the road seem important? Thus, even though the *colonia* was now politically united, economic differences emerged to separate households from each other. In addition, most of the early squatters were young couples with children. Over the years, as the children became old enough to work or enter into studies for careers that were different from those of their parents (such as careers in health, education, and the military), these households began to be able to meet their general needs on their own and no longer felt it necessary to be unified on general issues.

Colonia Linda Vista has changed from a community of poor folks to a community in which people with limited but variable incomes live in the same area (Mahar 1986). Instead of community members gathering on Sundays to work together on community projects, they now pay quotas to the

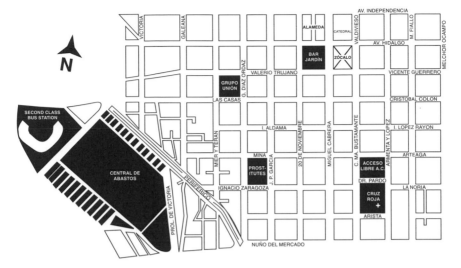

Map C: Center of the City of Oaxaca. Map by Purpura Disño of Oaxaca.

mesa directiva and the funds are used to hire laborers for the projects. In a structural sense, the *colonia* has been successfully incorporated into the city—the streets have even been paved—but socially and politically, the residents have lost any sense of community cohesiveness, and the colonia is now a residential area of various social classes, though the majority of the residents still have limited resources.

The *colonia* has also physically changed over these four decades. When people first moved into it, they would make temporary housing that became the base for further expansions. Roads were unpaved, and as one went higher up in the *colonia*, they turned into paths. During the rainy season, getting in and out of the *colonia* was always a hassle. There was no bus service, and folks were just getting access to water and electricity. There was also a vertical form of stratification; those who lived in lower sections tended to be better off than those living in the higher sections. Now, all the roads are paved; the residents have access to all basic municipal services, including buses; and the *colonia* is one of hundreds of such communities that surround the whole city of Oaxaca. More than half of the original settlers have moved on to other areas, and the social stratification of the *colonia* is still somewhat mapped out—the "better-off" residents living in the lower sections and the "less-well-off" residents living in higher sections, with those who are thought to be really "poor" squatting above the defined limits of the *colonia* itself (see Maps B and C).

THE FOLKS FROM COLONIA LINDA VISTA

Doña María Elena de Sosa and Her Family

> I do not give a fuck what anyone thinks because I am cursed with the behavior of always telling people frankly what I think. I guess you can say that I have a lot of balls.
>
> —*María Elena de Sosa, a woman in her early sixties, sitting at a table on her patio in Colonia Linda Vista and explaining her views on life*

María Elena de Sosa is an urban poor woman who has lived in the city of Oaxaca most of her adult life. We have known her for more than thirty years, and we have shared with María Elena and her family many experiences of happiness and sadness. She has seen us through major rites of passage in our lives (births of children, divorces, being *compadres,* and just getting old), as we have in hers (the death of her husband and two adult children, several miscarriages, and her children growing up into adulthood). She is truly an amazing person, with a keen intellect, an earthy and crude sense of humor, an unwavering belief in the righteousness of her way of life and a corresponding belief that the world would be much better off if it would only take her beliefs into account. She has worked hard all her life, has proudly raised her children to adulthood, and still maintains her life as she wishes. She is a great cook and has turned that skill and talent into one of the many mini-enterprises that she has used over the years to maintain herself and her family.

MARÍA ELENA'S BACKGROUND

María Elena is from the coastal region of Oaxaca. She grew up in the area around Candelaria, which is about an hour from the coast. A small town located in the coastal hills of Oaxaca, Candelaria has been a coffee-growing area for years. She has memories of her father as a small landowner who seemed to be involved in local political fights. Her memories of her early childhood are quite idealized, and she remembers it as a time of plenty, when there was always enough to eat. One only had to pick the fruit from the trees or snatch fish from the streams. For her, childhood was a time of happiness and tranquility. With this, as with many of her remembrances, however, she is quite selective in how she composes her various stories of the past. For example, her mother was not married to her father but was his "second woman," or mistress. Further, when he was killed (María Elena was ten at the time), life for her and her mother became very difficult, despite this idealistic countryside.

Her father died in 1938. She says that he was some kind of *cacique* in the coastal area and moved between Candelaria, where María Elena lived with her mother, and Puerto Angel on the coast. He was shot over a land conflict while he was on the coast. Her father had left them some land, which was taken from them by her father's brother, so they had to move into the town of Candelaria. Her mother maintained the family by turning her various domestic skills into small enterprises—cooking, sewing, washing clothes, and so on—the same strategy that María Elena would use later in her life. In her early teens she met her husband, José, who was a construction worker. He was working in the area of Candelaria, and they met, courted, and began living together. They first moved to Acapulco and then to the city of Oaxaca, where José had family. They were one of the first families to move into Colonia Linda Vista after the land scandal.

When I (MJH) first met this family, they had been living in the *colonia* for about ten years. They had a large lot, on which José had built a house. It was a single-level house with a cooking area, one large bedroom, and an open patio area. Over the years, the house has been improved upon, and it is currently divided into three apartments, one for María Elena, one for Víctor (her youngest son) and his wife and son, and one for Teresa (one of the younger daughters) and her husband and two children. When we met them, they were living quite humbly. José had constant work, but wages were low and they had eight young children. María Elena had had another daughter from an earlier relationship, but at this time that daughter had already died while giving birth at the age of seventeen. María Elena and José each had only a few years of primary school education; however, they encouraged their children to study and attempt to have a better life than they had. José worked hard and did not seem to run around or be abusive, although he did like to spend his weekends drinking. Those weekends caught up with him, for he died about twenty years ago from his drinking. It was María Elena's responsibility to bring the children to adulthood, and she did.

MARÍA ELENA'S CHILDREN

María Elena's children have attained lives somewhat better than she and José had, not through education per se but through a combination of having the same kind of grit as their mother and coming into their young adulthood during perhaps the last economically open period in the Mexican economy.

María Isabel, or Chabela, is the oldest child. She is now forty-two, has three children of her own, and has been married twice; she is divorced from her first husband, and in 1995 her second husband, Mario, died from drinking while only in his late thirties. Chabela is quite an attractive woman and was a very striking beauty in her youth. She went through secondary school and then started working and married her teenage *novio* (sweetheart), César, when she was eighteen. César also lived in the *colonia*, but his family felt that they were somewhat better off than the Sosas—not a good position to take with the Sosas, especially not with María Elena. César had gotten work in Tuxtepec, where they had moved. Chabela did not like it there, and she returned to Oaxaca. César and their son stayed, and that was the end of that marriage. They have stayed close over the years, and her son moves back and forth between Tuxtepec and Oaxaca. Several years later, she married Alberto, who was a bus driver and was younger than Chabela. She had two children with him, both of whom are now teenagers. Chabela, along with her younger sister Rosa, has been involved with various merchandise enterprises, including taking clothing, jewelry, and cosmetics to the coast to sell.

Jorge was María Elena's oldest son and was also quite attractive and charming. He always wanted to be a truck driver. It was his passion in life. María Elena even asked the Virgen de Juquila to get him a job. This turned out to be one of the many tragedies in this family. He did get his job driving a truck—a tanker. The job lasted for about six months, until the tanker went off the side of a hill and he was killed. María Elena has found the loss of her son and daughter to be among the hardest things she has had to deal with in her life.

Rosa Elena is the next offspring. She is currently forty years old, married, and has one son. They all live directly above María Elena. Rosa is much like her mother, quick-witted, insightful, and very hardworking. She did not want to get trapped into marriage and household work as her only option in life. Rosa worked in various retail stores in Oaxaca and then went into sales herself. Along with Chabela, she has been involved with selling various types of quality merchandise outside of Oaxaca. She got married about ten years ago to Flora Iberto, and they have one son and no plans for more children. Flora is a chauffeur for a government agency; thus he has steady work with good pay.

José Alberto, the next of the children, is thirty-eight years old and lives with his wife and three children on the coast of Oaxaca. He works for the state public works, doing construction work like his father. He did not finish primary school, and he has felt that he has been left with the *cargo* (burden) of being the oldest male of the family, not an easy chore in this family. He has worked hard to maintain his own family on the coast, and he sees himself carrying on the family tradition of being *costeños*.

Arturo is now thirty-six years old. He is the star of the family, or at least to María Elena, for he has become a professional military officer. Somehow, amid the confusion of the Sosa household, Arturo developed an academic bent, did well in school, and wanted to go to the national military academy, which he was successful in doing. He is now a captain in the army, has received a law degree, and works within the military justice system. He married a very middle-class woman from Mexico City, and they have three children.

Teresa, who is thirty-four years old, is the sixth child and was less talkative and more focused on getting herself a career as a nurse. She went to the nursing school in Oaxaca, received her degree, and worked in different parts of the state as a public health nurse. In this process she met Alberto, whom she married. He was a medical student, also from Oaxaca and a working-class family. Alberto has finished his degree and residency, and they have opened a doctor's office in Colonia Linda Vista, below their house. They now have two children.

Víctor, the youngest son, is thirty years old, married, and has one son. He was not much interested in school and always wanted to be a fireman, which ironically he became and did not like. He has worked at various jobs, and interestingly now works in the crafts production of wooden animals from his wife's village. They share the house in the *colonia* with María Elena and Teresa.

Alma is the youngest living offspring. She is twenty-nine, married, and has one child. Alma was always the kid who had to do the shit work around the house and run errands for her mother or siblings. However, she ended up marrying a lawyer, moved into a more middle-class *onda* than the other members of the family (with the exception of Arturo), dresses in quite up-to-date and costly clothes, and visits the family when she has the time (see photos 4 and 5).

4. *María Elena de Sosa.*
Photo by Joni Kubana.

5. *The Sosa family,*
1982. Photo by
James Haug.

MARÍA ELENA'S REFLECTIONS ON HER BACKGROUND

Growing Up on the Coast of Oaxaca

When I was young, living on the coast, we did not have that many
diversions. Once in a while there would be fiestas or dances, like a
wedding or a Fiesta de Santos. There were not a lot of dances; we lived
out in a rancho, in between Candelaria and Pochutla. On Sundays we
would go into Candelaria to the market to buy things; Mondays we
would go into Pochutla for more shopping, but that was about it. I
had a lot of siblings. I was very close to them. I was also close to my
parents; however, my father died when we were very young, just kids.
It was my mother who worked very hard to maintain us. After my
father died, there was no work for my mother in the rancho, so after
about a year my mother moved us into a house near Candelaria, and
she began selling things and doing domestic work. While we were

away from the rancho, one of my father's brothers said he would watch our land and take care of the coffee plants. However, when my mother tried to get our land back later, he said it was his and would not give it back to us. He robbed us. In fact, it was just last year that he sold the land. What an ungrateful person he is. A while back I saw him, and he acted like he was real happy to see me and he went, "Oh, didn't you know? I sold that plot of land." I asked him, "How did you sell without papers? Who signed for it?" I am sure it had to be something very crooked. I told him that I did not want anything to do with this land conflict, nor did I want my children getting involved. I know that this could be a lot of trouble, and if my children got involved they could end up in jail. But I told him he was more fucked than us. All his children [have] left him, and he now lives in an old shack near Pochutla. He has to beg for work and food. God has punished him for what he has done to us.

I began working for my mother when I was about ten. My mother would make food to sell, like tamales or tacos. My job was to take this food to the school and try to sell it. The director of the school was a friend of our family, so he let us sell things in the school yard. It was a good little business because things were so cheap then. You could make maybe three or four pesos a day, but that was enough to buy your own basic necessities; things were very cheap. My mother was also a seamstress; she would make clothes that we sold in the local store. For these reasons I only have four years of schooling. I was the oldest and could not stay in school because my mother needed my help with all this work. When my father died, my mother still had one little baby to take care of, but she died very young from the harshness of our living conditions.

My first love? Hell, I cannot remember. How did I meet my husband? He was working on a construction project out on the coast. I think it was at church. We met and started courting, and then he asked me to live with him. When we were first married we lived in Acapulco for a short time period because he had work there. Those early years were very happy; we were young and just starting out. We would spend Sundays going to the plaza or out to the *playa* (beach). We were like all other young couples. Living in Acapulco was fun; we lived with his family, and there were a lot of young women there my age. When my husband was working, we would all go down to the *playa* and play. That was a good time; then we came back to Oaxaca.

I have been living alone now for about twenty years. I have never had a lover since the death of my husband. I like living alone; I do what I want to do. If I want to go to the coast, I grab my things, and I go. I do not have to ask anyone's permission for what I am doing. I am alone and I am free. Sometimes I leave the house in the morning around nine o'clock. I go to the center, visit with my *comadres,* or I do other things and come back when I want to, without anyone asking me where I have been and why. If I am late, that is my business. I do not want any bastard telling me where I can go and when I have to come back.

I have never missed having sex; it was getting kind of boring with my husband before he died. It is not necessary to have a husband. I missed my husband, and his death was hard for me, but I have my children, grandchildren, and my brothers and sisters. This is what the family is for. In the early part of our marriage my husband and I had good sexual relations. We had a good sex life; we were equal in that sense. When we wanted it, we both wanted it! But since his death, I have not had any interest in sex or having a lover. When you have older children you have to respect them. What would they think if I had some bastard who mistreated me? I would be putting my children in a difficult situation, and they may feel that they did not have to support me because I would have this new bastard to take care of me. For example, if I am sick I can now use Berto's or Rosa's social security health plan, or if I am really sick I can go up to Mexico City and get in the military hospital because of Arturo. But if I was with another man, I would not have access to all that; it would then be the responsibility of the bastard I was with. And what if he did not give a shit and had no health coverage? Yes, the body asks for this or that, but the motherfucking body is not as important as one's obligations to one's children.

One has to respect one's children when they are adults. I respect my children more than anything or any other person. They call my attention to the fact, though it is an embarrassment to me, that once in a while I do need financial help from them. They tell me not to worry, that I have worked hard over all these years for them, and during those times they did not give me much money to help out. That's what they say. Who would take care of you if not us? You raised us, took care of us for all those years; it's our turn now. We are grown now. They say it would be ungracious of them if they did not give me something once in a while, five pesos for a taco or something. But I tell them not to give me very much, only once in a while, and when they have the money. I get help from them for some of my household bills like the phone, gas or water, things like that. If I had another man, I would not have this kind of respect from my children. Why bother? What if I had a bad man who mistreated me, and my children had to get involved, perhaps to kill the bastard? Then they would have to dirty their hands in my business. No!

Living in Colonia Linda Vista

Do you know about the history of the past president of the *colonia*? His name is Arturo. All he ever wanted from us was money, money, money for this and that. These assholes here in the *colonia* would give him money without knowing for sure what he was up to. One day I went to talk to him about getting the water connection to our house fixed. He told me that we needed a new connection for drinkable water and that was going to cost us several thousand pesos. But something went wrong, because we still did not have water, except for the water that I have tapped from the house above. The next day I went to talk with the president about where our water was, but before I got to his house, I ran into a friend. She told me that I had been treated like a fool. The president and his friends were not going to use my money for the water connection but to put an alley through my land to the house above because I did not have clear title to my land. I went to the president and told him that first I would gather my people together and we would take the water from the pipes that we needed and that nobody would use my land without my permission unless they wanted to face me with a gun in my hand. Because he dealt with people this way, we—the total *colonia*—got rid of him.

After this, I ran into Doña Milka [the woman who lives above her and was wishing to build the alley] in the *molino* (a mill for corn masa). She wanted to know why I was so upset. I told her nobody can mess with my land; it's mine. I will do anything to defend it. I told her to guard my words, for when I say something I mean it. If I promise to do something, I will do it. So when I say that I will borrow a pistol to defend my land, you'd better believe that I will. I am no *yope* (fool or Indian). I learned that *onda* a long time ago from my father; he was a very great man. Doña Milka and her husband want to make an alley so they can drive up to their house, which is fine, but they want to go through my kitchen! If they had no access to their house that would be different, and certainly I would help. We all have to help each other when the needs are legitimate. We are all children of God and he requires that we share what we have with others who are in need. But these *hijos de la puta* (sons of a whore), they have access to their house from two different streets! And now the bastards want to come through my *cocina*! Never! They think they can do this to me because I do not have legal papers to my land . . . yet. With the help of my son Arturo, I will get a military engineer out here, and with their help, I will have the survey work done so that I can get my papers. I have papers from the person that we bought the land from. It says that this is my land. Doña Milka keeps trying to tell me that it is not very much land of mine they will have to use. Such a small amount, huh, like my *cocina*! I told her before that I would not let her send anyone to take any of my land and if she did I would take their balls off! Now I will give them nothing. Fuck 'em. Yes, we should help each other, and I do. For example, recently, when I was waiting for the bus, I saw two boys ganging up on a smaller boy. People were walking by and doing nothing. So I said, "Hey, you two, why don't you leave him alone; it is not fair for you two to gang up on him." I told them that I might be a woman, but I was a woman of stone, and that I would make them stop beating up on the boy, which they did. And then other people started to support me. The boy who had been attacked thanked me, and I told him that you had to help other people in times of need and that if he wished to make a complaint, I would be his witness. In fact, I told him that I would tell the police that the two boys did worse things, like I would tell them that they threatened to throw [him] under the bus. But you know, he never made the complaint.

People here in Colonia Linda Vista are very envious. If I start to make some tamales or tacos to sell, then everyone else starts selling them. Though they try to sell tamales, they never can make them as good as mine. Marta [a woman who lives down the street from María Elena] started to sell tamales, but they were real plain ones, not the fine ones like I make. Everyone got envious; even those who do not have an economic need began selling things. For example, Doña Chula is now selling tamales. What does she need? She and her husband have everything, cars, houses, et cetera. It is all because of envy. What is envy? While, for example, if I have a burro, then you might get mad at me because I have something that you do not have. Thus, you start saying bad things about me and you start having fights with me over things. This is how people are. One day I was selling stuff down below in the streets here in the *colonia*. A *señora* tried to tell me not to sell in front of her house. I told her she had no right to tell me anything.

Worldviews

God, the Virgen de Juquila, and the Días de los Muertos

God does punish wrongdoers. That's why I always attempt to receive forgiveness from God for the things I have done wrong. It is God who will judge all of us. I used to fight with people a lot, for any old reason. But now, no. My priest told me during confession not to do or say anything to other people that was judgmental; he said leave that to God. God hears and sees all, and he will punish wrongdoers; they might not understand how and why, but God will quickly punish such wrongdoers. That's why I am scared to do things against God's will. You do not want to cheat or get God angry. Here in this world we are all fools! This is what I try to tell those evangelists who are always trying to get you to change your religion and seek their salvation. But I will not change; this is my religion that I have received from God through the Virgen. I will not change. I tell these bastard evangelists that in this world we are all born assholes and only God knows all. These evangelists think they can understand the way of God, but it is not true. If God wants to punish us, he can send a huge earthquake that kills thousands. He can be kind and patient, but he will punish for wrongdoings. Look at all those people who were killed in that gas explosion in Guadalajara; there was no prediction about that. We think things are fine, but at any minute God could send an earthquake and we would all be finished. As my grandmother used to say, I do not have to fear if there are going to be wars or whatever. It is whatever God wants. What I have to fear is the punishment from God, for without warning, suddenly, he can punish you.

The Virgen de Juquila is the mother of Jesús Cristo, thus she is part of our ethereal Father, who sent us Jesus as his only son. Because the Virgen is the mother of the Son of God, God has empowered her to be able to help us in times of need. All the different virgins throughout Mexico are more or less the same thing. It's just that they have different names. There is only one mother of God, who of course has been represented by different names. Mexico is a very religious and a very Catholic country, with many virtues. I assume that you do not have this in the United States.

Let's remember one thing about here. Though there are many poor people here in Oaxaca, none of them are dying of hunger because God has given us the protection of the Virgen. But up there in the United States, look how you kill your children on the streets, these children who are hungry and are sick, with many other kinds of problems. Yes, there are children here who are sick, live in the street, and have no money to get a cure. However, here you can take that child to the Virgen for help and a cure, and it will take place. There is no reason for more suffering if you have a strong faith, that is, faith in the Virgen Madre. Nothing will pass and things can be taken care of. But the thing is, there in the United States, because you do not have this kind of faith, you have all these kinds of problems. Here we learn from the time of our infancy about the power of the Virgen. Here you know that you can have help if you do your prayers and keep your altar and maintain the faith. Then you do receive her help. But up there in the United States, these things do not take place.

The children suffer more than we old folks. My God, some of the children on the coast are living only in their underwear. They are poor; they only have beans to eat or what they can catch, like fish or lizards. But even for them, God does not leave them without something to eat. They have a sad and hard life, but it is one they are accustomed to. But they are healthy, and they do not have an incurable sickness because with the help of the Virgen there are ways to cure them. Here in the city or up there in the United States they try to give poor kids some kind of pill so they can eat. It is a matter of those who have money can get themselves treated better than the poor. What we poor folks know is that if one of our kids gets a cold from playing in the water and then being in the sun, it will not last, for God will help us.

God works to solve political problems also. Take those problems

going on in Chiapas. There was supposed to be more fighting, things
were going to get worse and the prices on all things were going to go
up! But no, now things are peaceful. It was the hand of God. Those
who are fighting in Chiapas are a bunch of criminal bandits. Yes, it has
been partially the fault of the government because they let the prices
of so many things go up and the Mexican peso is not worth anything,
so what can we do? We thought because of this conflict and all that
other political stuff, that the prices of everything were going to go up,
but through the help of God, the president said things were not going
to get more expensive. If prices had gone up that would be very bad.
Everybody wants to raise prices, even here in the *colonia* all the stores
want to raise their prices, but so far they have not. This is because
God is taking care of all this.

I remember three stories about what happens if you do not believe
in the practices of the Días de los Muertos (Days of the Dead).

There was once a young man in the Candelaria area who was
skeptical that all of his dead relatives would come back to visit him
on the Días de los Muertos. On his altar he put only one candle and
espinas (large branches with very thick thorns), and then he hid
behind the wall where he had set up his simple altar. He was waiting
to see if his dead relatives would show up and to see what they would
do when they saw only his small offerings. He spent a whole night
behind the wall, and in the morning his living relatives found him
behind the wall, dead.

There was this other man who lived near my village. He was a
good man, but he was just a very lazy person and he did not work
very hard; thus, he and his family did not have very much money or
many things. One year, because as always he had not worked very
hard, they had very little to put on the altar, so he put only one candle
and one piece of fruit on the altar. On the afternoon of the Day of
the Dead when one's dead relatives were to return for their visit, this
lazy man was out in the fields, and he fell asleep. He woke up to find

himself surrounded by ghosts who were dancing and singing. Then he saw his dead mother, who was carrying the candle and piece of fruit from his altar. The ghosts danced all around him but did not harm him. He fell back to sleep and when he awoke all the ghosts, including his mother, were gone. Everyone in the village told him how lucky he was that the ghosts had not killed him. Everyone thought that he was not killed because, though he was a lazy man, he was still a good man. Next year he worked very hard to earn more, and he did put up a large and beautiful altar for his mother and her friends.

Also, there was one time, during the Días de los Muertos, when a group of kids were playing around an altar close to the time that the dead relatives were supposed to come. The children were being noisy and felt that the ghosts really did not come back. All of a sudden, the children could not see anything, but they heard that all the dogs in the village were barking, that roosters had started crowing, and all the birds were singing and that fruit was falling off the trees. Then a strong wind swept past the altar and the children. All the children were stunned into silence. That was the last year they played in front of the altar during these days.

Race and Class

There is little racism against Indians here in Oaxaca that I know of. However, it does seem that there is some; the rich Spaniards or gringos will treat poor people badly. What is this *gente de razón*? Well, that's about those who can reason, reasonable people. This does not mean that Indians do not reason. For example, if you are trying to explain something to me, and I understand that explanation, and I can do what you have explained to me, that makes me a reasonable person. However, those Indians, this is not the way they understand things. For example, if I give you a piece of candy, you would say thanks, but if you give an Indian a piece of candy, they will ask for money instead. These Indians like to say I have a lot of things and should give some of my stuff to them. I am under no obligation to give them anything. You should give things away because of the kindness of your heart, not for some assumed obligation. That's the way those people are, look at that *yope* (fool) who does my laundry, who has for various reasons left her fucked-up village. She always wants me to give her this or that. I tell her, "Why would I give these things to you? I bought them because I needed them and they are not for giving away to you." I like to have my things; I do not give things away, maybe something that's old and not useful, but my things . . . I hold on to them. All my pots, pans, and dishes are for when I don't have the money, I then can make things to sell, like my tamales. People always want to borrow my things; they come in their cars to borrow my pots. I say to them, "Listen, you fuckers, if you can afford to buy a car, buy your own fucking pots." I do not have a car and many things; I am poor, but I have my dishes. Here in my *cocina* you can find my herbs for cooking, like oregano and many things. I always keep these basic things in stock; when I go to the coast I bring back chiles for special meals. My daughters ask why I buy all these things . . . because I want them, that's what I say.

Why are there poor people here in Oaxaca? Because they have big families, and what they earn is very little, which then does not cover all the cost. Poor folks can only afford to buy the basic things like soap, sugar, beans, just basic things; their money does not cover all their needs. *En mi rumbo*—where I used to live, in the *ranchos* or on the coffee plantation, people earn only what the *patrón* (boss) wants to pay them, and he pays very little. He will give folks a little shack to live in and some dishes. That's how poor folks out in *mi rumbo* live; they do not have to pay for their little shack that they live in but make very little money.

I am a very proud person; I may be poor and I may be an asshole, but I am very proud; nobody orders me around; I do what I want! The only person who could order me around was my mother, not even my husband could order me about. I would never work under the balls of someone who was more of an asshole than me, never! One time I went to help a woman friend of mine; I was supposed to make her some tamales. When I got to her house, she was not there, and while I was waiting, her housekeeper tried to get me to help her with the laundry. I told her if my friend had asked me over to help with the wash I would, but I was here to make tamales, that's it. When my friend showed up, I told her I was leaving, that I did not take this kind of shit from anyone; it was just fucked.

Gender Relations

Why are women so mistreated here if there is a God who protects all of us? Because women are just *pendejas* (assholes). If I were living with my husband and he was not taking care of me and was hitting me, I would be an asshole for accepting that. Men hit women because the women let them get away with it. If a man is maintaining another woman, it is the fault of the woman for accepting this behavior in the first place. If one of my sons-in-law had another woman and was mistreating one of my daughters, I would demand that he stop or he would have to leave my daughter. It is fucked. No, men do not have the right to hit women, and women do not have to accept this behavior.

But now women hit their husbands, do not make their meals, and run around with their friends, or even have their own lovers. With such behavior it is no wonder that husbands will hit their wives. Women have the right to defend themselves or hit their husband back, but look, most of the time it is the fault of the woman. Unfortunately, in this world the men have more honor than women, because men are men. They are the ones who are supposed to maintain the family. A woman has the right to have fun and do different things, but she has to fulfill her obligations to her husband and family. These obligations are the basic things, like cooking the food, washing the clothes, ironing, having things ready for her husband to go to work, and having meals ready when he returns. Also, a woman does not have the right to have another man, but a man can have another woman because that's the way they are; that's the way God ordered it. I would not like it if my daughters' husbands kept another woman. It would be a great dishonor to our family; we would lose respect, and I would not like that.

If women want to do the same things as men, who then will fix the meals? Many women do work outside the house, and it causes them to have to work double shifts, both working and keeping the house, but that's because they want to. Yes, I worked at the same time as my husband, but I was always in the house. I did laundry, ironed clothes, et cetera, but I was always in the house, thus I never left my husband or children unattended. I would make them all their breakfast, then do some work, then make the *comida* (midday meal), and if I did not finish what work I was doing, then I would do it at night. But never, never did I not attend to my children, and I never worked outside the house. I am still that way, even though my children are grown. Last week a woman wanted me to make more than fifty tamales for her birthday, and she wanted me to make them in her house, but I said no, I only work in my own house.

Do my daughters have the same views about the obligations of women to their husband? I think so; they all take care of their houses; their husbands do not cook or do much around the house. However, all my children—the boys and girls—know how to cook basic things and do basic housework. All my daughters know how to cook; they do not like to do it all the time, but they do know how.

Political Views

Well, there are a lot of political parties here in Mexico, but as far as I know, the PRI has always won and will win again. And if they do not win, everyone says there will be a revolution or civil war because the PRI does not want to give up its power. They have been in power forever. They will not leave. Even though other parties win more votes, the PRI still wins. The PRI is better known and they have not lost any elections. No one tells me who to vote for; I vote for whoever I want, though, in fact, I have never voted in my life. Why? Because whether you vote or do not vote, you still have to work. And no matter what, the PRI wins. If you voted for Cuauhtémoc Cárdenas, the PRI still won. Last time Cárdenas had more votes, but the PRI won. So it doesn't matter if you vote or don't vote. But this time I am going to vote. I have my voting card. If you do not vote, you get a lot of shit when trying to get something from the government. I have to get my land papers in order, and so that I do not get shit from them, I will vote. I tried to vote once, but I only had my national defense card, and they would not accept that. It was no big deal to me, if they would not accept that card, fine with me; I did not vote. I told them with or without my vote, Salinas was going to win. But now I have my voting card, and in fact this time I will vote for the PRI. Why? Because I have two sons who work for the government, thus we eat from the table of the government. I need to maintain this government even if it is run by the PRI because it maintains my sons.

I have been fighting with the city tax collector over what they wanted me to pay in taxes for soft drinks that I sell here from the house. Because I sell a few sodas they say that I was supposed to be paying some kind of taxes. I told him, "Look, how come you want to tax me; I am poor and live in this poor *colonia,* and I do not sell that many sodas; I have six or seven cases which I sell cheap; how am I supposed to have something left over to pay taxes?" I told him that I would not pay. If one is running a *cantina* where you would sell a lot of soft drinks, yes, you should pay taxes but not a small enterprise like mine. It's because of these kinds of hassles that I think these little government officials are like rats or thieves. When you are poor and have nothing they want to take what little you have. You should not take this kind of shit from these government authorities. He would not talk to me and he ran off. I do not know if he will come back!

SAZÓN

One area of creativity for many urban poor women, like María Elena, is their skill at cooking the various regional dishes of Oaxaca. The ability to cook well involves the quality of your *sazón*. *Sazón* refers to the seasonings that one uses in the preparation of food and the magic quality of your seasoning. María Elena sees her *sazón* as a personal gift from God. Because of the creative quality of this cooking, we will include in these ethnographic portraits the favorite recipes of each household (though most often these are recipes of the women).

MARÍA ELENA'S RECIPES

■ ■ ■ ■ ■ ■ ■ ■ ■ ■

TAMALES DE CALABAZA

Ingredients
2 kilos corn masa
large green or red squash
½ kilo brown sugar
1 kilo cooked black beans
several dozen corn husks for the tamales
Also, you will use some dried chile, avocado leaves, and garlic.

Preparation
1. Make your corn masa.
2. Cook squash until soft, remove skin and seeds, and mash into a pulp.
3. Cook beans with a large onion.
4. Mix corn masa and cooked squash together with brown sugar and a little salt.
5. To cooked beans add dried chile, garlic, avocado leaves, and then mill it all into a paste.
6. Soak corn husks to make them soft, then line the insides with corn/squash masa and in the middle add a strip of bean paste and then close.
7. Place tamales in a steamer and cook for an hour or until done.

■ ■ ■ ■ ■ ■ ■ ■ ■ ■

MOLE COLORADITO

Ingredients
1 kilo chicken or pork
200 grams *chile ancho* (dry)
100 grams *chile guajillo* (dry)
50 grams sesame seeds
½ fried bread roll
½ banana *macho* (plantain)
50 grams raisins
25 grams almonds
small roasted clove of garlic
small roasted onion
½ kilo tomatoes
cinnamon as you like

Preparation
1. Boil and peel tomatoes.
2. Roast garlic, onion, and sesame seeds.
3. Fry raisins and almonds.
4. Take seeds out of chiles, toast them, but not as long or as dark as
   for *mole negro*. Soak chiles in water.
5. Blend all together and then fry in oil, stirring all the time to
   make a paste.
6. Boil either chicken or pork. With the broth from meat, thin
   the paste al gusto. Make sure to stir all the time.[3]

Victoria Bustamante and Her Children

> Now, I enjoy not working so hard. I have worked hard enough being
> a mother and father to my children. Now they are all raising their own
> children the way they wish. I do not interfere, nor do I help very
> much—a little bit, and only when I want to.

> —*Victoria Bustamante, sitting on a log in the patio that is in front of
> her house in Colonia Hidalgo, Oaxaca and talking about her views
> on life*

Victoria Bustamante is another urban poor woman in her early sixties who
has suffered through a life of hard work and sacrifice to raise three sons and
to enjoy the free time of being a grandmother. Victoria grew up in a village
in the neighboring state of Puebla and moved to the city of Oaxaca with her
first husband. However, she was the second wife, with no legal or economic
rights. Her husband died when she was in her early twenties, leaving her
with a young son and no means of support. Several years later she remarried and had two more children. However, again she found herself to be the
second wife.[4] This time she was aware that the world was not a fair place.
Because this common-law husband drank a great deal and was abusive to
her, she ended their relationship by throwing him out. Thus began her hard
and long journey to raise her children alone. She constantly worked in the
home and outside of it, until her oldest son, Víctor, graduated from the poly-
technic university in Oaxaca. He was able to get a professional job and began to provide support for her and his brothers.

VICTORIA'S BACKGROUND

Victoria is from a village in the region of the state of Puebla that borders on
Oaxaca. She left her village when she was about sixteen. Her mother and her
family were interesting and hard-edged folks. Her mother had two children
by two different husbands and was the second wife for both of these husbands, a pattern that Victoria would repeat. Victoria's memories of her childhood and the context of her growing up are not seen in the same idealized
terms that María Elena had about her youth. Victoria's memories are of hard
times and of cold and harsh emotional treatment from her mother. She did
not know her father as a father, but as the man who was said to be her fa-

ther. He died when she was a young girl. She attended some school but had to work very early in her life. When she was sixteen she met the man who was to be her first husband, though she was his second wife. She got pregnant by him and was then thrown out of her mother's house for repeating what her mother had done. She moved with her husband to the city of Puebla, where he put her up in an apartment and provided her with support. Her son, Víctor, was born during this time, and so was her daughter, who died in early infancy. Though Victoria was the second wife of her husband, the relationship was not abusive and he did provide her with financial support. Tragically, he died several years after Víctor's birth, and since she was the second wife she had no claim on what, if anything, he had left behind. She knew that he had relatives in Oaxaca, so she took Víctor and they moved to Oaxaca to seek help from his relatives. They received no such support and in fact were rejected by his family and lost contact with them over the years. She found some cheap housing in the city, found some work, and began her long journey as a single parent.

During this time she met the man who was to become her second husband and the father of Gabino and Claudio. It was with this husband that they all moved into Colonia Linda Vista as squatters. José, her husband, had a good job with the federal highway construction department, which, though it did not pay much, was steady and had health insurance for dependents. He did claim Gabino and Claudio as his natural children so that they would be covered by the health insurance. However, again she was the second wife; José was already married and had other children with his first wife. Since he worked on construction sites around the state he was gone a good deal of the time, and this work also gave him the means to move between his two families. He drank heavily and was abusive to both Victoria and the children. During one of his absences, Víctor (who was around ten at the time) suggested that Victoria get rid of this guy because he was drunk, abusive, and a poor provider. Victoria concurred and threw him out, and since he had claimed her two sons as his to get medical coverage, she was able to get his wages attached. Until the children were eighteen, she received a little bit of money for their support. Since that time, she has devoted herself to her children, and to a certain degree, she has been rewarded for this struggle in that her sons have grown into adulthood and she has a tribe of grandchildren who adore her.

VICTORIA'S SONS

Víctor, Victoria's oldest son, is now in his early forties and is a quite remarkable person. Drawing from his mother's struggles as he was growing up, he has developed into a man with a keen sense of fairness and a willingness to work hard. Since he could first work, he has done so and has shared his earnings with his mother while continually going to school.

When Víctor finished his secondary school he was able to get into the new university that was being formed in Oaxaca, the Instituto Tecnológico de Oaxaca. Luckily for him, the campus was just down the road from the *colonia*. He continued going to school and working. He completed a degree in electrical engineering and got himself a job with the Federal Electrical Commission, which is the national supplier of domestic and industrial electrical energy. He now has been working for them for more than twenty years. He married a young woman from the *colonia*—Carmen—who was studying for a degree in nursing. She has worked in nursing over this same time period. They got married about the same time that he went to work for the electrical commission, and they now have four children, three girls and one son.

GABINO AND CLAUDIO

For better or worse, these two young men have always been treated like twins in terms of this family. Because Victoria worked (though it was generally in the house) and Víctor was also either working, going to school, or studying, these two brothers spent a great deal of time together and still do. Their journeys through the school system and their teen years illustrate that they were pretty ordinary teenagers in terms of having problems in school and running around with their friends. Victoria suggests that both boys ran with what now would be referred to as gangs, though very tame in terms of either Mexico City or the United States. Though neither developed the same kind of academic discipline as Víctor (Gabino did want to go beyond secondary school, but it did not work out), they showed the same respect for their mother in terms of abiding by her rules of behavior, and they both always worked and shared their earnings with her. Through various routes, they both became plumbers, which has been their main employment in their adult years. Both are married. Gabino's wife has one child from another relationship; he has had two children with her. Claudio is married to a woman from a Zapotec village on the coast, and they have two boys (see photo 6).

6. Doña Victoria Bustamante and her grandsons. Photo by Johanna Liebsch.

Victoria's Life: Her Grandparents

I only knew my mother's mother, and I only knew a little about my grandfather. It turns out I am a mixture of *raza Oaxacaña* (folks from Oaxaca) and *raza Poblana* (folks from the state of Puebla). My grandmother married a man from the Mixteca Alta of Oaxaca. The priest in our village kept in contact with a priest in Santiago Tilantango in the Mixteca. Once when the priest from Tilantango was visiting our pueblo, a member of his group was a man who became my grandfather. My grandparents had a big wedding, both civil and church, and they went to live in Santiago Tilantango. And this is a story my grandmother told me.

It turned out that my grandfather had killed a man during a drunken brawl in Tilantango. He and another man, who I don't think was drunk, got into a fight and my grandfather stuck a knife into his chest and killed him. In fact, my grandfather passed out and woke up several hours later lying on the body of the man he had stabbed, the knife in his hand. He then came home and asked my grandmother for some clean clothes, for his were all bloody. He threw his bloody clothes away and changed into clean clothes. But for some reason he decided not to run away and simply waited for the village police to come get him. They did. First, he was put in jail in Tilantango, then he was taken to Nochixtlán, then to the city of Oaxaca.

This was around 1910 when the revolution was just starting. My grandmother told me that her father-in-law (my great-grandfather) went to Oaxaca to see if he could get his son out of jail. I think he was in the Cárcel de Santo Domingo (the jail at Santo Domingo). There he saw his son at the jail. A captain at the jail told him, "Listen, sir, the money you brought to try to get your son out of jail would be better used for his wife and his children. Because these young *muchachos*, whether they want to or not, are going to fight in the revolution." Thus, my great-grandfather returned to Tilantango and told my grandmother that her husband had gone off to war.

Because of the contacts between the two village priests, my grandmother's family learned of her situation and sent her a letter telling her to return to the village to live. She took her four children and started her trip back to the village. One of these children was to be my mother. My grandmother traveled by horse, and she had to put the kids in a basket strapped over the horse. They went from Tilantango to Nochixtlán and then from there they took a train to Tehuacán, where her family met her and took her back to her village. There she stayed for the next forty years, raising her children by herself.

One day, when I was about eight or nine, I was home by myself. My mother was in Orizaba (a city in the state of Veracruz) visiting her brother, and my grandmother had gone off to do errands. I saw this old man walking down the street and he came into our yard. He asked was this the house of the Mendoza family? I told him yes. It was very strange; he started asking about all of my older relatives, knew them by their names and wanted to know how they all were. I had to tell him that many of them were dead or had moved away. All my grandmother's brothers and sisters were dead and only my grandmother was left. Then he asked about my grandmother's children, including my mother. I said they were all alive except for the youngest, [who] had died many years ago. I still didn't know who this man was and how he knew about our family.

He asked when would my grandmother be back. I said I didn't know but if he wanted to wait out on the patio he was welcome to. Sometime later my grandmother returned. She came in and sat down and asked who was this man waiting out on the patio. I replied I didn't know. He was someone who had come to see her and he knew an awful lot about the family. She went out to the patio and asked the man who he was. He asked her, "Don't you remember? I am your husband." She did not believe him because she had been told through her brother-in-law that he had been killed in the battle around Monterrey. Further, she was suspicious because she had tried to confirm his death through the secretary of defense and had never gotten an answer. She felt that this just meant that he was dead. Further-more, he had never written or communicated in forty years. There were still some older people in the village who were of my grand-mother's age; they remembered him and convinced my grandmother that, yes, he was her husband! Since my grandmother had been raised a proper Catholic and they had had a real wedding, she consented to take him back in.

Now wouldn't you know it, this had no happy ending because it turned out they couldn't stand each other because, like my mother, he was a very difficult person. Further, a little while after his return they did nothing but fight because he thought he could order her around. My mother never accepted him and would not recognize him as her father. Only my aunt and uncle accepted him as a real relative. Eventually, because they were fighting so much, he went to live with his daughter, my aunt, for several years. After many years, he got very ill and he came back to live with my grandmother. Though she still couldn't stand to be with him, she attended to him until he died. Those people from Tilantango are very hard people. My grandfather and my mother had that kind of character; I have some in me, and Gabino is like that too.

Victoria's Mother

When I was fifteen or sixteen, I was pregnant with Víctor. My mother was very upset with me and didn't want me to have the child. At this time I was living with both my mother and my grandmother. My mother was a very difficult woman. One night she got me up at about four or five in the morning and started beating me with a wet bamboo cane. Fortunately, my grandmother was able to stop her. Later in the morning my grandmother warned me that once my mother started beating me she probably wouldn't stop, and she couldn't always count on my being able to stop her. So I left home. And with the help of the father of Víctor, we left first to Orizaba and then later to Puebla, where I stayed five years and then came to Oaxaca. During this whole time I had almost no contact with my mother, but I stayed in contact with my brother.

It so happened during this time that in the Tehuacán hospital there was a young woman who was very ill, and no one knew who she was. Someone suggested to my mother that it might be her daughter, me! My mother went to the hospital, and though this woman was sick and delirious, my mother took care of her and claimed it was me. When the woman died a short time later she brought the body back to the village and told everyone that I was dead. But my uncles and brother, after seeing the body, told my mother that that wasn't me and that they wouldn't have anything to do with burying this person as me. But my mother refused to listen to them and continued the plans to bury this person as me.

I knew nothing about any of these activities at the time, and for some reason unknown to me, I decided to send my mother a letter to reestablish contact, and would you believe it! That letter arrived to my mother the very day she was burying this other person as me.

Although this was a shock to my mother, she continued with her plans and buried the other person as me.

Some time later, I went to the village to see my mother since she had not answered my letter. When I returned to my house, my mother said absolutely nothing to me about these happenings. A woman with whom I grew up saw me in the street, and she ran up to me and started hugging me, laughing and crying all at the same time. I couldn't understand why she was acting this way. I kept asking why was she acting this way, why was she crying? Then I spent the entire night at her house, and she told me everything about my mother's activities.

The next day, I ran into more people in the village who had the same reaction when they saw me, and they also told me the same stories. I don't know how I felt—just that my mother is a very strange and difficult woman. And I guess that she so disapproved of my affair with Víctor's father that this was her way of purging me from her life. And you know until the day she died, she never explained any of this. She acted like we had all forgotten about her burying another woman as me!

She died about eight years ago. The year before she died she had been very ill and in fact had a broken leg. My brother asked me if I would come home and take care of her. Víctor didn't think that was a good idea and suggested that we bring her to Oaxaca so that she could get better medical attention and that we could all take care of her. Though she never approved of my pregnancy with Víctor, they had a strong affection for each other. He liked his grandmother very much. I had never told Víctor what had happened in terms of conflicts with my mother.

So we went to the village, and we brought her back here. This had to have been about seven or eight years ago because that was the year that Miguel was born, Claudio's son. My mother was very ill, and we were all taking care of her because she couldn't walk because of her broken leg. We finally got her into the hospital, where she was able to get an operation and she recovered enough to be able to walk again. She spent about another three months with us and then began telling my brother that she wanted to go back to her village. My brother told me this and I told Víctor about it. Víctor talked with his grandmother and asked her if it was true. She said yes, that she wanted to go back, so she could begin working to pay Víctor back for all he had spent to cure her.

Imagine a woman over eighty years old trying to go to work! What was she going to do? That was my mother. So we took her back. I thought maybe I could stay with her for a while, but at the time Gabino wasn't married yet and I still felt I had my obligations to attend to him. That was January, then there was February, March, and April. Four months later I was not feeling well myself; I had been sick with something, so I was staying over at Víctor and Carmen's. And my brother had called the person in the *colonia* where he could leave messages for me, and that person told Carmen, who told Claudio, but not me. That night Claudio came over carrying a duffel bag, and he asked, "How are you, Mother?" And I said I was fine. And then he asked, "Well, are you feeling fine from your illness?" And I said yes. But he was acting very strange and I didn't know why he was asking me these questions. And then Víctor came in the room and suggested that maybe Claudio and I should take a trip to Tehuacán. They said they had already bought the bus tickets. Then I knew what was happening. Something had to be wrong with my mother. So I asked them, "Is something wrong with my mother?" They then told me, yes, my brother had called and that my mother was very ill. Even though my mother had been a very hard woman and had done horrible things to me, I knew I had to go to her. What could I do? She was and is my mother. So Claudio and I took the bus to Tehuacán, and then from there we took another bus to my pueblo. And wouldn't you know it, when we got to my pueblo, they told me that my brother had taken her to the hospital in Tehuacán. So we went back to Tehuacán. And we found my mother in the hospital; she was very, very ill. In fact, she was vomiting blood. It was clear that she was not going to live. She was delirious and hardly recognized anyone, although she called out to me. Claudio and I thought that we should take her out of the hospital and take her back to the village so that she could die at home. And anyway it would be a lot cheaper, too. My brother wasn't in agreement, but we convinced him it was the best.

We talked to the doctor. He agreed, and we were able to bring her home in the ambulance. We got her home and into bed, and she was hooked up to an IV. My brother wanted to go get the doctor in the village and see if he could give her something to help her. I told him no, we should just let her go, that it was best to just let her die.

And following the last drop of the IV solution, she passed away. That's how my mother died. And she never explained to me why she had buried this other person as me.[5]

Victoria's Father

I never knew my father. He was supposedly from the Mixteca Alta, and my mother always said he was dead, dead, dead! She wouldn't tell me anything about him. But when I was in school, my classmates and even the teacher said they knew who my father was. He lived in the village and his name was Sr. Bustamante. He lived with this other woman and his children. At that time I took his name, which made my mother very angry. Though I never talked to him, I knew who he was. His wife told me when he died, when I was about sixteen, he was calling out for me.

I also never knew the father of my brother. He was killed when we were young. He was a drunk. They say that he was harassing a woman when a group of people began attacking him with stones and that he fell down in an arroyo and died after being hit in the back of the head by a rock. They thought he was just acting like a fool, but he was dead. My brother says he remembers a little bit about him. From this history I have arrived to where I am today.

Her Early Life with Husbands and Children

I have only seen the ocean once, for two hours, after visiting the shrine of the Virgen de Juquila. I keep an altar to the Virgen, I have a strong faith in her. That photo is of my daughter; she died when she was about three. I was living in Puebla, with Víctor's father. We lived in a *vecindad* and I worked at cleaning houses. He was a traveling salesperson.

My daughter was always sickly; she had problems with her stomach and diarrhea. We never could cure it. She would be fine for a few months, and then it would come back. The last time, I had left her with my *comadre*, while I went to visit my mother-in-law, and when I came back she had gotten very bad. I went back to the doctor that always treated her, but he could do nothing. That was thirty-eight years ago. Then they did not know as much about treating babies as they do now. There were no tests or special treatments. After her death, I separated from Víctor's father and then later he died. A friend of mine was going to Oaxaca, so I decided to go also. I met Gabino's and Claudio's father through his cousin, who was a friend of mine.

The first years of being the only parent were very hard, especially the first year after the accident with the house and the fact that the two boys were quite ill from that accident. While we were getting our new house we lived with one of my *comadres*. The first couple years I made tortillas and washed clothes. Later I made clothing for Doña Chola, which she sold in the market. I made 2.50 pesos a dress. I would work at night, after ten when the children were sleeping. Sometimes I would work until three or four in the morning. Those were very hard times.

I think Mexican men still run around and keep other women. I think men who take a lover when they are married are doing a bad thing. They are taking money away from the wife who takes care of their children. Do my sons behave this way? I'm sure they may. But it would be wrong. I stress to them to remember how hard their lives were, and do they want to do that to their children. But, they are adults, and they will do what they want. I tell my daughters-in-law that if they feel they are not being provided for, then they have to bear the burden, but it is not fair.

I never married either of the fathers of my children. Víctor's father was older than I and had another family. He helped me out a lot, but he died. The father of Gaby and Claudio was horrible. He was a drunk and was abusive. And he only wanted me as his lover, which I didn't want. I don't regret having been with him because I have two sons so that Víctor was not an only child. And though we all suffered, we have arrived at a good place.

The only problem is that Gaby, like my family, has that character from being from Tilantango and he has had problems with his wife. I think she has bewitched him. She is very contrary and won't obey him and he treats her badly at times. He won't believe us when we tell him, but she has had other relationships with other men and was doing this when they started going together. Now, in fact, you've seen Gaby's oldest child, you know he doesn't look a thing like Gaby. That is not his child. The other two look just like him. We all know this, but Gaby won't accept it. His wife blames me for all their problems, but I've done nothing. He was going to leave her. But I warned him, "Do you want your children to suffer the way you suffered? You have to make sure you take care of your children no matter what you do."

Now, Claudio was a horrible teenager. He would not stay in school and only finished the second year of secondary and ran with a very bad crowd. He even kept the police away once; he and his friends were standing up on the hill and throwing rocks down at the police. I did not know how he was going to turn out. But since he has gotten married and has had children, he has become much more responsible, and he has settled down.

Living in Linda Vista

I remember when the house fell on the kids. I was just going out to get my corn ground for the next day. It had been raining all afternoon and it was about five in the afternoon. Gaby and Claudio were on the bed, an old metal frame bed, and on the headboard was a shelf for books or a *santo*. Gaby was sleeping, and Claudio, who was sick, was awake. He was only a year and a month, and Gaby was a little more than two years old. Víctor, who had not wanted to go to work that afternoon, had gone because I warned him that if he did not go he would not get paid. I had just left the house and I was going down the road a bit, when the foundation from the house above began falling. I remember it all, but during the event itself everything became dark and I was frightened. I ran into the house and found them under all the rocks and blocks of cement. Gaby's lip was cut open and Claudio was more dead than alive. The man next door gave him mouth-to-mouth resuscitation, and he started to breathe. We got them to the hospital and they were all right. However, Claudio was quite traumatized by this event, and we had to take him to a psychologist at ISSTE (health service) for a while. It was very weird luck. The boards from the roof fell over the headboard of the bed and created a space between them and the falling debris. A huge cement block fell and rolled off these boards. If those boards had not been there, they would have been killed. If I had not just gone out to the *molino*, and had been in the house, I would be dead. If Víctor had not gone to work and had stayed at home, he too could have been killed. It was the darkest day of my life.

Gabino's and Claudio's Memories of These Times

GABINO

I had my first job at fourteen as a mechanic. Growing up in the *colonia* when we were little seemed normal. It is not until you get in your teens that you begin to understand how hard things are or how hard your mother has worked for you. I had a hard time my first year in secondary school and dropped out for a year. Then I decided that I wanted to go back. I was able to work and go to night school. I got my secondary school degree.

CLAUDIO

I did not like school. If I worked hard, I did all right, but it could not keep my interest. My mother urged me to continue, but I told her that I did not want to stay in school and got a job as a mechanic in a shop that worked on big trucks and trailers. I had that job for about six months. Once when the boss went off, we all starting fooling around and drinking. He surprised us and came back. We were caught and fired. Later a chauffeur offered me a job as his helper, but I would have had to go to Salina Cruz and my mother would not let me go. I was only fifteen. It was later that I became a plumber. But I have always wanted to be a chauffeur. I think driving long distance is great; it does not bore me like it does others. Actually I have only been driving for about six years.

No, we did not belong to *bandas* (gangs), nor did we hang out with guys in *bandas*—never had time. We also never worked when we were little. In those times not as many kids work in the streets as they do now. Our mom did not want us to work until we got older.

How Victoria Sees Her Life Now

Now, I enjoy not working so hard. I have worked hard enough being a mother and father to my children. Now they are all raising their own children the way they wish. I do not interfere, nor do I help very much—a little bit, and only when I want to.

All three of my daughters-in-law have had tubal ligations. I think it was very smart of all of them. The boys should get them too, that way there can be no gossip about other children. That is one of the reasons

I did not want to continue with Gabino and Claudio's father; he wanted more kids with both of his women, which meant everybody would have less!

Victoria's Worldviews

The Virgen de Juquila and Other Beliefs

I became a strong believer in the Virgen de Juquila after the accident with my house in Linda Vista when Gaby and Claudio almost died. Claudio had to receive mouth-to-mouth resuscitation in order to save his life. I asked the Virgen to save them, and since then I have been faithful to her. She helped me during those hard times, she helped me get over my sexual desires at that time, and she protected us. I have made many trips to her shrine, and if I can I will go before this current operation.

Well, my sons, two are married by civil law and the church, but Gaby and his wife are *unión libre* (free union). His wife is a very difficult person. He at first wanted to get married, and she did not; then she did, and he did not, but he has registered all the children as his. Is there a difference between a civil and church wedding? While a civil wedding makes one's children legal instead of natural (out of wedlock), a church wedding involves one's beliefs as a Catholic. However, nowadays, you see young people having their big church weddings. The bride is in white, then several years later the couple separates; it is like a game with them. My brother was married for twenty-five years by a civil and a church wedding. He took good care of his three daughters, sent them all to private schools, yet they all encouraged their mother to leave him. I do not know whose fault it was, both in different ways. And you know that his daughters will have nothing to do with him, will not even see him. They were married in both the church and civil wedding and what difference did it make? Now there is not even a legal difference between legal and natural children. I am glad I never married.

I do not believe in using either witches or *curanderas* (healers).
I do not believe in many of these beliefs, but *susto* (fright) and *mal de ojo* (evil eye) do affect kids. One day one of Gabino's kids picked up *mal de ojo* from somebody on the street, and my daughter-in-law cured him with an egg, but I am not into these things. For me if you have to choose between using your money in these things or meeting your daily needs, it is better spent on the daily needs.

Once, Carmen was worried about whether Víctor was seeing another woman. They say that out in Zaachila, there are witches who can divine these things. She asked me if she should use one of these witches. I asked her why? Are you suffering? Was Víctor providing for the kids? What would happen if you found out? What would you do? Would not this information make you unhappy or make Víctor unhappy? I told her better to take the money you would spend on the witch and buy something for the kids or yourself. I do not know what she did. Does Víctor have another woman? I do not know, but there is no reason to assume that he is not like other men—that is to say, they are all alike in these affairs.

Views on Gender and Sexuality

I was never sexually abused by the men in my mother's life; she was very strict about that. Further, none of my sons have ever used any drugs. My second husband, one of the few good things that you can say about him was that he did not treat Víctor any differently than his own sons. He did attempt to hit me once. He was drunk and he had heard some gossip about me from the neighbors, and it was not true. He pushed me against the stove and I cut my forehead. I still have the scar. I went into a rage, he grabbed my wrist, and I bit his wrist as hard as I could. I'm sure he still has the scar on his wrist from where I bit him. That was the only time.

Life is hard on women and women have to work very hard to bring up their children. I have told my daughters-in-law that if they are left by my sons, better to continue by themselves than seek another man, for a new man will most often be worse. That is my view. The current economic situation is very bad—wages are low and prices are high. The rich of this town do not invest in industry because they make their money from tourism. They pay very low wages to their workers and prices are very high in Oaxaca, so it is hard on such workers. These rich folks do not understand that they are screwing the hen that lays their gold eggs. This situation of low wages and high prices encourages people to rob the rich tourists, which in turn scares away the tourists, making things worse for everyone.

Often women will enter into the world of prostitution. I think this is for three reasons. One, some women are lazy and do not want to work, and this is easier. Second, many women simply like this kind of work, and, third, there are women who do this work out of necessity. Many women who have several children and cannot make ends meet from other forms of work go into prostitution. This gives them a way to take care of the needs of their children. We know this woman who left her children in her village and came to the city and has worked as a prostitute. Her plans are to make enough money in a short time and then to go back to her village and start a small business. Though I would not do that, I see nothing wrong with her idea. Often women will try prostitution, crime, or working in the cantinas with the drunks. I could not do any of these. Sex with someone I did not know . . . ick! If I tried to rob someone, the first time I would end up in jail, and I could not stand working with drunks. My way was hard but clean.

My first husband died, and with the second, I was his second woman. I knew if I stayed with him I would only get half of what he had, which was not very much to begin with. There was another man in the *colonia* who was interested in me for a while, even talked with Víctor, but I did not want to get involved. If I had stayed involved with Gabino's father, I would have ended up with more children and who knows what kinds of problems. I feel proud of my children and my grandchildren, and that has satisfied me. Further, if I had become involved with another man, there would have been problems with him wanting to rule me or hitting my children, and I would not allow that.

I forgot about men through dedicating myself to work and taking care of my children. That has consumed all my time and I soon forgot about men. Some nights I would cry because I felt so lonely, but my children would comfort me. Sex was OK, normal. With my second husband, he worked away, and I only saw him every other week or so, so I got used to not having a man in my bed. Though I thought about men and sex at times, I do not repent the choices I have made. I have a good family, I get along, and I have love from my sons and all my grandchildren. They love and respect me. That might not have been so if I had become involved with a man. Thus, as my life has turned out, it has been for the best. And anyway, at my age it is best not to think of men and sex.

Race

This question about the admiration that we have for *güeros/as* (people who are perceived as being fair-skinned), that you see in toys like dolls or in soap operas, I have not thought of it before. But it is true, and it does make us reject our own heritage and color. I am going to have to think more about that. That is a very important issue to think about.

Politics and Personal Behavior

There was a shooting today of a PRI official somewhere, I did not understand the news very well. [In fact, Francisco Ruiz Massieu, the national secretary of the PRI, had been killed in Mexico City that morning—September 19, 1994.] It is like the killing of Colosio [Luis Donaldo Colosio, the PRI presidential candidate who was killed on March 23, 1994]; who knows who killed him? Some think it was people from other parties or people inside his own party. I think that Cuauhtémoc Cárdenas [opposition political leader] might have planned it, he wants so bad to be president. But the people did not want him; that's all there is to it. If the people really wanted him, he would have won. This time he did very badly. My sons think that had he been elected he would have tried to make some changes that would have done the country harm. Salinas has been a good president and has done many beneficial things for the country, but the changes have to come slowly. Cuauhtémoc is like the others; it is all a fight for power. I do not feel that I lack any civil rights, and I can talk about anything I want. I am not much into politics and not that well prepared, but I have my views.

Am I conservative or liberal? What do these terms mean? If conservative means to protect one's customs, then I am conservative because I do want to protect my customs. More than anything, I do not like to be told what to do. I want to do what I want to do or have to do. I do not like to have others do this for me. Once, years ago in Linda Vista, I had a big problem about money. I owed some money to the water commission, I think. Doña Chola told me to go talk to the president of the *colonia* and get his help. But it was not his problem but mine. What could he do? Nor did I want to tell him about my problems. I went directly to the commission and worked out the arrangement. This surprised Doña Chola that I did it that way, but that is how I work things out. Of course, sometimes you have to use what *palanca* you may have.

When Claudio was in secondary school he had a horrible year. All his grades were low and they were not going to let him continue. I went to a *compadre* that worked in SEP [Office of Public Education] and told him my dilemma. He came up with the idea that we could tell the school director that I had been sick for the year and that the reason that Claudio did so poorly was that he had to work to support me. I was not sick, but he wrote the letter for me. I took it to another office of the SEP and the lady there believed the story and wrote a

letter to the director of Claudio's school saying that she should let
him in. So they did and he returned to school. However, he continued
in his ways, and by the end of the first term he was failing again. I told
him that was it and that I had done all I could for him—he was on his
own. He would now have to work. About three weeks after quitting
school he found work as an apprentice to a plumber and has been
doing that ever since.

Gaby was somewhat different. The year I worked in the governor's
house as a maid, which involved very long hours, Gaby ran wild and
practically lived in the streets. In fact, both of them at different times
were in *bandas* (gangs). He also flunked out of school. The next year
I quit that job, and he said that he wanted to go back to school and
work. His boss at that time told him that he needed either to work or
go to school, not try to do both. He found another job as a mechanic
that would allow him to work and go to school. He went to school in
the mornings and worked in the afternoons and did his school work
at night. He worked very hard and did finish secondary schooling.
He tried to go to preparatory school so that he could get into the
Instituto Tecnológico like Víctor, but it was too hard and I should
have kept working to help, but I had to quit. I regret that he could
not go on with his schooling, but his life has turned out all right. He
has a trade that he does all right at

Like I said, I like to do things directly. I like to look the person in
the face that I have to deal with. I dealt with meeting each one of my
sons' wives' families. I went with Víctor when he told Carmen's father
that he wished to marry her. He said that they would just run off if he
refused to give them permission, but there was no problem. Claudio
had been involved with his woman for more than two years before
they started living together. In fact, she was three months pregnant
when they got married. Claudio said that he was not sure he wanted
to marry her, but she was pregnant. I told him that it was his responsibility and if he did not want kids he should have used protection; that

is his responsibility. Also I stressed to him to remember how hard his life had been growing up with only me as the support and that he did not want to do that to his children. We met her family last year.

Social Class, Poverty, and Women and Children

It is very sad that small children are working in the streets or living in the streets. I see these kids that are washing car windows or eating fire. They have a very hard life. However, in my view, this is the fault of the parents, not the children. Children do not ask to be brought into this world. We brought them into it, and it is our responsibility to make sure they grow up right. When kids become drug addicts, criminals, or other bad things, it comes from the lack of good supervision by their parents. Some parents think that since they could do nothing in their lives, then it will be the same for their children, and they convey to them those kinds of values. Some parents just want to live off the labor of their children. There is a man who lives near Gabino's house. He sends his little daughter each morning into the market to sell plastic bags, and it is her earnings that they eat off.

I have always felt that it is the parents' responsibility to pass the values of hard work and education on to our children. One has to develop strong discipline—the belt—and strong care and love. I never found it hard to make children behave. Gabino was the worst of mine. He would go off and not tell me where he was and what he was doing, and when he got home he would get a beating for sure. Some parents just let their kids wander off and do what they want. Or unfortunately often parents drink, or they fight, or the husband hits his wife, or one or the other has lovers. These behaviors give bad examples to children. Or if a woman is abandoned, then she will take up with another man who is often worse. If you have kids from one man, the next one most often will not treat them well. If you have a *niña,* you always have to worry that the new man will sexually abuse the girl. This does happen a lot.

There were two cases from my pueblo. There was a woman in the village, and her husband died. She took in another who beat her and abused her daughter. One night the daughter killed her stepfather and then left the village and was never heard from again. There was another case in which a woman was abandoned by her husband, and she had one son who was *loco* in the head and she was drunk. They ended up having sex together!

VICTORIA'S SAZÓN

■ ■ ■ ■ ■ ■ ■ ■ ■ ■

ESTUFADO (OAXACA)

Ingredients
2 kilos chicken
1 ½ kilos tomatoes
125 grams almonds
125 grams raisins
olives al gusto
capers al gusto
small clove of roasted garlic
1 small roasted onion
pinch or dash of parsley, sugar, salt, and chocolate
1 toasted or fried bread roll

Preparation
1. Cut and boil chicken until done and save the water for chicken stock.
2. Boil tomatoes, roast garlic and onion, and toast bread. Bleach almonds and peel off skin. Chop up olives, capers, and raisins.
3. Blend together tomatoes, garlic, and onion and then fry them in oil.
4. Mix tomato mixture with chicken stock and then blend chopped-up olives, capers, chocolate, salt, sugar, and raisins and add them to the stock.

Put the cooked chicken in the sauce and serve. Serves sixteen.

INTERMISSION: HOUSEHOLDS AND ECONOMIC CYCLES

The two previous sections of this chapter were portraits of the Doñas María Elena and Victoria that were composed to give a feeling for their life histories and how they have maintained themselves and their families. In the following section we will present more of a narrative account of how two particular extended households in Linda Vista have composed and recomposed themselves over the nearly three decades that we have known them. Selby and Murphy have often written about the cyclical development of household economics. That is, when households are in the cycle of their beginnings with young children, household costs are expensive, whereas in later cycles when the children are older and can work, household costs are lower, and households tend to be better off economically (Selby, Murphy, and Lorenzen 1990). We will present contrasting narratives of the households of the Rodríguez family, a family that was always somewhat better off than others in the *colonia*, and the Alvarez Guzmán family, which was always one of the poorest families in the *colonia*. The Rodríguezes seemed to be a family that would move beyond the material limits of the *colonia*, which they have in a sense, although at the high price of tragedy and separation. The Alvarez Guzmáns have also moved beyond these material limits through hard work, luck, and a willingness to grin and bear their difference in order to be able to move ahead. Further, each narrative will also give some ethnographic texture to the dynamics of extended families. Sometimes there is an element of romanticism in the belief that extended families work better than the standardized nuclear middle-class families of the developed world. Each of these households could be classified as extended, but they have operated in different and hardly romantic ways.

The Rodríguez Family

Love is important, and I have lived too long in this relationship without it. I have tried to talk to Doña Lucía and see if we could work something out, but she did not want to talk about it. She just wanted to get out of the house. I did not help her or stop her—it was her choice. Now I have someone who loves me. It will not last, but I will enjoy it while it does.

—*Juan Rodríguez, a commercial artist in his mid-sixties, longtime resident of Linda Vista and the separated husband of Lucía, speaking about his marriage*

Love, it has so many definitions and each one is different, so I do not know what it is.

—*Lucía Rodríguez, a housekeeper in her early fifties, mother of seven children, former resident of Linda Vista, and separated wife of Juan, giving her views on love*

We have known the Rodríguez family for more than thirty years. For the majority of that time this family seemed to be oriented around the dominant but tolerant will of Juan—the father—as he attempted to lead his second family toward a better life through his honesty, wit, and consideration for his wife, Lucía, and their six children. This family theater had its weak spots. For instance, this was a second family for both Juan and Lucía, and although Juan spoke of care and consideration as part of love, he never seemed to know that for Lucía it was something that she could not define for herself or for their relationship. In addition, even though the siblings seemed to be a creative collective of personalities, they often expressed frustration at Juan's controlling manner and at the emotional distance from each other as they entered their teens. Nothing, however, could have prepared them for the set of joys and tragedies that would consume their future as the "happy family" unit. Juan had hoped to script an outcome for the family that would move them beyond their popular-culture context through the attainment of cosmopolitan values that could transcend that context and be the means for the family members to guide their everyday lives. Unfortunately, he did not fully convey these plans to Lucía and the rest of the family.

The family began to unravel as the children became adults and began leaving the homestead to marry, only to find that various tragedies would bring them back home, as that home was falling apart. Lucía, through her quiet strength and formidable willpower, said she would stay with Juan through the marriage of her two older children, and then that was it for her. She now felt that the marriage had been a fantasy all along and that no real love had ever been present. Juan, hurt and emotionally vengeful at this news, felt that he was always the one attempting to give love but that Lucía had become incapable of responding or recognizing how to love him or the children. Lucía, true to her word, after Cristy (the oldest daughter) married, moved out of the house and left Juan. She went to live with Alma, her second oldest daughter, who was in the first year of widowhood. Her husband had died in a most tragic manner. Two years previously, as Alma was giving birth to her daughter, her husband—Alberto—fell ill in the same hospital, and several hours later he died, never having seen their baby.

Juan stayed in the house with the two youngest children—Solya, who is in her early twenties, and Octavio, who is seventeen. The other children had already moved out of the house: America, who is in her mid-twenties, had moved in with her boyfriend, and they had a child; Cristy was living with her husband; and Nesto, the oldest, was living with his wife. Within six months these living arrangements all began to change. Solya went to live with her boyfriend, and Octavio just stopped coming home. Juan was living with a new woman, Julia, who was in her early twenties and had three small children. Juan, Julia, and her children had moved into what had been the bedrooms of Juan and Lucía's children, and Alma was living in the main house with her daughter and her lover. Lucía had moved in with Solya, America, and America's child, both of whom had left their boyfriends. They were all living with Cristy and her baby because tragically, several months before, her husband of less than a year had been killed in an auto accident.

BACKGROUND

We met Juan and Lucía and their family during our first summer in Colonia Linda Vista (1968). They lived in the higher part of the second section of the *colonia*. We were wandering through this section trying to meet folks and see if they would agree to do an interview with us that involved doing a census. We were walking by Juan's house, and he was outside working on his house. Juan "stood out" in the *colonia* at this time for several reasons—he was quite youthful-looking, he had a beard, and he was a *güero* (fair-skinned). Also, as we came to know Juan, we found him to be quite a literate, insightful, and witty person. He is very impressive, and it has always been delightful to have the time to visit with him. At this time he was living with Lucía, his wife, four of the children—Nesto, Cristy, Alma, and Solya (America and Octavio were not yet born)—and his father, an elderly gentleman who had been in the revolution of 1910 with the forces of Villa in the north.

Juan had met Lucía on a train ride from Mexico City to Oaxaca. Juan's father was from northern Mexico, but through his experience in the revolution and the army, he had traveled and lived in many parts of Mexico. Juan had spent much of his youth and adulthood in Jalapa, Veracruz. At this time, his father was stationed in the valley of Oaxaca, and Juan was going to visit him. On the train he found himself sitting next to Lucía. Since the train ride from Mexico City to Oaxaca can take anywhere from eighteen to twenty hours, they had a great deal of time to visit and get to know each other. They must have done so, for at the end of the ride, they decided to begin living together. Juan had just recently been abandoned by his wife in Jalapa, and he had left Jalapa and his four adult children. Lucía also had been in a previous relationship and had a child from that relationship. They began their union by moving into Colonia Linda Vista and started on what looked like the happy and fruitful building of a family. Juan was and still is a fine talker and has a delightful presentation of himself. He sounds reflective and somewhat self-critical. However, even in those early days Lucía suggested that life was hard and that Juan was quite demanding. She claimed that after the birth of one of their children (Solya) in the morning (she gave birth in the house), Juan demanded that she get up that evening to make the dinner.

JUAN: THE FATHER

Juan has worked for more than four decades as a graphic artist. His primary work when we met him was painting advertisements on the back of the local buses in the city. During the 1960s this was apparently a reasonably good-paying job, and it continues to be so currently for Juan. When we met the family, Juan was the only wage-earning worker in the house, and neither Lucía nor the children had to work to bring in extra income. The children didn't have to start to work until their late teens, when they had finished their schooling or had gotten married. Lucía never worked until the children were all in their teens, and when she did go to work, it was not to support the household but to begin supporting herself. Though the house they lived in was physically quite simple, they always had good appliances and furniture, and over the years the house was expanded into several more rooms, with bedrooms for all the children. In terms of household budgets and household inventories, they always were somewhat better off than other families in Colonia Linda Vista (Higgins 1974).

Juan is quite conversant on many subjects, ranging from politics to the current state of the *colonia*. Like others in the *colonia*, his worldview is a mixture of themes related to his own everyday life. Juan still sees himself as someone who believes in God, and he still respects the traditions of the Catholic Church, though he rarely attends. He strongly feels that everyone has to show tolerance for each other's views, especially in terms of religion. He finds Protestant missionaries to be too aggressive and slick in the manner in which they attempt to get people to change their ways. Juan does not have a lot of religious imagery in the house, nor was there much when he was living with Lucía. Though he is aware of the beliefs about the Virgen de Juquila, he has never expressed an interest in her, nor does he speak of folk illnesses or the use of healers or witches. Juan believes we make our own realities, and those are the ones we have to live with. He believes that respect and tolerance are how one should guide one's personal behavior with others. Though he is himself a *güero*, he does not think that is important nor that it should give anyone an advantage over someone else. He likes to watch television and will watch educational programs about other countries, and he enjoys these a great deal. He has attempted to be cosmopolitan about the issues of gender and sexuality, though his current separation has caused him to rethink his views on love and caring. He now feels that he has been unloved by his children because of how their mother treated him, though he still claims support for the equality of women and does not seem to be concerned with issues of gayness. He has always stressed that he likes sex and has suggested that in the past he and Lucía had an active and creative sex life. I (MJH) asked him years ago how he would describe good sex, and he stated that it was like the feeling you had after a great meal—mmm, that's good. I then asked him who should be the one to initiate sexual interaction, and he stated, "Whoever is hungry first."

Juan is quite verbal about the current political and economic crisis in Mexico and Oaxaca. His political views are a mixture of conservative and radical ideas. He has maintained casual contacts with leftist political parties in the state. Once he had his younger nephew invite over several young folks who were involved in oppositional politics through a leftist alliance. He said that after talking with them for several hours he was frustrated by their lack of understanding of the everyday lives of working folks like him or others in the *colonias*. More important, even if they did understand, they had no real model or plan of what they would change or how. In the last presidential elections, he voted for the PAN ticket. Juan said that he did not believe in any of that party's positions—only that one had to vote against the PRI—and he felt that you might as well vote for the group that might have a chance. Like many now, he feels that anyone or any party was better than the one they had currently. He sees political corruption as one of the main sources of Mexico's economic and political problems. He thinks that most politics is a game that those in the popular classes do not have time for because they have to work and work very hard just to get by. He thinks the Zapatistas are interesting but not a real national force. He does not know where things are going, but he has some hope that things will get better—but not much. He thinks part of the problem is that the majority of the people, like him, are constrained by the continuing crisis but that they are getting by. He holds that, as in the time of his father, it is not until folks are not getting by that the forces for radical change will emerge, perhaps another revolution. But he also sees that day as a long way off.

Juan likes to watch television, especially sports programs. He still likes to play sports like volleyball or basketball when he has the time. He does not go to movies very often, nor does he go off to drink in *cantinas*. His tastes in music are very traditional and mainstream. He does like to cook, and we put his recipe for chiles stuffed with bananas in this section.

LUCÍA: THE MOTHER AND THE SEPARATED WIFE

Lucía is from the Oaxacan valley town of Miahuatlán, which is about thirty miles from the city of Oaxaca. She is in her early fifties now and currently lives with Cristy, Alma, and their children (Cristy's son, Andrés, nine months, and Alma's daughter, Jessica, who is now three years old). When Lucía left their relationship she took basically nothing from the household. She seemed to feel that just getting out of the relationship was reward enough. She has several housecleaning jobs and felt confident that she would be able to take care of herself. She first went to stay with Alma, who was living in a little house outside of town where she had lived with her husband. After Cristy's husband died, Lucía moved in with her. Alma had returned to share the house with her father and his new little "chickens," as they all referred to Juan's new family. One of the tensions between Juan and Lucía was always their different backgrounds and the fact that Juan, from Lucía's point of view, acted as if his background and family were more important than hers. Though Juan was always more talkative and more willing to offer up a wide range of views on different subjects than Lucía was, she, in her own quiet way, was as insightful as he.

Lucía also has a popular-culture orientation in her various worldviews. She believes in God and the Church but does not attend church much, nor does she have the same kind of faith in the *Virgenes* as María Elena or Victoria. Because she was always the least talkative one in the household, we do not know as much about some of her views. When she was living with Juan, she did not express her own position on public issues, and now that she has left the relationship, her new working arrangements make it harder to find her to be able to hear her new voices. During the relationship, she never expressed her views on sex or sexuality but was concerned that her daughters receive equitable choices in life. She accepted a parenting division of labor in which Juan worked outside the house and she maintained the household. Though quiet, she was never docile, and she liked to talk about family things. She has expressed feelings of liberation and happiness at being on her own now. She at times seems to like to hear gossip about Juan and his new woman, though not with much bitterness (see photos 7 and 8).

THE SEPARATION

LUCÍA

I just felt that I had done enough over the years that was not really appreciated by Juan. I do not think that we ever had very much love in the marriage, and I could not and would not keep living that way. I know that I should try to get my share of the house or get some kind of support from Juan, but I have what I really want—I am free from that reality and that is more than enough. I can support myself, and I do not need to be a burden to my children. I am not sure if he had other women before I began thinking about leaving; however, that's not why I left and that's not why I do not want to go back with him.

7. *The Rodríguez family: Solya, Juan, Alma, and Jessica. Photo by Tanya Coen.*

8. *Cristy Rodríguez and her son, Andrés. Photo by Joni Kubana.*

He has his little *pollita* (a little hen) and I do not care. It's kind of funny to hear the gossip about them, but he can do what he wants. It is over. I am now going to live my life.

JUAN

It is still hard for me, this separation with Doña Lucía, because of how my children have reacted. They are now beginning to understand why we are separated, but it is just the beginning. Last week Cristy was here, and she told me that she had a problem that I was living with Julia, who has three children and is some thirty years younger than I. I told her that she should not worry about that. Julia and I are only going to be together for a short time. Now Julia needs a place to stay, and I need to be with someone who can show me love. It is a matter of convenience. I must say that we do know how to treat each other well; I attend to her and she attends to me. But I know that someday—perhaps soon—she will encounter a younger man that she will fall in love with, and that will be it for us. I understand and accept that, so my children do not have to worry about Julia being their stepmother or something else. It will not last that long. Though again I must say that she does know how to love me, and after so many years living with Lucía without love, this is a wondrous experience for me. I know that it will not last, but now at my age I just want to enjoy being loved as long as it does last.

Also I know now that my children respect me but do not love me. Now that the children are learning that the reasons that Doña Lucía and I are not together are more complex than they thought, maybe we can begin to get closer and begin to learn how to love each other. Now that they have children, they will learn how hard it is to be a parent. But how do I know that they do not love me, and why would I say that? Well, to be frank with you it comes from their mother, who never taught them how to live in a house with love for their father. Because she never loved me she could not teach them how to love me either! It is the mother's role to teach children how to love in the house. The father is always at work or doing other things, even sometimes getting drunk. The mother is always saying to the children, "Now wait until your father gets home, and we can do this or that." The mother should teach the children how to love their father, but if she does not love the father, she will not pass it on to the children. This is what happened to me.

THE CHILDREN

NESTO

Nesto is the oldest child of Juan and Lucía. As a young boy and as a teenager he was very sweet, somewhat quiet and always very helpful. He was slight of build as a child, though he was very physically active. When he entered the university, he began playing volleyball and working out with weights. He now is a large man who has maintained his new size through continued weight lifting and working out. At the university in Oaxaca, he studied accounting and public administration. While he was attending the university, he got a job working in the city government for a *político* (politician), a man whom we had known through our other contacts. We wrote a letter of reference for Nesto, which he felt helped him get his job as well as a job for Cristy later on. This job with Jorge—the *político*—has been Nesto's entrée into the middle-class professional and political world of Oaxaca. Jorge has used Nesto as his office manager, helper, and confidant. Through this contact Nesto has matured into an intelligent young man who knows the political and social ropes of the city. He likes to hang out with his male friends in hip places like the local bar called Liverpool in the Colonia Reforma. He is reasonably well informed about current political events, both local and national; however, since his patron is a player in the local PRI structure, Nesto's views are quite mainstream.

In the fall of 1994, he got married to a young middle-class Oaxacan woman, Julia, and they now have two children. They had a church wedding followed by a large reception. Those attending the reception tended to be Nesto's friends and work acquaintances more than folks or friends from the *colonia*. In fact, the only other people at the reception from the *colonia* besides his family were the members of the band. Nesto seems to have kept his distance from his parents' marriage problems and attempts to see both of them when he can.

CRISTY

Cristy is now in her late twenties, widowed and a single mother. She finished secondary school and then attended a professional secretary school. She has worked for Nesto's patron, where he was in charge of the office of regional political affairs, a governmental agency that helped coordinate political programs and projects between the city government of Oaxaca and the village governments in the valley. Jorge has moved on to the state assembly, taking Nesto with him, but Cristy has stayed in the office. Cristy is a very intelligent young woman who had hoped that her marriage would be the final addition to her self-proclaimed middle-class status. She has her own *onda*, which combines her attractiveness with her own style of assertiveness, though she sees herself as a timid person. She married a young architect,

Andrés, who was from the Istmo de Tehuantepec. Her wedding dress was a traditional-style gown from the Istmo. She was outfitted in the traditional huipil and skirts, the large white lace facial veil, and numerous gold necklaces. Their reception was a little smaller than Nesto's, but more lively, since Andrés's family was from the Istmo and they knew how to give a party. The wedding reception included the women dancing with pots on their heads, which they all smash on the floor after the dance. This was followed by her mother-in-law dancing with the mescal bottle on top of her head. This event had an undertone of sadness for Cristy, for she knew that this would be the last time her parents would be together, but what she and no one else knew or even thought about was that within six months she would be a widow. We saw Cristy on this Christmas Eve (1996). She was home on vacation and was getting ready to move back to Colonia Linda Vista into a rented house. Though she was friendly and did not seem to be depressed, she had no plans for Christmas Eve other than going to bed early.

Below is a summary of an interview with Cristy that was done a few months before her wedding. She talks about life in the *colonia*, her understanding of her parents' marriage problems, and her reflections on a range of social issues that were framed in terms of her perception of herself as a middle-class woman about to move into a loving marriage. It seems too soon after the death of her husband to ask her if any of her views have changed.

> I feel that my life here in Oaxaca is not that interesting. I get up, I go to work, then I go home, and then I repeat it all over again the next day. I like my work and what I do, but I don't know if any of it would be very interesting to other people. I do not have many friends here in Oaxaca. It is very hard to have real friends here, most people are nothing more than false friends. I do not know why Oaxaca is like that, but it is. People just like to treat you badly, so I do not have much of a social life.
>
> My biggest worry right now is my parents. They just do not get along, and they do not know how to communicate with each other. They use me as their sounding board—back and forth. Papi keeps asking me what my mother has said or is doing; my mother asks the same about him. They are just used to living with each other, but there is no love in their hearts. It hurts me a great deal because I am

put in the middle of this anger. They are both good people, but not for each other now! I do not know what is going to happen with them or what I should do. They do not talk to the other kids about these things, only me. My *novio* understands what's going on here and that helps me a lot. But I get scared—what if something like this happens to us after we are married? It worries me.

The rich people in Oaxaca are referred to as whipped cream, they are the "society" folks who fill up the newspapers. Most of us here in Oaxaca are in the middle class; we work and we are able to pay our way. However, there are far too many poor people. Oaxaca is one of the poorest states in the country. This is from a lack of economic development and modern communication. I do not think there is much racism here in Oaxaca, but there is a lot of concern about class differences. I have not felt much class prejudice directed toward me because I am from this *colonia*. People seem to judge you on your merits, not where you are from. Currently I do not like to be in the *colonia* because of the family situation involving my parents. Plus, I have always been somewhat timid, and I do not make friends very easily. I did not like high school that much because I am not too social and also because my father was very strict about letting me go out a lot.

Many people in Oaxaca are pretty uptight about sex, and they think that a girl should be a virgin until she is married. I had a friend who was almost raped, and her biggest fear was that she might not be able to get married. I enjoy sex; however, I do not think it is the end all of everything. It has to be a deep form of communication, and it should never be forced or pressured. I use birth control pills, and I only want to have two kids. Gay people are okay, and I think that they are given respect if they do not flaunt their gayness too much.

I like my brothers and sisters, but we are not close, like friends. I do not confide in them very often. I wish I had more time to talk with my younger brother. I think that he is being affected by the troubles here at home, and it is affecting his studies at school.

In the future I want my marriage to work, and I want to continue working, and I want to help my parents. Ever since I have worked I have put part of my earnings into the household funds. I make about 1,800 pesos a month [at the time of the interview (in 1995) about $240 USA] and once in a while a little more on commissions. My boss is a good person, but like all bosses, he has his defects. I wish I could help my parents through their troubles. But how? I have my own life to lead, and their life is theirs. I do not know what to do.

ALMA, AMERICA, AND SOLYA

Alma is in her mid-twenties and, ironically, she was a widow before her older sister, Cristy. Alma seems to have a more rough-and-tumble personality than her two older siblings. She was always laughing and presenting a happy face. She continues this *onda* in her widowhood. As we stated earlier, several Christmas Eves ago while she was giving birth to her daughter Jessica, her husband was dying in the same hospital. Alma has a degree in accounting from a private secretary school. She is currently working as a secretary and receives a small pension from her husband's death benefits.

America is a quiet young woman who did not get married but went off to live with her boyfriend to get out of the house. They are living in a free union relationship. They have one small child, and she works. Her husband is a chauffeur. They live with his family. Like Nesto, she has kept her distance from the family troubles and comes around once in a while to visit.

Solya is in her early twenties and had been studying for a degree in hotel and tourist management. She has a very open and cheery personality. She was feeling the most concern about her parents' separation, for she was staying at home with Juan and Octavio, and she did not want to be the substitute mother in the house. In fact, she avoided this by moving in with her boyfriend instead of waiting to get married. At one point she had left him and was living with Cristy. She is currently again living with her boyfriend, and they have one child.

Below is a summary of a discussion we had with Alma and Solya about the family, life in the *colonia*, and a range of different social issues.

> SOLYA: We knew that something was wrong between our parents because there was so much tension between them, but we never

expected that they were going to separate—it was a total surprise. One day she was going to Miahuatlán to visit her family, and the next thing we knew was that she was not coming back. Cristy knew what was going on—she went to visit with Mama and came back and told us she was not coming back. It was very hard to understand at first, but they both seem to be a little less stressed now that they have separated. Also, since we are all grown up now it is not that hard. It would be a lot harder if we were all still kids.

ALMA: I think if they are both happy with their lives, then it is okay. In a strange way it has made all of us a little closer, and we see more of each other now, since we have to get together in order to understand what's gong on. We now all live separately, but we are seeing more of each other than when we were all living together. I think it will be the hardest on Solya because she will be the only woman in the house and our father and brother will assume that she will do all the cooking and taking care of the house. In fact, she has been doing all of that work for the last six months. She has been trying to go to school and take care of them. It is not fair.

SOLYA: Oh, it is not that bad, and it will not last much longer because I am getting out, too—either my *novio* and I will get married or we will just start living together.

ALMA: Mama has been working as a domestic worker for about twelve years. She makes about forty pesos a day, and she works there two days out of the week. She is not going to take any money from Papi or anything from the house. She says that it just makes her feel more independent. Also, she is mad about the little *pollita* that he is seeing now. Also, Mama will not come to this house if Papi is here. Neither one of them will talk with the other.

As a kid I liked living in this *colonia*. It was great. There were always a lot of kids to play with, both boys and girls. It felt like everyone was living in close families and the times were good.

SOLYA: I hate living here in Linda Vista. The walk from down below up to here every day is horrible. But in life you can get used to anything.

ALMA: Oh, we have encountered a lot of machismo in our lives. My marriage was good, and my husband did his fair share around the house. I have a neighbor whose husband will not help her with anything. She cannot even talk to anyone unless he is there. For me, a *macho* is a man who is very jealous, will not let "his" women do anything without him, and if she does anything that he does not like, he will beat her.

But we do think things are getting a little better, there are more opportunities for women to look for a career than in our mother's times.

SOLYA: I think that there is a kind of racism in the area of tourism. Some of the teachers in our program of studying tourism stress that it is important that you look a certain way, like a *güera*. They, the teachers, say this is because of the foreigners investing in tourism here. It is more than that. I have a classmate who is very *güera*, and she does not like dark-skinned folks. She says that she would never marry a dark person. One time we were playing Ouija board with her and she started talking about how if you married a dark-skinned person you would have *"mono"* kids (monkeylike) and it horrified her. I know that I am somewhat of a *güera*, but that does not mean anything, nor does it make me special. This is what my parents have taught me and I agree. Also, in my group we run with everyone.

I guess we are middle class, like most of the kids in my school, though some are very upper middle class. But I think it is better to be sincere and basic than to try to be elitist and think that you are better than other folks. I never thought living in Linda Vista meant we were poor or working class, and I do not think that my friends thought that either. We were not poor because we always had things and always had plenty of food to eat. My friends are a lot like me in terms of social class. We have the same kind of *onda* in terms of tastes and values. I have friends from all over the city.

There are a lot of gay guys in Oaxaca, and there must be a lot of lesbians too. You just don't see them as much. It is easier to pass as a woman if you are gay. Some folks say that lesbians are bisexual; I do not know, but I think that they get very jealous in their relationships. I do know some gay guys. There is a gay guy in our class, and he is always joking around. But he never talks about being gay or we never have talked to him about discrimination or the kind of stuff that he might face. I think gay folks are just like anyone else—it is not a big deal. He has a lot of friends in the school and nobody seems to be hassled by it. Some folks do get upset, but I do not know why. I think some people think that if you hang out with gay folks that you are going to be gay—that's silly. It's really silly when so many men will choose to have sex with *locas vestidas* (drag queens). That's what a *mayate* is, a man who likes sex with gay men.

I think relations between men and women are changing. Look at my parents. Before, whatever the man said went. No woman had a real say. Now we can get important jobs and do more. We now talk much more openly about sex and our desires. Now it is more common for men and women to talk about things that they are going to do in a relationship and in terms of sexual pleasures. Abortions are very expensive and sometimes hard to arrange. There are doctors who will do abortions, but you have to know how to find them. It is common enough, though, to get an abortion. A couple of my friends have had them.

We are getting a lot of information about AIDS in school. They send medical teams to the school that give us *talleres* (workshops) on these issues. They give us folders with a lot of information about AIDS, but it is still pretty basic. Most of my friends, in fact, do not know too much about AIDS, such as how you get it or how to protect yourself. Some do not seem to be concerned. Most guys still do not use condoms, and they still accept that it is the woman's responsibility to deal with birth control. I feel that in the area of sex and birth control it is again something that a couple should talk about together, in an open fashion. In terms of AIDS, using a condom is for the protection of both persons, not just the woman. Also, some men like to use prostitutes and not use condoms. That is stupid and it endangers the wife or girlfriend. I know of several young girls that got pregnant (fifteen- to sixteen-year-olds) because they did not know how to protect themselves and they believe these *macho* guys when they say to them everything will be all right. Sometimes these girls have to leave school and their families are very upset. Most of what I have learned about my own sexuality I have learned from my friends, not my parents or sisters. Among my friends, most drink a little and a few have even used *mota* (marijuana). I know that some of the kids on the street are sniffing glue or other things. Some of the kids in the *colonia* have played around with that stuff. They like to hallucinate with it. But not me and my friends—we like to have a beer or *cuba libre* (rum and Coke) once in a while.

Mexican politics are in real bad shape and something has to change. Soon! Some of my friends have voted for the PAN or other parties. I did not vote. I really do not know too much about the Zapatistas, nor do we talk about it much with my friends.

The last devaluation hurt everyone. It was very bad. Now all the prices are higher again. In my future, I hope to work in the hotel business. This degree takes about three years, and I am almost finished. I need for some reason to take a physical education class and English. With this degree you can work in hotels, tourist agencies, restaurants, et cetera. Except there are a lot of folks getting these degrees and not that many jobs in Oaxaca. I might have to go out of state to get in the hotel business.

I like all kinds of music, especially old-style salsa, meringue, cha cha cha, and *tríos*. I am not too fond of *norteño* style and just a little bit of rock. I'm not a big movie fan, but I like to read novels that attempt to say something important, not just romance novels. I do not read magazines or newspapers too much. I like fashion—casual clothing that is loose-fitting. I have some of my clothes made here in the *colonia*. I like to wear a miniskirt once in a while. I think it's funny that when you are wearing a miniskirt you spend all your time trying to pull the skirt down, but the point is to show off your skin and legs, no?

I have kind of a mixed personality. Here at home because of all the family tension, I get tense and I find myself getting very irritable at times. Away from home I am very mellow with my friends at school or in other places. In fact, most of my friends think that my home life must be very positive since I am so mellow—if they only knew! Some folks like to bring their private lives into their social life. I do not. I am a fairly serious student and I want to do well. When I started at the preparatory school I would spend more time on my social life than studying and my grades were affected. I had to drop out of school for a while, and I felt very bad because I knew that I was as good or smarter than some of the students that were still in school. I decided to change my ways, and when I got into this program, I picked friends who were also serious about studying and doing the work.

OCTAVIO

Octavio is in his late teens and has just moved to northern Mexico to work with a cousin of Lucía's who owns a small company. He is quite a handsome young man and he seems to have decided to sow his wild oats in the context of this family confusion. He was finishing secondary school when the family hassles began, but when his mother moved out, he sort of dropped out and started staying at the house of his sisters or wherever his mother was staying. He has not suggested nor has anyone else felt that he has problems with Juan. He just felt like it was time to move on.

SAZÓN OF JUAN AND LUCÍA

This is one of Juan's favorite dishes, which we have enjoyed many times at his home. He claims that this is a recipe from Veracruz; however, Lucía claims he knows nothing about cooking and the recipe is from Oaxaca. Either way it is a fine meal.

■ ■ ■ ■ ■ ■ ■ ■ ■ ■

CHILES RELLENOS DE BANANAS (PLANTAINS)

Ingredients
chile poblanos, as many as you are going to make
sweet plantains, also enough to stuff the chiles
some raisins
eggs
flour
oil

Preparation
1. Toast chiles so as to be able to peel off skin.
2. Cut chiles open, remove seeds, and clean.
3. Mash plantains, put in some raisins, and fry until soft.
4. Stuff each of the chiles with plantain mixture.
5. Whip up egg whites until stiff, then beat into egg yolks with a little flour.
6. Roll stuffed chiles in flour, then in egg mixture, and then deep-fry in very hot oil.
7. Chiles can be served with or without tomato salsa.

The Alvarez Guzmán Family

I never encountered racism or discrimination because I am Indian or because I am a Zapotec. *Yope* is a word that is used negatively against Indians who cannot speak Spanish. You know what? I am sure that some people have seen me as an Indian or have called me a dumb *yope* at some time, but I do not pay attention to that kind of thinking or behavior, nor do I let it affect me. I know what and who I am. I am a very smart person, and I know how to handle this life, and that's what counts. What I think about myself, not what others might say, is what is important to me.

—*Francisca Guzmán López, fifty-year-old sierra Zapotec, co-owner of Popsicle workshop, and wife of Arnulfo*

I never encountered any racism that I can remember.

—*Arnulfo Alvarez Cruz, sixty-six-year-old Mazatec Indian, co-owner of Popsicle workshop, and husband of Francisca*

INTRODUCTION

We have known Francisca and Arnulfo as long as we have been working in Oaxaca. In all the years that we have known them, Francisca and Arnulfo have dealt with the ethnic and racial realities of Oaxaca as indicated by the above statements. A very class- and race-stratified society is evident in the city and region of Oaxaca, although the discourse of social anthropology of Oaxaca (Bartolomé 1997; Bartolomé and Barabas 1986) does not often deal with those issues. The dynamics of the racial discourse and discrimination in the city of Oaxaca are focused on access into middle- and upper-class status. This system works like the colorism that Lancaster talks about in Nicaragua (Lancaster 1992), with the addition of language as another mark. Colorism involves how social actors rank themselves and others in terms of the lightness or darkness of skin tones, with lightness having a higher value than darkness. This is a relative classification system, in that someone is always lighter or darker than someone else. The higher the social ranking, generally, the lighter the skin. In the case of Oaxaca, language is also a marker in that system. Being a monolingual native speaker will not get you beyond the humble classes, and an adequate command of Spanish is required for even the most minimal class advancement. Though in the academic/political world of Oaxaca having command of an indigenous language is highly valued and marks one as an activist for indigenous rights, beyond that world the value of such skills is not appreciated. For Francisca and Arnulfo, because their world is that of the urban popular classes of Oaxaca, where class marks folks more than race, they feel that they have not encountered racism; however, they are quite aware of class limitations. And if they were to desire entrance into the middle-class world of Oaxaca, they might find the racism that they feel they have so far missed.

BACKGROUND

Francisca is fifty years old and is from a Zapotec sierra community that now is only a few hours by car from the city of Oaxaca. She came to the city in her early teens and worked as a domestic servant. Her whole immediate family had also moved to the city. She and Arnulfo met in the city, began courting, and have been married and living together for more than thirty years. In this time period, they have raised their five children to adulthood and now have a small army of grandchildren. They have moved from a one-room adobe house with no water or electricity, on the very last street of Colonia Linda Vista, to a small housing compound with water and electricity in a new *colonia*, about five miles down the road from Linda Vista. Arnulfo has worked many jobs, but he was a Popsicle street vendor for more than thirty years. He left his Mazatec village in his teens because he wanted to find some kind of work that was easier than growing corn every year. Francisca also held various jobs, primarily in the area of domestic work. When we first met them, Arnulfo's brother's wife had died and the brother and his six children were living with Francisca and Arnulfo, and Francisca was caring for and feeding eleven children on fifteen pesos a day. Even given that this was twenty-some years ago and inflation and prices were different, it was quite an impressive job of household management by Francisca. About eight years ago Arnulfo's patron decided to retire and offered to sell the Popsicle business to them. At that time, two of their sons were looking for work, so they were able to get a bank to lend them some money, and they bought the business. Now the former vendor is the boss and owner, along with his wife and two sons. This impressive career move—like many among the popular classes over the last decade of economic crisis in Mexico—did not increase their economic level per se but provided them with the means to hang on to their limited gains. Like Victoria's and María Elena's families, Francisca and Arnulfo's increased well-being over the years that we have known them came about because their adult children were able to enter the labor market when it was still economically open.

FRANCISCA

Francisca is a woman of strength and a quiet wisdom, with a gentle sense of humor and the stamina to raise five children to adulthood, maintain an extended family of sorts with her sisters and parents, and stay in her relationship with Arnulfo for more than thirty years. Francisca has worked very hard most of her life. She speaks flawless Spanish, and is quite proud of her cultural heritage and her continued skill in speaking Zapotec; however, she does not wear indigenous clothing. She likes to tell stories, exchange gossip, and tell jokes. She feels that her greatest achievement has been keeping her family together and attaining enough economic security so that they now can cover the cost of their basic everyday requirements and have a little left over. She is proud that they all still live together and that they have all learned to live in harmony. She says they have attained this through being honest with each other and accepting that everyone makes errors.

She does not talk much about politics and does not have much of an interest in it. She finds Oaxacan politics to be a game played by the affluent, who have no real interest in poor or working-class folks. She contends that when she or her family have gone to different political parties for help in terms of concerns about the *colonia*, it is not forthcoming. Like most, she is quite skeptical of the PRI, but she does not involve herself in any kind of oppositional politics. She has no real interest in or understanding of the Zapatista movement. She strongly identifies with her village history and culture, but she does not project her indigenous identity beyond her village or involve herself with the various movements of indigenous rights in Oaxaca. She and Arnulfo have built a little house in her village, and she now goes often to the village. Though she is proud of her own speaking skills in Zapotec, she has not taught any of her children to be fluent in the language. As stated in her quote, she is aware of racism but does not see it as affecting her because she will not let it. She does have a concept of herself as coming from humble origins, and she hopes and feels that her children are moving toward a more middle-income lifestyle. Her primary political concern is similar to that of many in the popular cultures—the economy and the inability of the current political system to do anything about improving it. For her these are the dynamics that generate the poverty found in Oaxaca and Mexico.

She is a strong believer in the Catholic systems of saints and virgins. She, too, maintains an altar to the Virgen de Juquila, but she does not make a regular pilgrimage like María Elena. She maintains an altar to the Virgen in the house, and there are various religious items kept throughout the house. I (MJH) am the godfather of her youngest son, Santiago. However, it is a very informal *compadre* relationship, one she refers to as *compadres de la vela* (coparents of the candle); that is, we went into a church (Soledad), went to one of the chapels in the church, and lit candles together to the saint of that chapel. After that we were *compadres*. What was interesting was the use of the Zapotec tradition of vertically extending kin relations to include co-parents, for after this ritual we were also *compadres* with her mother and father (Mahar 1986).

Francisca migrated to the city in her early youth with her mother and father and four other siblings. The family is from a pueblo in the sierra named Teococuilco Marcos Pérez Islar. When we met Francisca, her mother and two sisters were living in separate houses on the same lot. They had a curious kind of extended family (Higgins 1974). They would all spend a great deal of time together—visiting, shopping, or doing household work together—and they would tend to help each other with child care, but it was not a form of economic cooperation. When they borrowed things—like money or food goods—it was expected that they would pay each other back. This would involve small items. For instance, if Juana, Francisca's sister, borrowed one tomato, she was expected to pay it back. They did not have any kind of co-operative budget between the households for buying food or household items. Interestingly, this pattern still holds between Francisca and her adult children. Her sons, Alejandro and Geraldo, and their families share the current house with their parents, and there is one common kitchen and bathroom. However, each of the familial units maintains its own household budget and expenses. They do not pool their funds, but they do rotate some common payments (like gas for the kitchen) and will share meals casually, but each household puts in its appropriate share. What they do share are the profits from the Popsicle business, but only in terms of who works there, not in terms of being family members.

Francisca is not particularly open about talking about the issues of gender and sex, particularly aspects of her sexuality, nor does she offer many views on the issues of sexism or what she feels about men. Like María Elena and Victoria, she suggests that there are traditional roles for women in terms of child care and household duties, though she (also like them) currently does not perform many of these roles. There is a sixteen-year age difference between her and Arnulfo. They met when she worked with her mother in the market. She was in her late teens, and Arnulfo asked her mother and brother for permission to court her. They courted for three years, and they had both a church wedding and a civil wedding. During the early years of their marriage, she was the "traditional" wife, though she also either worked in the house or did some domestic work outside the house. This was also the time when they were the poorest. About five years ago, according to their daughter, Berta, Francisca was ready to throw Arnulfo out of the house and seek a divorce. Berta suggested it was because he was getting distanced from the family and not showing Francisca any concern or affection. Neither Arnulfo nor Francisca has mentioned it to us, and at least in terms of public presentation, they act as if they enjoy each other's company.

ARNULFO

Arnulfo is in his early sixties and comes from a Mazatec village called San Bartolomé Huautla. The Mazatec are famous for using hallucinogenic mushrooms and for having developed a whistle style of communication. In most ethnographic writings on the use of hallucinogenic drugs, such drugs are always spoken of in terms of ritual use, not as a recreational drug. Years ago I (MJH) asked Arnulfo if, when he was young, he or his friends ever just took the mushrooms for the fun of it. He said yes, and it was fun. Since the Mazatec villages are in the northern mountainous region of Oaxaca, they are often separated by valleys or deep ravines, so in order to be able to communicate over the distances, they have developed a complex messaging system that uses whistling as a means of communication (Weitlaner and Hoppe 1969).

Arnulfo, like Francisca, does not perceive that his indigenous background has been any kind of hindrance to his life or well-being. He does not feel that he has been a victim of racism but that he has had to learn how to live through very harsh economic conditions. The hurdles he has had to confront have been class differences, not race. Arnulfo's use of social class in his stories is in terms of his own experiences, which is not necessarily the same as the political concept of class used in Marxism or leftist politics in Mexico, though there is some similarity. When we asked him years ago why there was so much poverty in Mexico, he said it was because of the greed of the rich, and his answer to why the poor did not rebel was that the poor did not own any tanks or airplanes. Arnulfo left his village because he did not see that he had much of a future there beyond continuous hard work in the fields for little or no economic gain. At that time, to leave his village he had to walk most of the way to the city of Oaxaca. There were no roads into the area of his village. He came to the city in his early teens, and although he left his village to avoid hard work in the fields, he ended up having to do hard work in the city in his early years. When he came to the city he did not speak Spanish, so he was limited to odd jobs, such as domestic work or construction. He learned a little Spanish while working when people would tell him to get something or go somewhere. Through these kinds of interactions, he began to learn more Spanish. At this time he was working as a helper in a company that bought and sold pottery. Also at this time he began going to night school. He said that he would have to get up about four in the morning and make coffee for all the other workers and the boss, then they would pick up and deliver pottery all day long, and then at night he would go to school. He said that this was a very hard and sad time in his life because all he did was work and go to school. He does not see that he was prevented from doing anything because he was an Indian; to him the problem was that he did not speak Spanish.

9. *Arnulfo Alvarez and Francisca Guzmán. Photo by Johanna Liebsch.*

10. *Berta Alvarez.*
Photo by Johanna Liebsch.

In his early twenties he got a job selling Popsicles in the street. He liked the work because it was outdoors, it was not physically too hard, and he enjoyed meeting and talking with people as he sold his goods. He thinks that this helped him become a better person because he learned how to communicate and to make a good presentation of himself. He feels that his greatest accomplishment is that he has worked hard and honestly and that he has been able to pass these values on to his children. He now feels that there is a great deal of poverty in Mexico because people have no hope and no means for change. He sees politics as a game of promises but not commitments or accomplishments. He tells a story of how when there was a conflict with the city over the land in the *colonia* where they now live—Colonia de los Maestros—he went to the PRD to get help. He said that he helped organize a barrio meeting that folks from the PRD were going to come to, and then they did not show up. He tried again and got the same results. Though, like many, he finds the PRI to be corrupt, he does not find that the opposition is any better in dealing with poor folks. He finds it very sad that so many men do not work and are drunks. He feels that he was always a good worker and salesperson because he knows how to be humble and friendly (see photos 9, 10, and 11).

11. Alejandro and Ofelia and their children, Alejandro, Manuel, and Carla. Photo by Tanya Coen.

THE ADULT CHILDREN

NICOLÁS

Nicolás is the oldest son of Arnulfo and Francisca. He is thirty-six and is married to María Cristina, who is thirty. They have three children— Marcos, age fourteen; Víctor, age twelve; and Marta, age eight. They live in the old family *"solar"* (a common housing area) in Colonia Linda Vista. Nicolás is an auto mechanic and has his own repair shop in the center of the city. When he was around ten years old he got a job as a bus driver's helper, and from then on he has been involved with working on cars and motors. In his early teens he moved to Mexico City to learn more about being a mechanic and then returned to Oaxaca to start his own business. His wife, Cristina, currently does not work, and all the children are in school.

Nicolás was a hard worker as a teenager, and he is not remembered by his parents as being a difficult child. Because he and his family still live in Colonia Linda Vista, he is not around the new housing compound as much as the others. He has an *onda* that is very much part of the urban popular culture of Oaxaca, especially in terms of male styles. His business has put him into contact with various sectors of the city and a mixed group of working-class and middle-class guys has formed around the repair shop for a late-afternoon drinking club. They get together to drink, bullshit, and enjoy themselves. This is a very male scene; the only "females" present are the nudes on the calendars decorating the walls. The language style of the club is a mixture of bravo stories about life in general and flights of fancy as to what they think women want and how they could give it to them. Often they will talk about politics, but more in the nature of how shitty the government is and how fucked up the economy is. There is no discussion of political action or involvement with political parties.

Except for his male bravo talk, Nicolás does not speak much about issues of gender or sexuality in terms of his personal life or in terms of his family. Also he does not speak about or see himself as an ethnic mixture of Zapotec and Mazatec cultures. He does, however, see himself as a working stiff getting stiffed by the bad economy. That is, he has a general social-class perspective that frames his various worldviews more than race or ethnicity does. He is a good-natured fellow who has put together a reasonable lifestyle for his family. He hopes that his children will do well, that they will be more than a mechanic, though he finds nothing wrong with his work—he just wants more for his kids. He does not talk much about his feelings toward his wife, either positive or negative. We know her only from interactions at family events, all fairly ordinary.

ALEJANDRO

Alejandro is the second son. He is thirty-three and is married to Ofelia, who is forty. They have three children: Alejandro and Manuel, who are nine-year-old twins, and Carla, who is two. Alejandro is the only remaining son who is involved in the Popsicle business, and Ofelia has worked as a cook in several local restaurants but is currently not working because they have no one to watch their youngest child. Alejandro, like other members of the family, is somewhat quiet but has a sharp sense of humor and often is more aware of current political and social issues than other members of the household. Several years ago he went to Los Angeles for a year to work and still has a wish to return. Though the Popsicle business makes enough profit to keep the family household solvent, it does not generate a large surplus. Alejandro would still like to return to the States to make more money.

During the last presidential elections in Mexico, he suggested that he was going to vote for the Green Party that was on the ballot. What made this comment interesting was not whether he would actually vote for the Green Party but that he knew something about this party and knew that the Green Party was interested in ecological issues. The Green Party in Mexico is a very small party, bravely attempting to develop an ecological voice on the national political scene. Its base is primarily in Mexico City, and currently it has no real base in the urban popular barrios of Mexico. Alejandro's expression of support for the Green Party is an illustration of his ironic sense of humor; the political system is so fucked up that one might as well vote for the most obscure party in the race. It is also an illustration of his interest in political issues: he was aware of this party in the first place.

Like his older brother, he does not talk much about gender and sexual issues and the requirements of safe sex; the fact that he has married an older woman suggests that he has views that are somewhat different from traditional "macho" assumptions. He is aware of the world of male prostitutes and understands the logic of active and passive male sex roles, though he offers no personal experience. The family's conservative approach to talking about gender and sex is somewhat amusing considering that their cousins on their father's side are the owners of one of Oaxaca's better-known whorehouses.

Ofelia is quite an open person; she likes to talk and likes to work. She has been a cook in several of the local restaurants over the years but found that working and taking care of their children is too much for her now. She wants to go back to work when she can, or she would like to put together a small food-vending enterprise in the *colonia*. She did not like the time that Alejandro spent in the States and is not too eager for him to return. She found that it was very hard on the whole family for him to be gone, and for all the effort that was put into that adventure, they did not gain very much economically from it.

BERTA

Berta is the only daughter in the family. She is twenty-nine, single, and a midget. She is very funny, quite articulate, and caught between a supportive family and her desires to go off on her own. The supportive-family context is not just the result of her being a midget; given the overall size of everyone in this family, she is not that much shorter, though it is clear that she is different in her body form. It is also the result of her position as the single daughter left in the household, and Francisca encourages her to stay at home to take care of it and some of the grandchildren while she works at the Popsicle *taller* (workshop) or travels to her village.

Berta attended primary and secondary school and has taken some computer classes, and she would like to take more classes if she had the money. She states that she has not confronted prejudice or discrimination because of her body size. She does not remember being teased or made fun of as a kid by other kids. She has a wide range of friends who are of regular body size. She likes to go clubbing with her friends and suggests she is quite a party person. In fact, she was the one who told us that it was her cousins who were the owners of Casa Blanca (a *cantina* and whorehouse). She is also well versed in the overall family gossip and history. She was the one who told us about the near-separation of Francisca and Arnulfo. She is aware of the complex sexual diversity that exists in Oaxaca and has no qualms about it. She does not offer many comments on sexism, but sometimes she suggests that her family's protective attitude toward her is more because of her gender than her size. She does not like to work at the Popsicle *taller* and thus accepts tending to the house in lieu of working there. She suggests that she would like to get a job in town and that's why she needs more computer classes. She also has stated a desire to go to the United States, either to Los Angeles or to Houston. She does not express any kind of indigenous identity, though she likes to go to her mother's village for the fiestas. Like the rest of the children, she does not speak either Zapotec or Mazatec.

SANTIAGO

Santiago is the second youngest son and is twenty-four, married to Minerva, who is also twenty-four, and they have two daughters—Beatriz, age eight, and Minerva, age two. Santiago works as a traveling salesperson for an auto-parts store. That is, he drives around supplying auto-parts stores throughout the state. Minerva currently is not working. They live with Minerva's parents, next door to Francisca and Arnulfo. They are building on to that house to have their own home. Though there is no tension that we have noted between Santiago and the family, they tend to spend more time in Minerva's house than over with his parents. What is interesting is that Minerva's family is Mixe, an indigenous group from the sierra of Oaxaca. As with his parents, this was not a marriage linking two ethnic groups; it was just a coincidence that both have an indigenous family history.

GERALDO

Geraldo is the youngest son. He is twenty-three and is married to Gabriela, who is twenty-one, and they have an eight-month-old son named Geraldo. Geraldo and Gabriela have been married for about two years, and they live in the family compound with Francisca, Arnulfo, Alejandro, and Ofelia. Geraldo had been one of the working partners in the Popsicle *taller*, but now he is working with Santiago in the car-parts vending business. He is quite a social and insightful young man. Gabriela is quiet, which may be because she is the youngest and newest member of this household.

   Here we would like to present some of Geraldo's views on growing up in the *colonias* and on current issues in the social life of Oaxaca.

> Sure, there are a lot of youth gangs, or cliques, in Oaxaca. They say that currently gangs put on punk rock dances by the general cemetery. Since the dances are in very *humilde* houses, these houses are called *cartonlandia* (the land of cardboard houses). In fact, I think that one of the gangs in this *colonia* uses that name. I belonged to a *banda* here in the *colonia*; we called ourselves Los Güeros. In fact, I still see guys in the group once in a while. We all had nicknames for each other, and we would just party or run around together, nothing

too heavy. We were not a very conflictive *banda*; we did not go looking for fights. The more conflictive groups hung around the market
area. You can tell the *bandas* that want to be seen as real tough; they
like to talk in *calo,* the slang they learn in jail. Though to be frank, our
banda would get into fights sometimes. A few years ago, here in this
colonia, the *bandas* started fighting over what each claimed was its
territory. If conflicting *bandas* were at the same parties or dances,
there were often fights. During this time there was a dance here in the
colonia where a fight broke out and a guy was stabbed and he died. I
was not there, but my cousin Juan was, and he told me about it. The
banda of the guy that got stabbed broke up after that. There were also
bandas around Linda Vista and El Fortín—they actually formed into
an association of some kind, but I do not think that it still exists.

Now, *poros,* that is something different than *bandas. Poros* are paid
rough guys who work for different factions within the university, and
they send their *poros* after the other *poros* to fight. That can get quite
heavy.

I like living here in the Colonia de los Maestros. This is where my
friends are from and where I met my wife. I know that some folks
think that people in the *colonias* are rough or crude, but it is not so.
I do not feel that I have encountered any discrimination because of
being from this *colonia.* The rents in the center of the city are high,
and people move out into the *colonias* because it is cheaper. For example, there was this woman who recently moved in near us, and she
thought that everyone here was going to be some kind of rough type,
but after a while she found out that people here were open and
friendly, and in fact now she has become friends with us.

I think we all live together fairly well; we had a lot of time to learn,
that's for sure. We have hassles or misunderstandings, but we know
how to talk about them with each other. I do not think that I will stay
at the *taller* much longer. I'll do some work where I can make more
money, maybe something in selling.

There is still racism here, or for sure discrimination against people from the *campo*. I think this is wrong; we are all equal. That's true of *jotas* (slang word for gays) also. They should not be hassled either. There are gay clubs now in Oaxaca—one is called the Cotton Club or something like that. I have gone there with my friends and there were no hassles. There are gay beauty contests in Oaxaca, and last week at a party here in the *colonia* a guy came dressed as a woman. He or she danced with everyone and we all had a good time—it was no big deal.

I am not too much into politics; it is all pretty shitty. The Zapatistas seem to be attempting to do something positive for the *indígenas*—at least they are talking to them and that's more than others do. But again, it is like I said before—stereotyping folks is wrong. Like that 187 [the anti-immigrant amendment] in California. That is wrong. It has generated an anti-gringo feeling for sure. You cannot put everyone in the same category—that just reduces our understandings of each other.

THE FAMILY SAZÓN
Recipe from Ofelia, the wife of Alejandro

■ ■ ■ ■ ■ ■ ■ ■ ■ ■

PORK COOKED IN BEER

Ingredients
1 kilo pork steak
1 or 2 large onions
salt
beer
peppercorns and oregano as you like

Preparation
1. Mix salt and oregano in oil and fry.
2. Chop onions and cook until onions are soft and clear.
3. Cut up pork and add to the mixture and sauté until almost cooked.
4. Add beer and peppercorns al gusto.

SUMMARY

How do we summarize these stories? First, we hope that these families seem ordinary in their own particular ways. For us, all of the actors here have struggled with composing themselves within what they hold to be traditional roles. Unlike social scientists (Rosaldo 1993), however, these folks have composed their traditionalism in an open and fluid manner rather than in a static or rigid manner.

María Elena and her family express many assumptions that could be viewed as traditional in some sense. Certainly María Elena expresses very traditional values in terms of gender, ethnicity, and class. Her assumptions about gender roles and social class on the surface seem quite traditional, and her views about race and ethnicity—to be kind—could be called traditional. However, the style and substance of her *onda* are not traditional at all. Her upbringing on the Oaxacan coast was a complex process of growing up in a highly class-stratified rural social setting, where she was part of the second family of her father. She married early and got herself out of that rural context into the emerging urban popular class of Oaxaca. She had an openly confrontational relationship with her late husband, and although she clearly states her love for him, that experience of marriage was enough for her. Her celibacy is not based upon respect for the memory of her husband but on her commitment to protect and maintain her relations with her adult children. She feels that her hard work in her life has earned her the right to tell the world what she thinks of it and to say it very loudly. Again, what she thinks is a mixture of various values and concerns. She is not political in a formal sense, but she has keen insight into the particularities of contested locations in everyday life. In fact, she approaches everyday life as a battle. Though her everyday speech can be cruel and condemning of others, her everyday behavior is cordial and respectful. In the popular classes of Oaxaca, race is seen more in terms of social class than as a biological reality. That is, it is thought that one's social status can change through migration and learning Spanish. This popular myth of limited social advancement is what frames María Elena's views on race and ethnicity. She has recomposed various different religious elements into her own reading of the Virgen de Juquila as her personal protector and Señor de Reyes (the Lord God) as an overall moral enforcer for her private and public life. Thus, she uses the traditional religious discourse not only for her now-emerging spiritual concerns but also as a pragmatic means of dealing with the material world.

She thinks that her children share her values, especially her daughters, and they do. That is, though they are somewhat different from their mother, they would suggest that they live ordinary lifestyles. And their ordinary lives are as confrontative and as innovative about dealing with everyday life as their mother's traditional ways have been. Her three living adult sons are quite diverse in their lifestyles: Alberto is a construction worker, Arturo is a captain in the army, and Víctor is now an artisan worker. Chabela got married and divorced young, remarried, and is now a widow. In both of these marriages she worked and led her own life besides that of being a wife. Rosa got married late, has one child and no plans for more. Teresa is a nurse and is now married with two children. And Alma—the youngest—has the most traditional marriage—if that means being taken care of and not having to work.

Victoria's *onda* on the surface looks very traditional and, as she has aged, she has come to look like the classic grandmother, which she is not. Victoria's birth was the result of her mother's being the second wife in her relationship with her father, and she ended up being the second wife in her two relationships, having three sons. She grew up in the rural area on the border between the states of Oaxaca and Puebla. Her memories are not of happy times, however, but of a harsh home environment with her mother and other relatives, whose lives were also filled with hardship. She suffered through a horrific experience as her mother buried another young woman as her, and then years later she helped her mother die a death that had some degree of dignity. Her first husband died and left her nothing, whereas she abandoned her second husband and was able to attach his wages. She has forged a level of solidarity with her sons that makes it hard for their wives to know where they fit in. She, too, has composed a life of celibacy as a practical solution to maintaining her relationship with her children, and like María Elena, she has used her spirituality as a practical discourse to help her in her everyday life.

Victoria has a popular-class worldview of politics in terms of the wealthy against the poor, but she, also like María Elena, supports the overall position of the PRI. She often frames her general opinions in terms of what one of her sons has said, generally Víctor, but expresses her own strong voice in terms of her personal concerns and achievements. She is righteously proud of what they have all accomplished, since they started with so little, but she does not show much solidarity with her daughters-in-law in terms of how her sons' behavior in these relationships could engender similar living conditions for the grandchildren. She does admonish her sons to remember how hard their lives were, and she asks them if they want their children to live like that, but the critique is about the outcome, not their behavior. She suggests that it is the wife's responsibility to prevent such negative outcomes.

Victoria does recognize that male privilege can engender harsher living conditions for women and children, and she also thinks that males can be persuaded to behave in such a manner that they use that privilege in an honorable way. However, she accepts that men—including her sons—will be men, and she encourages her daughters-in-law to put their needs as secondary to the needs of their husbands. Yet she herself accepted one relationship as the second wife and ended her second relationship because she no longer would be the second wife.

Víctor, Gabino, and Claudio struggle with the identities they have composed. Víctor fits very few of the Mexican stereotypes about macho men, but he is uncontestably Mexican. It's not that Víctor is so different from other men but that perhaps the male stereotype is more atypical than it is the norm. Gabino has an *onda* of being frustrated in terms of his quests for achievement (wanting more schooling) and his efforts to earn enough money to maintain his extended family obligations. He is funny, well informed, and articulate. Like his brother, Claudio, he expresses an informal style of presentation of self that struggles with the emotional dynamics of being male in the context of shifting sites of gender and sexuality within the popular sectors of Oaxaca. Claudio is quite similar, except he does not seem to express a frustration of achievements; rather he seems frustrated from not understanding the quest of intimacy and family obligations. At this writing, he and his wife are struggling to maintain their relationship. She is demanding more autonomy for herself, which is criticized by Victoria, but at least Claudio, within all his confusion of behavior, is attempting to listen.

Both these stories are about what sociologically could be referred to as female single-headed households. But as should be self-evident, that would be only a bare-boned metaphor for what are two very diverse tales of the social history of urban poor households (Finkler 1994; LeVine 1993). None of these folks has consistent or fixed identities—like everyone else in this postmodern world, they are struggling with their identities within the contested sites of their everyday lives. They navigate their way through the terrains of the situated knowledges of sexuality, class, race/ethnicity, gender, and age like everyone else does. And for them, as for many others, these contestations are framed in the material history of their social conditions. They move back and forth between general and specific understandings of their behavior, which they use to interpret the struggles of social composition in their everyday lives.

The Rodríguezes' household looked like a family that was on the other side of poverty and seemed to be a family that would have an easy time as they moved toward a more middle-class lifestyle. However, as their stories suggest, life is full of twists and turns that one cannot anticipate. The children thought they were growing up in a household that was stable, only to learn that in fact their parents were staying together only for them, and then only for the oldest ones. Though they were a family that did a lot together, the children felt that there was an absence of closeness in their personal relationships and that their parents' separation has actually made them feel closer. The children looked to marriage and leaving their household as a means of moving toward their own lives, but in the case of Cristy and Alma, tragedy shattered that hope, and they, like many others, have learned that marriage brings many new dilemmas that they had not anticipated. Clearly, all the children from this household have developed a sense of tolerance in the areas of racial and sexual issues, whereas their concerns in terms of public political issues are very mainstream.

Juan married Lucía, hoping that he would have a loving and simple wife; however, he never seemed to ask Lucía if that's what she had in mind. They both feel that they have endured a difficult relationship that fell apart for lack of love. Juan now feels he has found a temporary love that he is gambling his emotions on, whereas Lucía is attempting to pursue her own life, interwoven now with helping her widowed daughters, but she shows no interest in having another relationship herself.

The persons in this household are all smart, very articulate, and cosmopolitan. They will endure these current crises of personal trauma and move in the directions that they have envisioned. However, they have certainly lost the assumption of ease with which they thought these journeys would transpire. Maybe they have made it into the ordinariness of middle-class lifestyles. Though this is the family that would have seemed least traditional in comparison to the others in the *colonia*, this is the family that is in fact living out what are perhaps the traditional patterns of household dynamics in the postmodern world.

Francisca and Arnulfo's household thirty years ago looked like a family that would at best survive while moving ahead, though in fact they have moved ahead and now struggle to maintain what they have accomplished. Ironically, they would have the most social material to use to maintain traditional values in terms of their respective ethnic heritage, but they in fact have merged such concerns into a general lifestyle of urban popular groups. They do not see themselves as victims of racial discrimination, nor do their children, who recognize racism as it affects people in the countryside, not themselves. As in the other families, their political concerns are centered more on economic issues than civil issues, and also like the others, their public political involvement is limited and in no way radical.

Francisca and Arnulfo's adult children have so far all been successful in their various pursuits. If the family expresses positions that are traditional, it would be in the area of gender and sexuality in that they do not talk about it much. In other social domains, however, their behavior does not fit into any particular patterns that would be traditional per se. Francisca and Arnulfo have a functional partnership at this point in their lives, but it is hardly a traditional one. Alejandro is married to a woman older than he is, and Berta has stayed single, whereas the rest of the siblings at this point in their lives are involved in marriage patterns that seem to be stable. Within all this supposed tradition, however, are cousins who run one of the better-known whorehouses in the city, and when one of these cousins died, his funeral was a major gathering for the sex workers of Oaxaca, and his mother, a monolingual speaker of Mazatec, attended in her traditional indigenous clothing.

These households can be labeled as extended families or households in terms of generational and residential connections. Again, however, such a label would be only a minimalist expression of the dynamics involved with these social actors.

There is not much that is similar between the two households except in terms of how they struggle to understand themselves in the context of their everyday lives. Both Francisca and Arnulfo, as well as their children, are proud of their indigenous heritage, but these are identities that they use to compose their futures, not to protect their pasts. Juan and Lucía have raised vigorous and healthy children to adulthood, not through some kind of tradition of togetherness but by living through its opposite.

One interesting theme, which will also appear in other stories in this book, is the absence of tales of being victims. There are many reasons for their choice of avoiding that theme in their stories. The persons in these stories know that they are to be part of this book, so it is possible that they could be wishing to put things in the best light, thus giving positive stories preference over negative stories. However, since we have known them for more than thirty years, we do not think that they are doing this. They are not telling only positive stories; they are giving accounts of painful and difficult periods in their lives. For various reasons of the social dynamics of identity composition among the popular classes of Oaxaca, the "trope" of being a victim is currently not a dominant mode of expression. From María Elena to Berta, their stories are neither tales of victimization nor sunny tales that everything is fine. What is present is their stories of how they confront the realities of everyday life as they understand them and then act upon those understandings. They are expressing, from our point of view, the ordinariness of their diversity.

CHAPTER THREE

We Are
Not Lesbians!

Grupo Unión: Homosexual
Transvestite Prostitutes in
Urban Oaxaca

Women are just lazy! They do not like to spend the time fixing their hair or doing their makeup right. It takes a lot of time, and you have to work very hard at it. It's all part of how you develop your look.

—Debra Blanca and Iracema Gura, male transvestite homosexual prostitutes, talking about their views on women while standing on their street corner waiting for clients

INTRODUCTION

The Días de los Muertos are during the last days of October in Oaxaca and the rest of Mexico. The city of Oaxaca is famous for having one of the strongest traditional celebrations of Días de los Muertos. These days involve various activities that range from cleaning the graves of relatives to large fiestas that take place in and around the cemeteries in the city (Norget 1996). We were visiting the new cemetery out near where we lived. There was a carnival with games, vendors, and large mechanical rides outside the cemetery. It was quite crowded inside the cemetery, with people cleaning the gravesites of family or friends and having small parties at the gravesides. As we were looking around, we saw a group of casually dressed "women" gathered around a gravesite. When we got closer, we heard a couple of them hollering at us, "Hey, *güeros*, come on over and have a drink of mescal." As we approached the group, it was clear that these "women" were guys in drag. Sitting down and talking with them, we quickly learned that they were indeed drag queens and that they were there to clean and visit the grave of their friend Cristina. They proceeded to inform us that they were passive gay men who dressed as women and worked as street prostitutes. Further, they stated that they were organized into a group that they referred to as Grupo Unión Lucha Prevención de Enfermedades Transmisibles—HIV-SIDA (Union for the Prevention of Transmittable Sexual Illness—HIV-AIDS). They had organized themselves into this group to struggle for the right to work the streets and to deal with AIDS education with their clients and in public forums. They were open and friendly and encouraged us to visit with them, indicating that they would be interested in working with us on our general ethnographic project. We said we would be seeing them, and so we have for the last several years. Since we were interested in including the gay world of Oaxaca in our research, being invited to hang with a group of organized male transvestite prostitutes seemed a fortuitous gift on this Day of the Dead.

GRUPO UNIÓN

Prostitution exists in a kind of legal never-never land in Oaxaca. It is neither legal nor illegal. To work as a prostitute either in a cabaret or on the street, however, one needs to have a health book from the public health service that certifies that s/he is in good health, including being HIV-negative. Grupo Unión claims to be the first group of male prostitutes to have gained the right to carry such a health book. How they gained this right is part of the story of this group. According to members of the group, drag queens started working on the streets of Oaxaca about ten years ago, where they met resistance from the police, the city government, and female prostitutes. This came to a crisis level with the death of Cristina, who was arrested by the police, severely beaten, and later died from the beatings—it was her grave they were visiting during Días de los Muertos. The police claimed that s/he had died of AIDS, but her friends had an autopsy done, and it strongly suggested that s/he had died from being beaten. This forced many of the drag queens to organize themselves against police harassment and to learn about AIDS in order to protect their health and ensure that it wouldn't be used against them. Under the leadership of Leslie, Grupo Unión was formed and has been operating for about five years. So who are the folks in this group that we came to call the *chicas*?

The group is composed of eight to fifteen people, most of whom have known each other over the last five years as friends and as sex workers. Leslie is the leader of the group. (Since they use feminine pronouns in their everyday conversation, we will follow that pattern.) She is in her early thirties, very articulate and cosmopolitan. She grew up in northern Mexico and has been living in Oaxaca for about ten years. She is quite attractive and is the uncontested leader. Leslie's roommate, Tania, in her mid-twenties, is quite verbally quick and likes to act as second in command of the group because she lives with Leslie. They are not lovers, a fact that we will explain shortly. Debra, who is from the Pacific Coast region of Oaxaca, is also in her mid-twenties; Vicky, from Northern Oaxaca, is in her early twenties and is about to enter law school; Iracema, who is in her late twenties, is from the eastern part of the state of Oaxaca and has been in the city for about five years; Alejandra, who is in her early twenties, grew up in the city of Puebla and has only been working the streets for a couple of years. Yanine is also young, in school, and has a very classy "look." Susana is the oldest member of the group and has been a prostitute for the longest. Susana proudly boasts, "I was born a whore and I will die one."

Though these *chicas* are part of the overall gay scene of Oaxaca, the fact that they are both transvestites and prostitutes gives them a particular *onda* in their everyday activities. They all define themselves as passive male homosexuals, which means that they do not penetrate their partners or clients; instead, they are penetrated by their partners or clients. They also all express acceptance and pride for their gender and their sexual orientation. When we first met Leslie and Tania at their apartment, we were thinking with North American sexual logic and thus we asked them if they were lovers. They both shouted, "No, we are not lovers; we are not lesbians!" Though they expressed acceptance of both their gender and their sexuality, they also said they all prefer to dress and act like women. And concurrently, they said that the best way to maintain such a lifestyle was by working as prostitutes (see photo 12).

12. *Grupo Unión, 1995.*
Photo by Jason Holland.

Working the Streets of Oaxaca

So what is an ordinary day like for the members of Grupo Unión? As one would guess, since they are prostitutes, their ordinary "days" involve nights on the streets of Oaxaca. Through organizing as a group, they have laid claim to a street corner about four blocks from the *zócalo*. They work from around midnight to five or six in the morning, depending on the number of clients. They do not work in competition with each other, and they have no *patrónes* (pimps). They take their clients to a hotel on the street they work, where they have a deal with the owner for special rates and protection. Each "trick" is for half an hour, and they claim that, depending on services performed and their particular skills, they can earn anywhere from 80 pesos to 150 pesos per client.[1] On a good night, they may have five or six clients. They will give oral sex (but will not receive it), masturbate a client, do *beso negro* (anal kissing), and *chapiar* (have anal sex)—the most expensive activity. They stated that only about half their clients request to penetrate them. They inform all their clients that they are males and that they will not have sex without condoms. For the right price they will do group sex, but not across gender lines; that is, they will have sex with several men or be part of sex with men and women, but they will not have sex with women. They are sometimes contracted for special events.

Before they go to work, there is a long process of getting ready, which in many ways is a transforming ritual for them as they make themselves over from their day look (which for them is looking like a guy) to developing the "look" that they will use on the street that night. They try to put on different outfits and looks each night. It generally takes three or four hours for them to get ready, depending on what look they are seeking for that evening. They tend to get up around midday or later. They use the afternoons to deal with necessities of the day: shopping, cooking, cleaning, visiting with each other, and drinking. Around six or seven in the evening they will take their showers and shampoo their hair. Then they proceed to deal with their hair. Most of the them do not use wigs, so they have to set, tease, and make their hair do what they want for that evening. While their hair is in rollers and drying, they begin the makeup/makeover process. This can take an hour or two, depending on the person's style and what she has to cover up. None of them have much facial hair, so covering their beards is not a problem. They first put on their base makeup, then toners; this is followed by doing their eyes and then their lips. They all have extensive makeup kits and feel quite proud of their work. When all the makeup is done, they decide on the dress and accessories for the night. They are then ready for the street.

For them this makeup/makeover is seen as a form of labor time investment. That is, the makeup/makeover process is viewed as work time, and it influences their pricing demands. In fact, Leslie states that she does not allow her clients to kiss her because it will ruin her makeup job and cost her time and labor to redo it.

When they have achieved the right "look," they then go off to work. The majority of the *chicas* live within walking distance of their street; the others get there by taxi or other means of transportation. In Oaxaca (also most of Mexico) people are paid bimonthly, so every fifteen days they have their biggest nights in terms of volume. Depending upon their own particular economic needs, most of them work five or six nights a week, generally taking Sundays and Mondays off. Depending on their preferences or moods, they will space themselves on the four corners of the intersection that they work. Most clients drive by in cars and negotiate the services they seek and the prices they would like to pay. Like many commercial interactions in Oaxaca, it is a barter system. When not with clients, the *chicas* stand on the corner joking and drinking with each other and whistling and shouting at cars going by to draw attention to themselves, something they really do not have to worry about.

While they are waiting for tricks to appear, they like to talk among themselves, and they love to talk about themselves and their work. They have a very bravo attitude about the future; they live for the now—life is to be enjoyed in the present; the future is not something to worry about. They offer a hedonistic justification for their work: it is a job that is not too hard, and they can earn the kind of money that allows them to maintain themselves in a fashion they feel is required for drag queens. They seem to think their options are either prostitution or some kind of working-class job.

They see themselves as real professional sex workers. Their style of sex work is based on trying to provide good services to their clients. They claim that they get pleasure from the work if the guys are good-looking or good at lovemaking. They admit that often you get really ugly guys, but that's part of the job also. Three of the *chicas* are in "permanent" relationships with men they refer to as lovers or husbands, and they claim there is no tension with their husbands or lovers over their work. Leslie says that her husband

(Adrián) knows that this is the work of her body and not her heart. Further, she states: "Since I met him as a client, he certainly knows what I do."

They also talk about the problems of violence and harassment while working on the street and take the view that it is just part of their lifestyle. They all have various stories of being in fights or being attacked by clients with guns or knives, and they tell of how they successfully fought such attacks. Their main weapon is their high-heeled shoes. One night when we were with them on the street, Susana, who is physically the largest and strongest of the group, provided a good example of their response to such problems. While we were standing around with them and some possible clients, a short male started hollering and wanted more attention; they told him to calm down and get to getting. He persisted, and finally Susana just picked him up and threw him out of the way.

Their presentation of self on the street is very positive. They are quite egocentric about themselves and their worldviews. They boldly state that they are very proud of who they are and what they are sexually. They do not express interest in sex-change operations. They state that they are comfortable with who they are. At times they will say that they are not men or women; they are homosexuals. For them, being gay means that they are the passive partner in sex between two men. That is, the one who is penetrated anally is the passive actor, thus the gay person in the activity. They do not penetrate or seek to have any particular kind of genital stimulation for themselves. They perceive those "gays" who are both active and passive as bisexual.

In terms of slang phrases, they will refer to themselves as *maricones, chotos, jotos,* and most often, when talking about each other, *putas* (whores). They refer to their clients as *mayates,* or *mariachis,* their diminutive word for *mayate.* The word *mayate* has a fascinating social history. It often means an active gay male or one who penetrates. It can also refer to a very masculine male who is involved in some kind of street hustle, including sex, crime, and sometimes violence. The *chicas* use it further to refer to their clients and sometimes their lovers. The actual word is a Nahuatl word for dung beetle, a bug that eats shit (Prieur 1996). Interestingly, among Mexicans and Chicanos in the United States, it is a negative word used to refer to blacks; it is, in fact, the slang word for "nigger." It is interesting that in Oaxaca *mayate,* a sexual metaphor that connotes an ambiguous sentiment toward gay sexuality, gets transformed in the migrant social context to a racial slur.

The *chicas* refer to the penis as *pene, pito, pájaro, verga, plátano* (a big banana), and *camote* (a sweet potato). They themselves do not masturbate, but they will masturbate a client or watch as a client masturbates. In terms of their own sexual involvement and enjoyment, they do not seek either erections or ejaculations, though sometimes that will happen during anal sex. They often express a kind of polymorphic sexual pleasure in terms of not being interested in their own ejaculations. They enjoy a wide range of sexual pleasures: kissing, hugging, and so on. Though they define themselves as passive actors in terms of penetration, they do not see themselves as passive in terms of their sexual encounters. They see themselves as very *caliente* (hot)—they enjoy getting sexually excited; they like to introduce their clients to new styles of sex (within their definitions), such as *beso negro* (anal kissing) and oral sex. They think that men are more attracted to them because they will do more things than straight women. They do not totally undress for their clients, or if they do, it costs a lot more and they will keep a towel over their own genitals. They think that female prostitutes have more options to offer men but that females are not better at sexual variety. Older female prostitutes sell sex for 20 to 40 pesos a half hour; the *chicas* say that they can get up to 150 pesos for the same length of time. They think that female prostitutes (or females in general) do not know how to value themselves very well. Female prostitutes, according to them, "don't put enough effort into fixing themselves up and creating an attractive look." The *chicas* think that female prostitutes think that just being a woman will be enough to attract clients.

They all have different preferences in terms of the type of client they like. Leslie is wild about *güeros* (light-skinned males), and she is especially fond of Germans. Iracema likes dark-skinned Mexicans best and thinks that *güeros* are too light, in fact almost translucent. They all think that blacks and Latinos from the Caribbean are very "*caliente*" and that the Japanese have been their strangest clients (see photos 13 through 18).

Events of Grupo Unión
THE SHOW

The members of Grupo Unión like to put on shows, as they call them. They dress up as one of their favorite singers and then perform by lip-synching the songs of the artist. We saw them perform in this style twice during our stay. One time was at the Ms. Gay Oaxaca contest, and the other was a show of sorts in Etla. They had agreed to do a benefit for Renacimiento, an openly

13. *Wendy talking to a client on the street.*
Photo by Joni Kubana.

14. *Vicky and client, 1996.*
Photo by Julia Knop.

gay group that works with people with AIDS. The leader of this group, José Antonio, was a friend of theirs, and they felt it was important to support his projects. Though José Antonio is a dear person who works very hard on helping people with AIDS, his organizational skills are not stellar, and events that he tries to put on do not always come off right. We will talk more about him and his group in chapter 4.

This show took place in April 1995. They had been telling us that they were going to do this show and that it was a benefit to help people with AIDS. First, it was going to be at a local secondary school; then it was going to be at a disco in town; and finally it was to be held in a movie theater/disco in Etla. This was a problem because Etla is about twenty miles outside of the city toward Mexico City. It is a small town of around 15,000, which is known for its weekly market and Easter festivals, not for drag queen shows. This would have been all right, but neither José nor the members of the group had any form of transportation besides us, and there had been no publicity beyond those we had told. We had to take José's group out to the theater (a half-hour drive) and return to the city to bring Iracema, Alejandra, and Debra out to the theater. José and the rest of the group came out in taxis, which were quite expensive. They finally arrived at the theater about an hour after the announced time, but since there had been no real publicity, this was not a draw-

15. *Tania and Iracema on the street. Photo by Joni Kubana.*

16. *Vicky on the street, 1996. Photo by Julia Knop.*

17. *Susana on the street, 1996. Photo by Julia Knop.*

back. As the *chicas* were getting ready, they noticed that they had left several of their costumes in the taxi. We took José back to Oaxaca to track down the taxi and get the costumes back, but we never found it.

After all this, the show did go on, though somewhat late even by their standards. All of the *chicas* except Iracema performed. They did Vicky Carr, Ana Gabriel, Selena, and several others with whom we were not familiar. They did solos and duets. The presentations were quite dramatic, and the performers attempted to be provocative as they sang or danced around. They wore very nice costumes, and some of them were pretty good at the lip-synching. Leslie was by far the most talented and professional in these styles. They did two sets that were well received, and then they stayed and danced with the disco crowd—or what there was of it. The show cost twenty pesos, which was not too high, but the only nonlocal people in attendance were us,

18. The hotel that Grupo Unión uses with clients. Photo by Julia Knop.

the group, and José Antonio and his friends. When it was all done, José had made only ten pesos for the whole event. The Grupo Unión's attitude was that "a gig is a gig" and it didn't matter how much money they made or how many people showed up.

THE MARCH ON CITY HALL

In the latter part of July in the city of Oaxaca there is the folkloric celebration called Lunes de Cerro, which is a large festival centered around the presentation of folk dances from the eight ethnic regions of the state of Oaxaca. This big event draws thousands of tourists to the city. During this year's celebration (1996) the members of Grupo Unión were forced off the streets by the city police. The police stated that it was no longer legal for them to work as prostitutes on the streets and that their health books were no longer valid. Well, the *chicas* did not take this restriction passively. They met with officials of the city government over the harassment, and when they did not get the support they were seeking, they staged a march and protest in front of the city hall.

The march was pretty casual, but when they arrived at the city hall, there were about thirty queens in their day look, carrying signs protesting discrimination against sex workers and gays. A meeting had been set up between them and various city officials. The city officials who were present included a representative of the mayor, representatives from the offices of health and human rights, and a liaison official, whose job was to act as a go-between for citizens bringing complaints to the city government. Inside the meeting hall, the city officials sat at a table in front of rows of theater seats that were filled with the queens. Most of those present were from Grupo Unión or from other groups or they were independent sex workers. The police had said that the transvestites were hassling people on the streets and causing public disturbances. The queens stated that maybe some were causing disturbances but they were not, and they wanted to know why the whole group was being hassled for the actions of a few. They pointed out that when some women prostitutes caused trouble on the street, not all of them were forced off the street. The meeting with the city officials was intended to clear up these concerns.

Leslie was not present, but the others were quite articulate and forceful in presenting their claims. They demanded to know why they could not work the streets, why gays in general were being harassed, and what the city was going to do about their concerns. They stated that they had the right to work the streets, that they were working within the legal boundaries (such as having health books), and that they were not hassling others on the streets or being disrespectful to those who lived in the areas where they worked. Wendy (one of the longest-employed male prostitutes in the city) stated that it was being said that they—the queens—should not be working the streets during Lunes de Cerro because it might be bad for tourism. Wendy stated quite forcefully that as a Oaxacan, she had every right to benefit from tourism as much as anyone else did. She also expressed the view that working the streets was their job and being forced off the street was putting them all in an economic bind. She asked why, with the current economic crisis in Mexico, were they being harassed for doing their jobs?

When members of the group address political issues in relation to either their work or their gayness, their main line of argument is that as citizens of Mexico they are due all rights and obligations granted by the constitution. They stress that the constitution of Mexico does not state that gays, prostitutes, or transvestites are not citizens. Thus, they do not seek any kind of special rights, just the rights that everyone else has. This makes the debate not about them but about the formal rights and duties of all citizens.

All of the city officials stated that the positions of the queens were, in fact, correct and valid. They said that if the queens had their health books and worked within the hours the city allowed (from midnight to early morning), then they were in no way attempting to block them from working. They admitted that groups within the local police were the source of the problem and that they had not been able to get a representative from the police to attend this meeting to clarify the police position. They told the queens that they could work that night and gave them phone numbers to call if the police hassled them. The queens said that they would test this arrangement by going back on the streets to work that night. They did, and nothing happened.

Leslie told us later that the problem involved a few officials of the police department and the city who were trying to hassle the queens and that by going public and using the city's system of filing grievances, they had worked out the problem, at least for now. She also thought that they would have to find a way to deal with these other officials to chill them out.

What was ironic about this event was that the current city government is from the opposition conservative party, the PAN, which ran on a platform that stated that it would be more responsive to citizens' concerns than had the PRI. We doubt the government thought that its campaign promises would be tested by a group of organized transvestite prostitutes seeking their legal rights as sex workers.

A Reflective Pause

In terms of doing fieldwork among the urban popular cultures of the city of Oaxaca, the *chicas* were an engaging and clearly fascinating group to get to know. During the entire period of establishing rapport, we visited with Leslie and Tania the most. We would go by their house often, and a few times we went clubbing. Later, as we got to know the rest of the group (we mainly hung around with Iracema, Debra, Alejandra, and Susana), we did the same range of activities with them. We also spent a few nights on the street with them.

Since one of our concerns in this study was to capture in ethnographic detail the patterns of gender and sexuality among the popular classes, the folks in Grupo Unión were quite an attraction. In terms of their everyday lives, they seem to live the kind of ethnographic expressions of socially composed multiple identities that are so vigorously debated within the postmodern discourses of anthropology and the social sciences. For them, however, these were not theoretical debates but expressions of how they use their personal agency to navigate these hegemonic terrains in their daily lives. Our other concern was to illustrate their forms of transgressive behavior without making them too exotic, that is, the new other of urban Oaxaca. They saw themselves as just ordinary folks with a lifestyle somewhat outside the mainstream.

How do we represent the reality of their everyday lives? They were all very engaging individuals, and interacting with them was always a unique experience. For example, though one knew they were men, they did not act like men; nevertheless, they did have access to some forms of male privilege. Though they acted like women, they were not, and they did not see themselves as women, especially in terms of dealing with the realities of being a woman in Oaxaca. They had little or no interest in the daily hassles that women confront both in the streets and in their homes. They did not think sexism or *machismo* was a problem for them. They felt that they were exempted from these problems, which, as men, in fact they were. Further, the type of woman they present themselves as being is a type of woman that many women in Oaxaca no longer desire to be: a woman who knows how to provide pleasure to a male and meet his needs over her own. In addition, even given the fact that they are prostitutes, the way they compose their "look" as women is again a look that many women in Oaxaca are trying to move away from. They draw their image of what women should be and how they present themselves as women not from the fantasies of women but from the fantasies of men—but then again, they are men. It should be noted, however, that when we would just hang out with them, joking, drinking, dancing, or talking, they seemed to be able to create a different gender space that was neither male nor female but simply themselves.

We were struck by how the transvestic component of their lives was composed through play. The amount of time that they devote to their makeovers and the way they enjoy presenting themselves in public spaces—whether in the street or at their shows—is very playful. They play at being women, they play at being men different from the norm, they play with their sexuality as sex workers, and they play at being singers and famous entertainers. Further, many of these social domains where they like to play are areas that many Oaxacans (and others) are often quite timid about entering. Most Oaxacans, when they play with their gender roles or sexuality, do so in the social space of parties or spectacles (carnivals), whereas the *chicas* use their everyday lives as playgrounds for gender and sexuality games. We are not suggesting some kind of infantilization of transvestic behavior, but we believe that this life-style offers to its actors the satisfaction of still having some space to play, in opposition to the restrictive behavioral options within consumer capitalism.

Lancaster suggests that "play is the very quality of action that both en-compasses structure and makes it possible." He asks if it is "so outlandish to suggest that play is the 'matrix of identity,' that very surplus of activity whose consequences entail 'subjects,' 'selves,' and 'groups'?" (Lancaster 1997a:569). He further stresses that play is exhilarating because it is an experience con-trary to routine; we play freely, though within various contexts of power and authority. Play is an actual physical and bodily involvement in the movement through the spaces of normative actions and other possibilities. This all clearly takes place within the material contradictions of everyday life, par-ticularly in terms of the realities of class, race, ethnicity, gender, and sexual-ity. Further, Lancaster sees transvestic behavior as the playground where these contested realities are confronted. He contends that we all use trans-vestic play as we negotiate these domains and test out our own fluidity of identity composition. The transvestites themselves push these social spaces to their most playful contours. Lancaster's argument suggests to us that per-haps in our wish that the *chicas* would have some sense of the actual mate-rial realities of the women they are copying and that they would have some general political feelings of solidarity with other marginalized groups, we were missing the point that perhaps part of what is involved in being a trans-vestite for them is not the actualization of what they are copying but a play-ful and profound demonstration that in fact we can all playfully go beyond the limits of the status quo in these domains, not in the future but now. For us this playing was an illustration of how their "politics of pleasure" ex-pressed forms of their personal agency.[2]

GAY MEN IN THE SEXUAL POLITICS OF OAXACA

Before moving on to present ethnographic sketches of a few of the mem-bers of Grupo Unión, we will explore some of the contextual and concep-tual issues that can be highlighted by their experiences. They are fond of saying that their lifestyles, or *ondas*, involve a "*rompiendo los esquemas*" (breaking of boundaries). But the question remains, Whose *esquemas* are being broken? Though they clearly are breaking some of the boundaries of male sexuality, they are reinforcing certain assumptions about female sexuality and behavior by the glamorous looks they compose. As a means of placing the *chicas* in a larger context, we will present what we see to be aspects of the sexual politics of urban Oaxaca.³

The boundaries between the gendered assumptions of heterosexuality and homosexuality are much more fluid in the context of Oaxaca and in Latin America in general than those usually assumed to be operating in North America (Lancaster 1992). We are talking more about sexual politics of maleness than femaleness. Clearly in talking about one, you are talking about the other, but in the case of Oaxaca, male sexuality is clearly composed on the borders of what North Americans see as the difference between being straight and being gay. Male sexual politics in Oaxaca is composed around the roles of active and passive participants. The active partner is the one who penetrates, while the passive partner is the one who is penetrated. Further, the active partner is not coded or stigmatized as gay, he is perceived as an *hombre/hombre*, a man's man: one who is so macho that he can have sex with both women and men. These active actors are also referred to as *mayates*, as stated earlier. The passive partner is coded as gay—*maricón, joto, puta,* or *vestidas locas.* Carrier (1995), Cornwall (1994), Kulick (1997), Lancaster (1992, 1997a and 1997b), Lumsden (1991), Prieur (1996), and Taylor (1978) have all talked about how in Brazil, Mexico, and Nicaragua, homosexuality is framed in these dynamics of male sexuality in terms of active versus passive partners. This is also true in the context of Oaxaca, where male heterosexuality does not stand in opposition to male homosexuality; they are both components in the general *onda* of male sexuality.

All the members of Grupo Unión describe their sexuality as that of passive gay men. This seems to be the strictest boundary in their sexual discourse. As passive gay men, they will not have sex with other passive gay men. They do not seek or desire genital stimulation for themselves, though they do enjoy providing such pleasure to their lovers. They often say that their penises are only good for peeing. In fact, many keep their genitals covered (sometimes with a towel) during the sexual act. Now, the role of passivity does not mean that they are sexually passive during the activity. They talk about various forms of sexual activities that they enjoy and how they are the instigators of novel sexual acts with their partners or lovers. They see themselves as hot and excitable sexual partners and seek to attain a wide range of sexual pleasures in their roles as the passive partner. For Lancaster, the passive concept is related to feminizing the gay male within this discourse of male sexuality, and it is this feminizing, as much as the gayness, that encourages the stigmatizing. For Lancaster, the social politics of *machismo* involves an economy of values that reinforces patterns of power and control in the terrains of gender and sexuality through valuing aggressive behavior and devaluing passive behavior, with femaleness being the form with the least value. Gayness and femaleness are correspondingly devalued sexual categories (Lancaster 1992). The gay male still derives more privilege than the female, however, for until quite recently, not only was female sexuality labeled as passive, but sexual practices by females were performed passively. The stereotype of women as being sexually conservative and as being the passive recipients of male sexual desire has had a long history. Clearly this is not just Oaxacan or Latin reality; the censoring of female sexuality within Western sexual discourse also has a long and violent history (Spivak 1988). What we are noting is that passive gay males like the members of Grupo Unión are not sexually timid, conservative, or passive during sexual activity. Their passivity is defined by their being penetrated, not by their being passive sexual actors. This discourse does, however, deny for them their own genital stimulation, and it does dictate that they will be coded and stigmatized as gay.

Ironically, this particular male sexual discourse of active/passive partners can be referred to as the "traditional" sexual discourse in the context of Oaxaca and other parts of Mexico. This *ambiente* or social space is where the role playing and game playing between *hombre/hombre, mayates, jotos,* and *putas* takes place. It encourages and feminizes gay males, who often express themselves in a transvestic style of presentation and find that prostitution is a means of maintaining their lifestyle with fewer hassles. This is also the same space where the *hombre/hombre* attains the privileges of sexual pleasure independent of gender and also encourages a form of street hustling that males can use to have passive gays take care of them, or they can use the easily crossed boundaries to hustle the folks from the other side—that is, those gay males who express their sexuality in a style that is referred to in Oaxaca as "internationalist."

The style of being gay as a transvestite does engender forms of social tolerance within the popular classes of Oaxaca. When we told our various friends in Oaxaca that we were working with drag queens, numerous folks expressed that they had either family members or friends who were drag queens and that they found them to be good people who just had their own lifestyle. The *chicas* themselves had wide-ranging social networks that involved many straight people. The current politics of the *chicas* revolves around their struggle to attain rights as sex workers without harassment, and they believe that there should be more social tolerance for their lifestyles. They frame these issues in terms of human rights. When they were lobbying to get the right to work in the streets, they sought the assistance of human rights groups in Oaxaca. We think that one of the reasons for this existing social tolerance of the more "traditional" *onda* of gayness is the fact that their concerns are expressed as human rights and not as either social or civil issues. They are not fighting against job discrimination or seeking legislation on particular civil issues, as is the case in the United States or Europe. Lumsden reviews the history of such civil rights struggles of gays in Mexico D.F., which emerged in the early 1980s and faded because of internal sectarian factions and the overwhelming domination of the economic crisis over all other issues (Lumsden 1991).

This form of conditional social tolerance for gayness has been discussed by Cornwall in terms of Bahia in Brazil (Cornwall 1994); Lumsden, Prieur, and Taylor also state similar ideas on male gays in Mexico (Lumsden 1991; Prieur 1996; Taylor 1978); and Lancaster talks about the same dynamic in Nicaragua. Lancaster's argument is also about the political economy of male sexuality; *hombre/hombre* versus the *cuchón* (the passive gay male in Nicaragua) involves coding male privilege through a hierarchy of values that places the gay male as better than a woman. That is, these boundaries are the edges of the hegemonic terrains that maintain male privilege in relation to capital accumulation, and within that context there are forms of both tolerance and stigmatization. The role of being gay is a stigmatized category that regulates sexuality without placing the actors in closed social categories, and the behavior of passivity carries the stigma, not the persons themselves (Lancaster 1992). It is this separation that allows for the social tolerance and the absence of the levels of hassles and violent expressions that are found in the United States. In the case of Mexico and Oaxaca, harassment of gayness in the public arena often involves the general corruption of police enforcement that allows the police to focus on the gays as a source of bribes in exchange for being left somewhat alone. Currently in Oaxaca, there are no governmental attempts per se at legally harassing gays, as there are in the United States. However, the category of gay—*joto, puta, maricón,* et cetera—is a stigmatized category that is applied to males who do not attempt to affirm their *hombre/hombre* status. We are not saying that there is no homophobia present, only that it is played out in the different historical/cultural discursive spaces of Latin sexuality and gender formation. Being gay in this context is different from, not better than, being gay in those spaces found in the United States. Given the style of this book, we do not wish to enter into a complex debate on these issues, but we strongly encourage readers to explore developments within the discourse of queer theory and the anthropology of sexuality being composed by many insightful scholars (Basilio 1996; Cornwall and Lindisfarne 1994; Greenberg 1988; Lancaster 1997a and 1997b; Leiner 1994; Lumsden 1996; Melhuus and Stolen 1996; Nagle 1997; Oliveira 1989; Phelan 1994; Rubin 1994; Weeks 1995 and 1997).

ETHNOGRAPHIC PORTRAITS OF GRUPO UNIÓN— DIVERSITY WITHIN IDENTITIES
Leslie, Tania, Adrián, and Iridiann

LESLIE

The first ethnographic portrait that we will present is of Leslie and what she defines as her family: Adrián, her husband; Tania, her roommate and friend, whom she refers to as her sister; and Iridiann Leslie—a four-year-old girl whom all three have adopted as their child. Leslie and Tania last year were able to adopt Iridiann from a friend. Tania has legally adopted the child, and all three accept a parental role and obligation to her. We will present a summary of Leslie's and Tania's backgrounds, followed by short narrative accounts about two events in their social lives, and then we will conclude with an interview in which the three of them explain their views on family values and gay lifestyles.[4]

Leslie is in her early thirties and is the leader and counselor for the group. Her strength, insight, and persistence have provided the push behind the members of Grupo Unión's organizing themselves for job protection and building support and cooperation among themselves—the latter part not being that easy, given the wide ranges of personalities that make up this group. Now Leslie has added being a mother and guardian to their adopted child to her responsibilities.

Leslie grew up in Chihuahua in Northern Mexico. She did not talk much about her background in terms of family or class position. The other members of the group told us that she came from a lower-income family. She stated that she was on good terms with her family, though she did not visit or see them very often. She says that she always knew that she was gay and that her first sexual experience was in her early teens. She began working as a prostitute in Chihuahua, and in her early twenties she moved to Oaxaca. She describes her early years as quite hard, both socially and economically. She tells of living in abandoned houses and of numerous hassles on the streets from other prostitutes and the police. It was these experiences and the death of her friend Cristina that provided the impetus for her to form the group.[5]

Currently, Leslie lives in a large two-bedroom apartment with Adrián and Tania, her friend and coworker, and their child. The apartment is on the lower end of the central part of the city, about four blocks from the street corner where they work. It's furnished like many working-class or middle-class households in Oaxaca. They have two large sofas, a large entertainment center with a TV, VCR, stereo, and radio. There are various styles of art on the wall, some quite hip and some very common. There is a large dining room with dining room table and chairs and a large cabinet for dishes. Most of the furniture was new and well within the taste standards of middle-class Oaxacans. The apartment was on the fourth floor of a large apartment building. Leslie and Tania had the nicest apartment of all the *chicas*. As you enter the hallway leading into the apartment, the wall is lined with stuffed animals. Both Leslie and Tania collect them and say that they receive them as gifts from their various clients.

Leslie is a very impressive person. She is very slender, fair-skinned, and quite an impressive dresser. She keeps her hair short, and generally within the color range of blond. Though her formal education is minimal, she has a strong intellect and is the most sophisticated spokesperson for the group. Though she is generally open about her work and her sexuality, her style of presentation is analytical and she, more often than the others, attempts to express her concerns—or those of the group of passive gays—within the overall social and political context of Mexico. She is public about her sexuality and her work. She has appeared on local television as a spokesperson for sex workers, and she has given lectures and interviews on these issues. She has won several beauty contests for drag queens in Oaxaca and Mexico City. Two years ago she got married and had a very large public wedding. She was dressed in white, and her husband was wearing a formal suit. The wedding and reception drew several hundred people and was reported in the national Mexican gay magazine. She does not talk about what she will do after her current career options become more limited with age and changing styles. She maintains her focus on the struggle of current working conditions, and she attempts to open up the social space in Oaxaca for more social tolerance for their lifestyles, or *ondas.*

Leslie considers herself to be a practicing Catholic, and throughout the apartment are the various religious items—saints or virgins, photos or statues—that can be found in many Oaxacan homes. She had a Nativity scene set up at Christmas and feels that her lifestyle is not a contradiction of her belief system. She seeks a quality of life that she feels she has earned by her hard work, the sophisticated manner in which she expresses her sexuality, and the public position that she takes. For her, this is not a position that seeks social or political space for either gays or prostitutes as identity positions, but it is a position that advocates that social and political spaces should include them as part of the overall diversity of these contexts.

Leslie sees herself as a person who is able to create her own social identity by crossing the boundaries of gender and sexuality—"breaking down boundaries," as she expresses it. She feels that she was always gay and, further, that she wanted to dress like a woman at an early age. Like most of the others, she does not want a sex change operation and is content with her sexuality. She likes to be composed as a woman, but she does not have an understanding of what it means to be a female in the context of "real" women's everyday hassles. She feels that everyone should respect women because we are all born of women, and thus we should respect our mothers. Like the others, she feels that in many ways she is better than straight women because she knows how to compose her various looks (her combinations of wardrobes, hairstyles, and makeup), which are more provocative than those of straight women, and she is not timid in terms of her sexual expressions. Regarding issues of domestic violence or the hassle of navigating public spaces that "real" women deal with, she has little experience with such concerns and holds them to be unimportant problems.

Leslie has very common views on certain issues of ethnicity and colorism. Like many Mexicans, she expresses a preference for light-skinned folks or, in her case, light-skinned clients. She herself is a *güera*—light-skinned—and she quite forcefully states that in terms of her own sexual pleasures, she likes light-skinned Europeans, especially Germans. She thinks they are very hot and sexy. She finds Mexicans to be all right since they are the majority of her clients, but she does not find blacks attractive and thinks the Japanese are the oddest clients she ever had. These preferences are in relation to sexual pleasure and the ranking of her clients.[6]

Leslie has a reasonable awareness of social and political issues currently happening in Mexico. She is concerned about the anti-immigration movement in the United States; she knew about the issues of Proposition 187 in California and considered it an affront to Mexicans in general. She was aware of the Zapatista movement and expressed sympathy and solidarity with its concerns. She finds the PRI to be a fossilized and oppressive political system and hopes that some kind of political alternative is emerging in Mexico. These thoughts of hers do not translate into any kind of political involvement in these issues, just an awareness and a critical read on them. She understands the reality of poverty and clearly feels that her current lifestyle is her best guard against falling into poverty herself. She expresses an understanding that her social and political concerns as a sex worker and as a gay person place her into domains of what is referred to as popular classes and she expresses her concern with these issues. In terms of direct involvement, she is only concerned with the issues of AIDS or protection for gays. What direction these various political trends are taking she is not sure of, at least, no more than most other Mexicans at this time are.

In terms of urban popular culture, Leslie has tastes and preferences that are pretty ordinary. She likes to cook and have dinner parties. Her style of cooking is from the north. For Debra's birthday party she made a chile beef stew that was her favorite. She likes partying, going clubbing, and dancing. Her musical tastes, again like those of many Oaxacans, are quite eclectic. She likes romantic music, traditional *ranchero* style, and the new *onda* of *norteño* music, like Tigres del Norte or the Banda Machos. She is not much of a movie viewer, though again, like numerous Oaxacans, she is a big fan of soap operas. She likes to shop for all the items that go into composing her look. For her, leisure time is hanging out with her friends or going out on picnics or other diversions. Once in a while, she and some of the others will rent motorbikes and go off on an excursion around the city. All of this is pretty ordinary stuff.

Leslie is married to a young man—Adrián—and this relationship is an odd mixture of traditional heterosexual assumptions along with an awareness of the limitations of this arrangement. As stated above, Leslie and Adrián had a large public celebration for their wedding. They rented a big dance hall, had a band, and invited hundreds of folks to attend. This was a symbolic act, for same-sex marriage is not legal in Mexico, though they were not hassled about their presentation. Although Leslie publicized this event to the point of having it covered by the national gay magazine, she did that not to argue

for the right of gays (for Adrián is not gay, but an *hombre/hombre*) but to further code this relationship in their heterosexual fantasy theater. Leslie expresses her role of wife as someone who should be obedient to her husband,
meet his desires, keep his house, and make his meals (it's doubtful how much
of this she actually does, considering her work requirements and other time
commitments); at the same time, however, she sees herself as Adrián's protector because he is young (he is in his early twenties) and has not experienced the world as much as she has. Adrián is a handsome, slightly built
young man who is somewhat quiet (a rare trait within this group) and quite
charming. He works as a chauffeur for a state government agency and says
that his family knows about his marriage to Leslie. His public presentation
when he is with Leslie is that of a devoted lover, and he is quite demonstrative with her. He clearly seems to be madly in love with her. Leslie claims that
it does not bother him that she is a prostitute, for he knows that it is just a
job for which she uses her body but not her heart. However, she does say
that he gets quite jealous if she expresses too much concern for *güero* men.
She has also said that since she cannot have children (that's where the heterosexual fantasy stops), their relationship could end anytime he feels that
he would prefer a "real" woman so that he can have children. Perhaps one of
the reasons for adopting Iridiann for Leslie was to diminish the chances of
this happening.

Leslie, again like most Mexicans, expresses a strong concern and commitment to her family, though we did not know what kind of contacts and involvement she has with them. She does maintain a network of fictive kin that
she uses as her family base in Oaxaca (see photos 19 and 20).

TANIA

Tania is in her mid-twenties, and she has been living with Leslie for about
six years. She often acts as Leslie's second in command and as her guardian
and front person. Tania is sharp-witted, verbally articulate, and a constant
tease and flirt. She is quite petite and is one of the more glamorous dressers
when they are on the street. She considers herself to be a passive male homosexual, and she is proud of both her sexuality and her work. She is open
about her sexuality and enjoys talking about her likes and dislikes in terms
of these domains, but about personal information she is more guarded.

She states that she is from the city of Oaxaca, had a normal childhood,
and is close to her family. Some of the others have suggested that she is from

19. *Leslie at her husband's birthday party, 1996. Photo by Michele Kelly.*

20. *Leslie and her husband, Adrián, 1996. Photo by Michele Kelly.*

the coastal areas of Oaxaca and comes from a very poor background. She has offered very little information about her youth or about how she got into prostitution or about her educational background. Although she is neither shy nor a particularly closed person, for her own reasons she does not want to talk about these aspects of her life.

She likes being gay and a transvestite. She has entered the Ms. Gay Oaxaca contest several times in Oaxaca, and every year goes to the national gay pride march in Mexico City. She considers herself to be very sexy, and when she likes someone, she is quite persistent in her attentions and often acts hurt or insulted if the person does not return her interest. She likes to be very *caliente* during sex. Like Leslie, she likes *güeros*, but prefers Italians to Germans. She also states that she thinks Cubans are the sexiest clients she has encountered. She will not penetrate nor does she like to take off all her clothes, though she will go completely nude for a price. She claims to make 150 pesos per client if they penetrate. She suggests that only slightly more than half of her clients request anal sex. She can be quite frank in discussing her activities; for example, when asked how she can handle having so much anal sex, she states that it's easy because you develop calluses on your anus. The idea of sex with women she finds revolting. She stated that once she was approached by a man who wanted sex but when they got to her room it turned out to be a woman in drag, and she refused to have sex. She has been involved in multiple-partner encounters, but she will not have sex with women in these encounters. To her this would be like being a lesbian.

She is quite aware that her style of gayness is one of several such expressions, and like the others in the group, she stresses the need for more social tolerance among gays for their own differences. She recognizes that the world of international gays defines the boundaries of active and passive differently than she does, but as of yet, it does not interest her. She feels that being a sex worker is reasonable work for her lifestyle and desires and does not express any plans or visions about what her life will be like after working the streets. She has interacted with lesbians at different conferences or workshops on sexuality and AIDS, but does not have any lesbian friends. Most women she knows are friends or wives of other males. She has no particular interest in or understanding of feminism, nor does she perceive sexism to be much of a problem for her. Though quite aware of contemporary political and social issues taking place in Mexico and Oaxaca, she does not express much interest. For recreation she likes to party, watch soap operas, and hang at home (see photo 21).

21. *Tania, 1997.*
    Photo by Joni Kubana.

Events in the Social Lives of Leslie, Adrián, and Tania

GOING OUT TO THE CLUBS

Once in a while, when the *chicas* take a night off, they like to go to local clubs to have a good time and dance. However, their access to many clubs is either restricted or they do not feel comfortable in them. The middle-class discos, frequented by the *fresas* (a local slang term for middle-class, affluent youth), are off limits to them if they are in drag—which is the same thing as banning them, since they will not go out at night except in drag. In fact, the one openly gay club in Oaxaca, called Club 502 (the address of the club), also will not let the queens in if they are in drag. They don't like to go to the *zócalo* because it is associated with another segment of Oaxacan sex workers—the Zócalo Boys, who pick up international men or women and work as their local guides during their visit to Oaxaca—and also because they think they might get hassled by the police on the *zócalo*. Thus when they do go out, it is to particular *cantinas* or cabarets, which are often also whorehouses.

One night in early January 1995, we went to Casa Blanca with Leslie and Tania. We were accompanied by John, a friend from the States. Casa Blanca is considered to be the upscale cabaret in Oaxaca. In this city, a cabaret is a club for dancing, for seeing striptease shows, and for contracting the services of prostitutes (generally female). Several of the *chicas* had worked at Casa Blanca as waiters and didn't say whether they were sex workers or not. It is a big club with a large stage and a runway on which the strip shows are performed and on which customers dance in between shows. When we arrived, the doorkeepers and many of the waiters seemed to know Leslie and Tania. They both stated that they liked this club because they did not feel the management showed them any disrespect, and because they were acquainted with the managers of the club, they felt that they were protected from being hassled while they were there.

One of the ironies of this outing, which in fact we did not learn about until after our visit, was that the two brothers who owned the club were the nephews of my *compadre* Arnulfo, whom I (MJH) have known for more than thirty years, though he never mentioned this to me and I never asked him about them. The nephews, Carlos and Pedro, like their father and uncle, are Mazatecas. Their father and uncle (my *compadre*) migrated to the city more than thirty years ago, and all of their children have grown up in the city. However, Carlos and Pedro's mother (their father is dead) speaks almost no Spanish and wears traditional Mazatec clothing. Sadly, Carlos died in 1996, and we never got a chance to meet him. But his *vela* (wake) was a very large gathering, and more than half the guests were prostitutes, both male and female.

Our night at the club was fun and certainly entertaining in many ways. Since this cabaret is, for all practical purposes, a whorehouse, most of the women on the premises were prostitutes. To dance with working women in the club costs ten pesos a dance. If one wishes other services, prices are negotiated, and there are rooms off the dance floor where the sexual business goes on. Because of this context, our table was an attraction, since there were three females, of sorts, who were possible free dances. Thus all three got frequent requests for dancing, which all three frequently turned down. However, all of us danced.

The striptease show was quite spectacular by Oaxaca standards. There were several dance numbers in a Las Vegas style of performance. Individual dancers danced and lip-synched to hit songs, and then there were big production numbers with men and women in chorus lines. It was an odd mixture of tackiness and strained provocativeness from the dancers and singers. The crowd, practically all male, was not into the level of talent or the attempts of the strippers to present their various exotic styles. They just wanted to see the naked women. Tania and Leslie watched the shows from their own particular critical points of view. They would either criticize the talent of the performer or talk about how tacky the costumes were and how their own shows were, in fact, much better.

LESLIE AND ADRIÁN'S WEDDING ANNIVERSARY PARTY

August 1998 was the second anniversary of Leslie and Adrián's wedding. They were planning to have a big bash, to which they planned to invite hundreds of folks, just as they did for their wedding. Because of some conflict that we did not understand, the event was scaled down to a smaller party, but one that was quite spectacular, as is often the case with them. Leslie had gotten the use of a vacant apartment on her floor, and that's where they had the party. More than fifty people attended, with the majority being their friends and members of Grupo Unión.

This was quite a formal affair. The main room of the apartment was lined with decorative lights and paper hangings. Metal folding chairs were placed around the room, with bottles of brandy or rum near each set of chairs. A sound system played music, and all the *chicas* were dressed in their best.

Vicky, Yanine, Iracema, and several others were in charge of greeting people and getting drinks served. We were told that Leslie was getting ready. After about an hour, Leslie and Adrián made their appearance. Leslie was wearing her wedding gown, a full-length dress covered with pearls and sequins. She wore her veil and carried a bouquet. Adrián was in suit and tie. As they entered the room, they were greeted with applause and whistles of approval. One of the reasons for the switch in the dates for the party was that they were able to get the priest from the gay church in Mexico to attend. He gave them a benediction for their anniversary celebration. It was like they were doing their vows over again, but this time with the blessings of the gay church. During the benediction, Leslie and Adrián held hands while the priest spoke of the importance of their relationship and its durability, stating that perseverance on their part was evidence of God's grace upon their relationship. After the blessing, Leslie and Adrián thanked everyone and expressed their feelings about the importance of this event to them and to other gays who might be thinking about forging stable relationships. The durability of their relationship had acquired new meaning for them since they now shared the responsibility of raising their adopted daughter.

After these events, the dinner was served. Leslie had supervised the cooking of the meal of meat loaf, beans, and rice. After the dinner the wedding cake was brought out, toasts were made to the couple, and then the cake was cut. The cake was a traditional wedding cake with the little *novios* standing in the middle.

After the serving of the cake, the show began. Susana and Yanine both performed a lip-synching show of their favorite artists, doing the songs that Leslie and Adrián liked best. This was followed by another queen, Veronica, singing several of Leslie and Adrián's favorite love songs. Then the dancing began, with Leslie and Adrián leading it off. We stayed until around three in the morning, and the party was still going strong when we left. After the party was over, Leslie and Adrián went to the beach for their second honeymoon (see photo 22).

A Short Interview with Leslie, Tania, and Adrián

LESLIE

My grandparents are from Oaxaca, they lived up in the Sierra Mixe, that's where my father was born. I was born here also, but when I was very young my father went to Chihuahua, and that's where I grew up.

22. Yanine at a party, 1997. Photo by Michele Kelly.

Why did I came back to Oaxaca? The nostalgia of returning to one's place of birth, where one's principles were formed. That's what made me come back, but there were problems with my life even before returning here. Something was missing. To me, the most important thing is the family. To have, I don't know, responsibility, someone to exist for, someone to achieve for, you know? And someone to strive for, that's what I wanted. I began my "family" with my colleague, Tania. Previously, I had my friend Cristina, may she rest in peace. That's how I began to have friends, and to me they were like sisters. And from there, well, every woman, like man, has the illusion to get married, to feel self-accomplished, as a person, it does not matter what is the sexual preference. I wanted to be married, I did not have *novios* or lovers, I do not know why, but I wanted to have a stable relationship so that I could form a family, and now I have it! I met Adrián, we liked each other, and we have been together for a long time, now more than two years, and we are happy. But our relationship needed to bear some fruit, but the fruit is not mine alone, it belongs to us, because it cannot be mine alone. The little girl we have adopted— Iridiann—belongs to all three of us—me, Adrián, and Tania—and she is a wonderful little girl. She is the joy of the home, she is the one who completed the missing part of the picture we wanted, and now we are all here together.

I am aware that some people might not think that I could be a
good parent because of my work and lifestyle, but you know what?
That would be a problem for such people who think that way, not me.
I ask you, what's more important: that a child has a home and is loved
or my job or lifestyle? This child would be living in the streets if we
had not adopted her. Is it better for the child to live in the streets or
be in a home with "*jotos*" that love her?

ADRIÁN

How do I feel about being married to Leslie? It's something unusual,
for sure, it is something different, but not a torment or anything. I am
not a homosexual, I see Leslie as a woman, no? I am a man, right? I
take her for a woman and she takes me as a man. I do not think about
her as a man, only as a woman. I am not gay, I just love Leslie. Yes, you
could say that I am an *hombre/hombre*!

TANIA

No, I am not Iridiann's aunt; like Leslie, I am also her mother. How
will we share this role in the future? I do not know for sure. Like when
she is in school, we will have to decide who will go to the school and
do those things that you do with the schools. It should not be a problem, I feel that in life everything is fixed by itself. I do what I have to
do in life, and problems just then tend to vanish, little by little, just
by themselves.

LESLIE

What is Grupo Unión? We are a group of homosexuals who work
as sex workers and we work on educating our clients and the general
public about AIDS. We always give information about AIDS to our
clients and we always make sure that they use condoms. Also, we try
to help people with AIDS by doing benefits and donating money to
help with medicine or rent. We also put our own money together that
we make as sex workers, to maintain a fund to help ourselves if we get
sick or cannot work for a while.

We formed the Unión because we were oppressed, discriminated against, and marginalized by the so-called "society" of Oaxaca. Now with the formation of this group of ours, we have become more acceptable, mainly because of our work on the issues of AIDS. The group was formed after one of our colleagues was assassinated by the police—well, not directly, but indirectly by one of the police officials. Though Cristina was HIV-positive at the time, she died from the beating from the police, not AIDS, as they tried to say. In fact, we had an autopsy done to prove that she died from the beating. That incident prompted us to form our Grupo to protect and attain our rights. We even went to the human rights commission here in Oaxaca to get help in the formation of our group.

What I hope for is that we can all be seen as equal, the only difference is our sexual preference. We should all have rights to form a family and to be happy, that is, enjoy all the rights that we deserve as Mexican citizens. I have, as you know, formed a family, I work as a sex worker, I live a normal life, or as normal as anyone else. I do not see anything "abnormal" with being homosexual or with having a different sexual orientation. My family life is not perfect, but then, who does have a perfect family? But Adrián, Tania, Iridiann, and I, the four of us are a family. I am happy with my present family, my gay family!

How is it living as gays in Oaxaca now? Well, there are several factors. We are sex workers, we have a bit more liberty than before: to dress up, to fix ourselves up, and to stand on the street corner that we have attained the right to work on. I am happy about my life now. I know that there are other *ondas* of being gay in Oaxaca, who dress different than us, and they are happy with their homosexuality. Currently there is a little more freedom for all of us. I think there seems to be less rejection or hostility towards gays now, I feel that we are now better accepted by that so-called "society" of Oaxaca.[7]

IRACEMA

"It is the price you have to pay for fame." This *dicho* of Iracema's captures her approach to her life as a gay transvestite prostitute. Iracema is in her mid-twenties and has been living in the city of Oaxaca for more than five years. During the last three years she has been working as a street prostitute. She has a very sharp wit, a keen sense of humor, and she likes to offer up many *dichos* that capture the *onda* of her lifestyle. She is short, a little on the stout side, and is often perceived as one of the more masculine-looking members of the group, though in fact she has a very fluid presentation of her composed femininity, more so than many of the others. She comes from the eastern part of the state of Oaxaca, near the border with Veracruz, close to the city of Tuxtepec. She grew up in a rural area, where her father was a small rancher. She says that there is a village near her home that is famous for the number of gays who live there and that the patron saint of that village is the saint for all the gays of Mexico.

Iracema lives about a block and a half from Leslie and Tania's apartment, in a little apartment in a *vecindad*. The apartment and *vecindad* are "*muy humilde*"; the residents are part of the working-class world of Oaxaca. She shares her apartment with Alejandra. The apartment has four rooms: a tiny bathroom, a small kitchen, a living room, and a bedroom. In the living room there are two sofas, a coffee table, and a large entertainment set with a TV, VCR, and stereo. The walls are decorated with posters, religious pictures, and stuffed animals. The apartment is a little dingy in that there is only one outside window, which they keep covered. It is a small and cramped apartment, made more so since it is also where several of the *chicas* like to hang out before and after work to gossip and drink.

In terms of the group, Iracema is one of the few who talks about life after being a prostitute. She is currently taking classes to learn how to be a seamstress, and she hopes to be able to save enough money to open her own dress shop. She defines herself as a passive gay male who found that working as a prostitute was the easiest work that she could do to support her current lifestyle. Her family knows that she is gay but not that she is a prostitute. She chose her current name when she moved to Oaxaca and starting hanging out in the gay bars. Her legal name is José, but she liked the name Iracema because it was the name of her niece. She said she was in a bar, and someone asked her name, and she immediately said it was Iracema. For her there are three domains of sexuality: *bugas,* straight folks; *jotos,* either passive or active; and *bisexuals,* gays who are both active and passive or those gays who go between men and women. She thinks bisexuals are hypocrites because they cannot make up their minds as to what they are or want to be. For her, bisexuals are choosing a lifestyle, whereas *bugas* or *jotos,* like her, are either born that way or have made a commitment. She does feel that both Debra's and Vicky's husbands are gay no matter what they say. However, like most of her group she does not like the crowd at Club 502 because they confuse the boundaries between active and passive roles, and the gay crowd there do not like to present themselves as women (see photos 23 and 24).

She likes to pretend that she does not like to use crude words for gays, such as *puta* or *joto;* however, her everyday speech is full of these words, and she and the others are always calling each other *puta* or *joto.* Following is a summary of how she tells aspects of her life:

23. *Iracema's "whore look,"
1996. Photo by Julia Knop.*

24. *Iracema's "day look," 1996.
Photo by Julia Knop.*

I do not have many childhood memories, not till I was around eight. My childhood was like any other *muchacho*. I had good family relations. I was always playing, I had a lot of friends, and I always got along with people. I liked school very much. It was easy, and I seemed to be able to get along with everyone.

I loved my family, and I still have very strong feelings for my family and love to visit with them. I always knew that I was gay. I always liked bright colors, flowers, cooking, cleaning the house, and wearing women's clothes and putting on makeup. My family knows, and did not seem to care too much, so long as I would act, as they say, "normal." My father was a small-time rancher and would not take me out to work in the *campo* because he knew I was gay and that I liked to stay in the house and help my mother. I do not remember dealing with any discrimination because of my *onda*. We lived in a little village near Tuxtepec, and there were other gays around; however, I did not hang out with them; they were older, and I did not understand their scene then. I left home early, not because I was not getting along with my family but because it was just too small a place, which in fact was full of all my relatives.

My father died when I was only six, and I was thirteen when my mother died. It was very hard when my mother died. Your mother is the only one you will ever have your whole life. I wanted more time with her. You really need someone with a lot of experience to help you out when you are growing up. My father was always working, so I did not know him as well. When he died, it was my older brothers and sisters who took care of the family and my mother. I have four sisters and two brothers, and I am the second to the youngest. My older brothers would always give me a lot of advice. They told me not to stop studying, to learn a career, to be careful not to hang out with people who did drugs, to work hard, and to use my time well. My older sister is married to a captain in the army and she is a housewife, and my other sister is married to a school principal, and my brothers are also married. My brothers work at ranching like my father. They do not know that I am a prostitute. I don't want them to worry, and I don't want to cause them concern. They are all married with kids and are getting along in life. I do not want them to worry about me. When I visit I do not go with my whore look, though I still look gay. They think that I have my *taller de costura* [dressmaking shop] already.

My first sex encounter was when I was eleven; it was with a friend from school. I did not think it was any big deal, just acting out instincts or early sexual urges. I had very little awareness of what I was doing, it was not that important. Later, I did develop more of a consciousness of the importance of sex, and then when I had sex, it was with someone I really liked or even loved.

I did not think of myself as gay then; at that age one does not think about that or analyze it. That started when I was around fifteen. In fact, I encountered my first true love when I was fifteen. His name was Gabriel, and he was a few years older than I was, maybe sixteen or seventeen. We went everywhere together. We were a very public couple. He would wait for me after school, and we just hung out and fooled around. The *pueblo* was very small and open, but nobody hassled us; maybe they thought we were just friends. We were *novios* for more than a year. During that time I would wear a little lipstick and wear very baggy pants.

I did not start wearing women's clothing until I came to Oaxaca, out of respect for my family. Still when I go home I do not go in drag or put makeup on, out of respect for my nieces and nephews. I left the Tuxtepec area when I was about sixteen and went to Mexico City and enrolled in a private military school. That was a pretty strange place. I went because that's what my brothers suggested that I do, but I was gay and did not like people telling me what to do. I did not stay there too long; in fact, I was forced to leave the school. This upset my family; they all thought that would have been a good career for me. Boy, were they wrong! So I left Mexico City, and came to Oaxaca City and started at the secondary school here in Oaxaca. I wanted to study medicine or nursing, but since my parents had died it was hard for me to meet all these expenses, and my brothers could not help me very much, for they had their own families to take care of. So I decided to quit school and go into prostitution out of economic necessity. It was very scary to move into this kind of work. I was young and scared. I was afraid of the police and the clients you had to deal with on the street. Drunks were always hassling me and I had to learn how to defend myself. I was working solo at the time, up the street from where we now work, in front of that little liquor store. Economic conditions forced me to choose this profession.

The first other transvestite prostitute that I met was Susana. I met her working the street also. She had been working for a while, and she began to show me the ropes and tricks of the trade, how to treat the clients and not get ripped off. She was like my godmother. That was about four years ago. We lived together for a while, and we were and are very close friends. We lived together for about three years in a different *colonia* in the city. Then Susana started living with her *novio,* and since I was now making pretty good money, I moved in with Vicky and we shared an apartment. Last year I got this apartment that I now share with one of the new *putas.*

The Grupo Unión was formed over the issues surrounding Cristina's death. She had been arrested and beaten by the police and later died from that, but the police said that she died from AIDS, which was bullshit. At the time we were all working different street corners. I was on Calle Mina, Leslie and Tania were working Calle Trujano, and Debra and Vicky were working on Calles Díaz Ordaz and Las Casas. During the *vela* for Cristina, we began talking about the need to work together so that it would be safer and we could work as a group to get health cards to work the streets. It is not good to work solo; as a group we could help each other with the hassles of the streets—how to deal with clients, how to negotiate prices and services, and how to handle all the drinking that goes with this work. At first there was one group, but some of them broke off because of fights with Leslie; they formed their own group. We remained with her, and there have always been between eight and ten folks in the group. Leslie has always been the *jefe* of our group. She likes it and is good at it. We all respect her for her hard work and willingness to continue fighting for our rights. It was through her efforts that we were finally given the health books that we have to have to work the streets; these books verify that we are healthy—including that we are HIV-negative. These booklets are given out by the public health services of the city, and we have to go for a monthly test to maintain our health status. With this booklet the police are not supposed to hassle us on the street. Since we have been organized as a group, we rarely get hassled by the police anymore, unless we get into some kind of trouble—like fighting with the other group of drag queen prostitutes or getting into fights with our clients, and the police try to press charges against us for assault or other things. We do not look for new members to our group. We are a small group and have known each other for quite a while. It would take a new person a long time to get to know us and work their way into our group.

I was born gay—I am sure. Though I am a male, I like that I am very feminine and love when I transform myself into a woman. I don't care for my male face much, but I feel very beautiful when I start to make myself up. You can feel yourself change as you begin to paint your face and change into dresses and other clothing of being like a woman.

I am a strong believer in the Catholic Church; I believe in God, the Virgins, and all the Saints. In fact, in the area near my pueblo, there is the Santo de Los Putas, who is the saint of the gay people in the area. The *santo* lives in the village of Jalapa, where they say that more than half the community is gay—though the saint himself does not look gay.

I like sex, almost everything. I am *pasivo,* much like a woman; in fact, I often think of myself as a real woman. I am kind of a tranquil lover, I like to give oral sex, but not the *beso negro* (anal kissing). What you do depends on how you are feeling, but when you are working you are doing it for money, so it does not matter whether you like it or not. Clients like to see you totally nude, but that costs more. Many of the clients like to get oral sex, and some do not want sex; they just want to have a drink and talk. I always make the clients use condoms. I charge between 80 to 100 pesos for anal penetration and 100 to 150 pesos for masturbation along with oral sex.

I do not know many *locas vestidas* [slang word for being in drag] of the older generation. One of the more famous ones is Maura Monti, who is in her late forties and lives in [a] *colonia* nearby us. She designs floats for fiestas and is quite good at it; she has won several prizes. She once was a prostitute but is not now. There is also Venus; he was once a street prostitute but now runs a bar, and there is Eloy, who now designs dresses for *jotos*.

I have a great deal of respect for women, since we are all born from women. I did not like to see men hit women; that is wrong. We get some of the hassles that women face on the street, but it is different for us. We do not do very much with female prostitutes; sometimes we ask them to help us on some of our issues, and other times we help them with issues that are important to them. I am not sure I understand what feminism is; a feminist is someone who thinks of him or herself as very special and does not like to talk to other women unless they are involved in the struggle for social rights. I do not understand women who do not like to create a look for themselves, who do not do their hair or wear makeup. For me they have not thought out their sexual preference yet or they are lazy and do not want to put the work in that it takes to make oneself pretty. For me there is always time to make yourself attractive.

My diversions are pretty simple and common. I like to listen to music, talk and party with my friends and neighbors, and I like to sleep. I do not know much about modern art; I like landscape paintings. I like all kinds of music, especially the classic *tríos* and the pop music of Alejandra Guzmán or Gloria Trevi. She is very good; she sings about real things, like being in love or when you get hurt because you love someone too much. I rarely go to movies. I like to cook, but I do not have any favorite recipes; I just like everything. Drugs? I have never used them; I like to drink, maybe too much. I do like my work; for one thing, I get to meet interesting people, like you all. I doubt that I would have met you [Michael and Tanya] if I had been working in some other kind of work.

I am not into politics very much, it is all pretty corrupt here in Mexico. There is a lot of poverty and misery here in Oaxaca, and I do not know when that will change or how we can change it. Life is hard.

DEBRA

Debra is in her early twenties and has been working as a prostitute in the city of Oaxaca for about five years. She grew up in the coastal city of Pochutla. Her family is involved with small mercantile enterprises in that city. Her father and mother run a clothing stall in the local market in Pochutla, and most of her siblings are also involved with market vending. She has seven brothers and sisters, and she is the second to the youngest. She went through secondary school in Pochutla, moved to the beach city of Puerto Escondido with her first lover in her mid-teens, and then moved to the city of Oaxaca, where she worked as a secretary in the city jail before she began working as a prostitute.

When we met Debra, she was living in the same *vecindad* as Iracema and Alejandra. Debra lived in a two-room apartment on the top floor of the *vecindad* with her lover, Eduardo. Their apartment had very little furniture in it—a bed, a few small end tables, and a radio and television. They felt that this was just a temporary location and that they would soon move to a better place. They had been living together for about six months at that time and were thinking about getting married, though later in the year they were going through a separation because Eduardo was concerned about Debra's drinking. He worried that it would lead him back into his former drug use. Like Leslie's husband, Eduardo does not see himself as gay, nor does Debra see him as gay, but as an *hombre/hombre*—a real man. Debra is a very attractive person, who composes herself into quite a striking woman. Like most of the others, she is quite intelligent and verbally quick, with a very biting sense of humor. She likes to play verbal games that are loaded with double or triple sexual meanings. It was from Debra that we learned the verb *chapiar,* which seems to mean to get a rash or chapped skin. They use it to mean that one has anal sex that is so good that one gets chapped in the process. She took delight in attempting to seduce me (MJH) with verbal games that she thought would also cause Tanya to react with jealousy, and the fact that neither of us would respond as she expected seemed to fuel her desire to keep finding new ways to tease us. She had some ideas of getting out of prostitution in the future and starting some kind of small business, like selling flowers. Her relations with Eduardo were framed in terms of the numerous contradictions, with the status of their same-sex relationship being the least difficult component for them. Eduardo, like Leslie's husband, met Debra on the street in a client relationship. He claims that he does not mind that she works as a prostitute, since that is only work, though Debra states that he is quite possessive and jealous. Eduardo contends that Debra's prostitution does not bother him, but the lifestyle of the *chicas* in terms of their drinking and partying puts pressure on their relationship. Other tensions in the relationship are that Eduardo has a former wife and child, and Debra thinks that produces divided loyalties for Eduardo. Eduardo runs a small taco restaurant with his family, and only his younger brother knows about his living arrangements with Debra. Following are Debra's views on her life and profession (see photos 25, 26 and 27).

25. Debra doing her "look," 1996. Photo by Julia Knop.

26. Debra's "whore look," 1996. Photo by Julia Knop.

*27. Debra's husband,
Eduardo, 1996. Photo
by Julia Knop.*

My childhood was quite normal. It was a time of fun, playing with all
my friends. It was quite a beautiful time. I was close to my parents and
to my brothers and sisters. I was about ten when I knew that I was gay.
I don't know why, but I just knew I was gay. I first told my sisters, and
they did not seem to mind, and then I told my parents; again, they did
not seem to be too shocked. They all seemed to accept it. I never liked
cars or football, guy things; I liked playing with my sisters' dolls more.

I had other gay friends at this time. I was around ten years old
when I had my first sexual encounter. It was with the boy next door,
who was then fifteen. He penetrated me, and he was not gay, but was
an *hombre/hombre*. At first, I did not like him, but I did like having
sex. I began to like him more, and we were *novios* for about four years.
When I was about fifteen, I left home to live with a gay who was older
than me; he was twenty-seven. We went to live in Puerto Escondido.
In fact, he was from there, and I had met him on the beach when we
were there on a vacation. At this time I started dressing like a woman,

and I stopped going to school. Not going to school made my parents quite angry with me. They do not like to see me in dresses too much, so when I was with them I would wear pants and a shirt and not use too much makeup. I used to enter gay beauty contests in Pochutla, and when I was seventeen, I won one.

I was then living with my older *novio* out in Puerto Escondido; we had been together for about two years, and things started to get boring. He was spending all his time working at his mother's store. It wasn't much fun for me, so I left and came to the city of Oaxaca.

I had a lot of friends in Oaxaca. My first job was as a secretary in the jail; I only had to work in the afternoons. After a while, I started working as a street prostitute. I look at going into prostitution as a kind of experiment to find out about that *onda*. I knew it would be full of *pendejadas* (hassles), but the money looked good. I found out that I like it a lot; in fact, I thought my first night of work was wonderful. I worked alone at first, but I had a lot of friends who helped me learn how to work the streets.

I am a passive gay male, and I like it that way! I would never want an operation to change my sex; God made me this way and this is the way I have to stay. It would be an offense to God if I changed myself through an operation. My *pene* (penis) has no value to me except for peeing, but it is here to stay. I enjoy having sex with my partner. It is very exciting. I do not get an erection nor do I ejaculate very often; it is not important to me. I love it when he penetrates me or when I give him oral sex or do a *beso negro.* However, I do not like those activities for myself; in fact, I do not allow him to touch my *pene*. I keep a towel over my *pene* when we are making love. The only time he sees my *pene* is when we are taking showers. I never let clients touch me there either.

I go to work around ten or eleven at night, and I will go until about four in the morning; I do not like to stay out too late. Most of my clients are kind of good-looking, and they are of every kind of person. The few ugly ones are good clients because they will pay more. Generally I can get 100 to 150 pesos for anal sex and up to 200 for oral sex. I do get a lot of clients who only want me to masturbate them. I have about three to four clients a night, with most of them wanting to have anal sex with me. I learned how to do my makeup from reading magazines and just doing it on my own; I did not learn from my sisters.

I met most of the *putas* in the group on the street while working, and it was after Cristina's death that we formally put the group together. I feel for women and respect what they have to do, but I do not know anything about feminism. My closest friends are all transvestites like me. I do not visit with my family too much. I do not want them to worry about my safety and work. I have encountered many violent hassles on the street—guns, knifes, fistfights; you name it, I have encountered it on the street. But that's what life on the street is like, full of *pendejadas* and *pendejos* (hassles and assholes).

I met Eduardo on the street. He is now my "lover/husband"; however, he is very jealous. He has always known that I was a prostitute and gay, but he says that he does not care. We live together and share *gastos* (expenses). In terms of my work, he would like me to quit—who knows—maybe. I could work as a secretary or something. I am not sure about that because I want to continue to dress like a woman, but if I worked in a normal setting, then I would have to adapt to those conditions or what the boss would want me to do.

I think that Eduardo and I will be together for a long time; he says he wants to, and I think that would be good also. However, we do not do many things outside the house; we do not go out to clubs or things like that. It seems too much of a hassle for him, and he gets jealous if I talk or dance with other guys. It is more fun for me to go out with the other *putas*. I have known a few older transvestites here and in Pochutla; they are my friends. I like romantic music like José José, whereas Eduardo likes salsa or discos. I have tried a few drugs but not too many or too much.

Several weeks after this interview with Debra, she and Eduardo were having a trial separation. They had moved out of their apartment to a nicer *vecindad* across from the main market. A few days after they moved into their new apartment, Eduardo moved out, saying that he could not tolerate Debra's drinking and that it was affecting their relationship. He was a recovering drug user, and he feared that the drinking context of Debra and her friends would encourage him back into drug use. He stated that if she would quit drinking, he would return to the relationship. Debra seemed at the time to be entertaining the idea of quitting drinking. She said that she had not had a drink for a week and was going to a psychologist to work on her problems. She and Eduardo went to see *When a Man Loves a Woman* (a movie dealing with an alcoholic woman), and she found the movie to be quite powerful and felt that she could identify with the woman in the film.

She seems serious about this change in her life and talked about the fact that her father was an alcoholic and also that the job of being a *puta* encourages you to drink just to be able to put up with all the *pendejadas* of the work. She thinks that she really has had a drinking problem since she was fourteen because of the harshness of her home life, where her parents were very strict, made her go to a nuns' school, and would not let her do anything but her homework. If she did not do these things, she was physically punished. She did comment on how this story was different from her memories of a happy childhood.

Debra and Eduardo did break up last year. In the summer of 1996 Debra said that she had not seen him for more than six months and that she was now going to live a single life; it was better.

During 1996 both Debra and Alejandra left the Grupo Unión. Debra said that she left the group because of fights with both Leslie and Tania. She had moved into a first-floor apartment in the building Leslie and Tania live in, and living that close together produced more tension than they could all handle. She said that she got into a pushing and scratching fight with Tania. She and Alejandra left the group and have joined with a few other queens to work a new street corner. She said that the quarrel bothered her a great deal at first, but that one has to move on and live one's life.

EDUARDO: DEBRA'S *COMPAÑERO*

Eduardo, at the time we met him, had been living with Debra for about six months. He was twenty-three, had been married before, and had one child. He and Debra lived in the same *vecindad* as Iracema, but later they had moved into a new apartment near the Mercado de Abastos. As we stated in the section on Debra, toward the end of our stay they were involved in attempting to figure out if they could make a go of their relationship or should end it. Eduardo felt that the problem was Debra's drinking. In his view, her job and her workmates constantly put her in the context of heavy drinking. Thus, he was putting pressure on her to think about quitting prostitution and not to hang out with her friends. For Debra it was a conflict between facing her drinking and her love for Eduardo. Further, she was concerned as to whether he was being honest about his commitment to her; for if she left the trade and her friends, how secure would her life be with him? Both claimed that the fact that they were a same-sex couple was the least of their problems, for as everyone knew, Eduardo was not gay, and Debra just happened to be the male/woman that he was in love with. Below are Eduardo's reflections on his life and his history with Debra. As stated earlier, their relationship has been over for about year.

I am twenty-three years old and I was born here in Oaxaca. My father died when I was nineteen, my mother remarried a guy who works in the government, and they live in the Colonia Reforma. You could say that I come from a middle-class background of sorts. I have two older sisters who are married and live here in the city. I have a brother who has been living in Los Angeles for about six years. I also have two step-siblings, a brother fifteen, who just moved into this *vecindad* so that I can keep an eye on him—he is having trouble at home—and a twelve-year-old stepsister. Except for my younger stepbrother, the family does not yet know about Debra and me.

I have pleasurable memories of my youth, and I always got along with my parents. I finished secondary school and then began working and partying, you could say. When I was seventeen, I went to Los Angeles to live with my brother. It was a wild time. I was working, sometimes making thousands of dollars a month, but I spent it all on parties and drugs. I was running around with Mexicans and Cubans, and we were doing a lot of crack and other drugs. I liked the money you could make in Los Angeles, but I never liked the style of how people lived there. I had two jobs, both as a busboy. While working as a busboy, I met a woman from Mexico City. We started dating, and then we got married and went back to Mexico. We had a child, a boy; however, the marriage did not last very long, and when we separated, she took everything. My son is now five.

I have always been a good talker, and I have never had problems meeting women or having lovers. I think they all like my hairy chest; it makes them think I am very sexy. Though I knew a lot of women, I never had important relationships. To be honest, I like the game of conquest more than having a relationship. Also, I was kind of a wild teenager. I liked to fight, and often these fights were with knives. I ran with a *banda* (gang), and we would have fights over turf, but we never had too many problems with the police. But then things got a lot heavier. At that time I lived in Xoxo, and was running with my *banda*. Some real violence was coming down, and I had to leave town and go stay in Mexico City for a while. Most of my old mates have been in jail, and some have been killed. I am still a little concerned about going back to Xoxo in case anyone is still holding a grudge against me. Actually, it has been my relationship with Debra that has helped me change my life and stop using drugs. I have not used cocaine in more than a year.

I am totally in love with Debra. We have a strong relationship and we do all sorts of things together. She is very pretty. When I first started going out with Debra, many people felt that I was gay, and in fact I started wondering about my own sexuality. But I started thinking that in fact Debra was the first man I had been attracted to, and I do not think that I am attracted to men, only Debra. I am not particularly attracted to transvestites; in fact, I still find myself looking at women (real women) on the street, and I find them very attractive. No, I am not gay; I have been with numerous women. It is just that I fell in love with Debra. In fact, I do not particularly like gays; it's just that I love Debra.

Will we stay together for a long time? I do not know. I want to have a long-term relationship with her, but we would have to deal with some concrete problems, like her drinking, or if she wants kids, we would have to figure out how to adopt kids. Because I love her, I am comfortable in this relationship. At first it was a little strange, but not now; it just feels normal. Plus these are more open times, and the hassles are fewer. In the past I have had many affairs with women, but when things were tough, they would leave me. Debra gives me support and tries to understand me. We make a lot of mistakes, but we try to work on them.

Having sex at first was a little strange, but not now. We have a very passionate sex life; it is great, though more often than not, I want to have sex more than she does. I think she thinks that I'm sex-crazed or something. Maybe because of her work, she is not always that hot to have sex. Yes, she does have a *pene,* but we do not think about it too much. No, she would not want an operation, nor would I ever demand that; it would not be right. Like she says, "I only use my *pene* to pee, but it is mine."

I do not mind that she is a prostitute; she does not do it for the pleasure, but out of necessity. Also that's her life, and I respect it. She does what she wants on the street, but at home we are a couple. I do not get jealous of her work; it's more when we are on the street or at parties, sometimes she can act a little too *puta;* that gets me jealous. It is strange; I was never jealous with other women, only with Debra.

How did I meet Debra? Well, one night, about a year ago, I was hanging with some friends of mine, and we all wanted to get something to drink, so we headed towards a liquor store, which was a block away from where Debra worked on the street. I was really a mess; I had not shaved, my clothes were dirty from work, and I had on an old baseball cap. As we were buying some liquor, Debra came up to buy something also. I was stunned—she was so beautiful. I knew from looking at her she was a prostitute and a transvestite, but I did not care. I fell madly in love with her at first sight. That night we just joked and talked, and I said that I would look her up later. It took two months of courtship before we had sex. At first we would just go out, hold hands and kiss, but nothing else. It was in fact the night of Leslie's wedding that we finally had sex together.

After that we starting living together. It was hard at first, getting used to the odd hours of her work. At first I would get angry and holler at her when she was late, but now I have learned that her work does not ever have exact hours. Some of my friends know that I am living with her, but most do not. I like having some kind of private life. My brothers know about us; my mother knows but does not say anything, and I think my brother in Los Angeles would have a heart attack. I do not feel that we are hassled particularly in public, though I do not like to be too demonstrative in public, so we do not offend people.

Oaxaca has many social problems. Both Debra and I come from families that were more or less middle class. But there is a lot of poverty in Oaxaca, which causes problems of alcoholism, drug use, and family violence. Most people only see the tourist things here and not how people are really living in the *colonias* or at the market. Most tourists do not think of the poverty here; they only look at the pretty things. I'm not too much into politics; I do not understand the Zapatistas. I am not for them or against them. I do know that the PRI and the presidents of this country are corrupt. The last one stole millions of dollars from us, which could have supported all of Oaxaca. If I vote, I think I will vote for the PAN; they seem more honest. I used to be into spiritualism, like my mother, but now I am just your average Catholic. Both Debra and I believe in God, and we go to church once in a while. I believe in God more, while Debra puts more faith in the Virgen de Juquila.

VICKY

Vicky is in her early twenties and has been working on the streets for about three years. Currently she is finishing preparatory school, and she has plans to enter law school. She is very open about her lifestyle and desires and has the most clearly defined view of anyone in the group regarding what she

28. Vicky doing her makeover, 1996. Photo by Julia Knop.

wishes to do after working the streets. Vicky is quite stylish, and her whore look and day look are hip and close to being the most tasteful within the group. She has an apartment on the other side of the city from Leslie and Tania. It is basically one room that she has separated into her bedroom and living room. Her range of material items is similar to that of the others, including the stuffed animals. Though she is not quite as vocal as either Leslie or Debra, she has a cosmopolitan outlook about herself and the sexual world she lives in. Following is a summary of her views on her life (see photo 28).

I come from a large family in Huajuapan de León, Oaxaca. Huajuapan de León is the largest city in the Mixteca Alta, which is near the border with the state of Puebla. My father is a primary school teacher in Huajuapan, and my mother is an *ama de casa* (housewife). I have four brothers and two sisters. My oldest brother is a civil engineer who lives in Huajuapan and is married, and my other older brother is single and lives in the Los Angeles area. I have two younger brothers, ages thirteen and five, who are in school. One of my sisters is twenty-four, married, and lives in Huajuapan, and my other sister is nineteen and is a lesbian. She lives in Huajuapan with a woman from there. She has had some hard times once in a while; it is a small town, but no worse than what gay men have to confront. We are very close because of our lifestyles.

My mother says she knew that I was gay when I was very young because all I wanted to do was play with girls. My childhood was very free and happy; I had a lot of friends and just played a lot. Sometimes I would get hassled, but nothing that was any big deal. When I was in secondary school, I hung with a group of about five other gays who were like me. There was Beto (or Roberto), whose family had some money, so he could study and did not have to work. He now is an accountant, and I see him once in a while. There was Juan Carlos, who now lives in Mexico City and works in a factory making plastic things. Galdino is in Pueblo studying agriculture, and Tino still lives in Huajuapan. We split up after secondary school; the only other one who came to Oaxaca was Beto.

I knew that I was gay in primary school. I was in my fourth year of school when I had my first *novio;* he was named Antonio. He was very manly; we would just kiss and do innocent sexual play. We stayed together until the sixth grade. Interestingly, it was my lesbian sister who encouraged me to be careful with having too many *novios.* She told me that I should not just go with anyone, that before I had sex, I should wait for someone I really cared for.

I had my first lover when I was in secondary school, and I was sixteen. He was a teacher, and his name is Gaudincia. It was with him that I lost my virginity. This is when I began dressing in drag. He was a social science teacher, and he was married. He, like my early *novio,* was very manly, and not gay. How did we get involved? Well, it was easy; one day I went to talk with him in his office about my school-work and the trouble I was having, and I made a pass at him, told him that I really liked him. He tried to discourage me, and in fact said no to my advances, but then a month later, in his house, we finally got together. He was living alone, and we became lovers. I moved to Oaxaca, and he would come to visit me a few times during the month.

He got transferred to Mexico City, and I have not seen him in several years. My next lover was also married; his name was Trinidad, and I really liked him, but after about six months we had a big fight and I left him.

I have been living with Alejandro for about two years; it is almost like we are married. I met him on the street when I was working, but not as a client. He worked just a block away from the apartment where I was living at the time. I would pass by his workplace on the way to going to work the streets. We would say hi to each other as I walked by. Later he approached me about going out together. At first I was not interested in having a new lover, but he persisted, and I finally agreed to see him. Now it has been two years!

He is really a very good man, and very manly. He is very sweet and attentive to me, but he is also very jealous, though he says he does not care about my work.

I really began dressing in drag (*loca vestida*) when I moved to Oaxaca about three years ago. I came to Oaxaca to go to the preparatory school, and there I met another gay. He told me he was working in prostitution. He said, "I work as a prostitute; why don't you come with me and try it out?" I said that I could not do that; it would be too scary. This was Wendy, who was killed recently by a crazed client. So I went to Wendy's house and she made me up to look very *puta* and I decided to try it. The first couple of clients were okay, and nothing bad or negative happened to me. However, in my second week, a client pulled a knife on me, then tried to get his money back. Luckily we were making a lot of noise, and the hotel manager came into the room, subdued this guy, and he went to jail.

My worst experience so far was after working for about a year. Wendy and I were taken by three guys out to the Presa de Huayapam (an area south of the city with a small reservoir and picnic area). It was a rainy night, and it was very hard to see. When we got to the *presa* and got out of the car, the guys pulled out guns and started shouting that they were going to kill the *putas*. We started running and they started shooting. They got back in their car to chase us, but it was too dark and rainy; we were able to get away. That is the worst experience I have had working on the streets.

Wendy and I were working together on the same block, but then she wanted to go to Mexico City, so I moved over to the corner of Calle Díaz Ordaz. It was there that I met Debra, and through her I met Leslie, Tania, and Cristina. We all began working the corner of Calle Trujano together. After Cristina's death we formed ourselves into a union. Prostitution is a good job; I make good money, and I can do what I want. At first it was scary, but now it is just work. I charge 150 pesos for anal sex or oral sex. Also, I like to be totally naked. You know what I would like to do is have some pictures made of Alejandro and me having sex; that would be great. Can you do that for us?

I love having sex. I am a passive gay; I like to be penetrated. I do get an erection and ejaculate, which is fine, but I do not like to have my penis touched nor do I like to get oral sex, but I love to give it. I also find *besos negros* to be very exciting. Alejandro and I are very passionate lovers, and I get totally naked with him. I am the first man he has had as a lover, but he treats me like a woman, accepts me as gay. He doesn't touch my penis because he is the active one. Our sex life is great.

My clients are all different and they like everything. Most are in their late twenties. I have a lot of clients, four or five a night. In fact, I think that we have more clients than the female prostitutes; that's why they get angry at us, for taking away their business. Some female prostitutes have made formal complaints to the city officials against us and have opposed letting us work on the streets in drag. They (the female prostitutes) want us to have to dress differently to work the streets, but the city officials said it was not their problem and there was nothing they could do about it. Personally, I have nothing against female prostitutes; we have to deal with similar hassles and perception of ourselves, but they are very hard to get to know. They seem to be a very closed group.

When I begin to change myself into my "look" for working the streets, it is a great feeling. I feel different, and I can feel myself changing as I put on my makeup or put out my outfit for the night. One feels different in a very positive sense; it is magical. I would never want an operation, I am a male homosexual and that's what I will stay.

When I finish preparatory, I want to go to law school. I have always been interested in the law since I was young. Hopefully I can work in the area of civil rights for gays. It will be interesting to see if, when I am a lawyer, I can keep dressing like a woman. I doubt it, but it would be great to stay in drag and be a lawyer. My future with Alejandro—who knows? We love each other, but it is very hard to keep a relationship going. Everything changes with time.

I am a good Catholic, a strong believer in the Virgen de Santa Marta—as is my whole family. In terms of feminism, I do not know much about it, except that it is something that encourages women to feel very womanish about themselves. My sister, who is a lesbian, also dresses in drag, but like a man. Through my sister I know that there are a lot of lesbians in Oaxaca, but I do not know many personally. Mostly I have met lesbians at the parties of my sister.

SUMMARY

In this chapter, we have presented a set of ethnographic portraits of a group of homosexual transvestite street prostitutes in the city of Oaxaca, Mexico. As with the other materials presented here, we are also trying to show the ordinariness of diversity within the urban popular cultures. Why the drag queens? We do not intend to exoticize urban popular cultures or to be trendy, but it does seem a fair observation to note that the domains of gender and sexuality have not been looked at extensively within the discourse of the social anthropology on Oaxaca. We clearly wanted to explore these issues of gender and sexuality, but the encounter with the *chicas* was one of those lucky events of doing fieldwork. To our great advantage, they were generous enough to give us access to diverse sexual worlds of Oaxaca that we were not aware of and that certainly were not part of the overall ethnographic presentation of Oaxaca. Further, since a construction of a more tolerant social context in Oaxaca was one of the *chicas'* primary desires, they and we felt that presenting them as particular actors in their own social context required working collaboratively to tell these stories (which we are doing with all the groups in this book). Also, we believe that in these short but intimate portraits, the diversity of their backgrounds and views about life illustrates what we mean by "the ordinariness of diversity."

One of the ordinary aspects about the *chicas* is how in their similarities and differences they nevertheless express their personal agency in their particular everyday lives. In terms of similarities, the common value they all hold to is the border between the roles and status of active versus passive sexual actors. They all define themselves as passive gay men, and they will not penetrate or cross this boundary. This is a boundary that is in a fluid state, and some passive gay men in Latin America are exploring moving between these two roles. As of now, the *chicas* seem committed to this division as a means of composing parts of their identities. Also, only Iracema expresses any interest in a sex-change operation. The rest of them feel that no matter what, God gave them a penis, and they are not going to change that.

Another similarity is that in telling their stories, none of them speaks in the language of a "crisis of identity." All state that they knew at an early age that they were gay and that they liked dressing as women. Further, they suggest that this awareness did not cause them any hassles with their families, and their memories of childhood are of a time that was normal and happy. In addition, they do not talk about their early sexual encounters in negative terms. They also all speak with confidence and acceptance about their current sexuality and lifestyles. However, within these tales of ordinary and happy childhoods, they make references to concerns about parents' or relatives' feelings about their current lifestyles. Though they all talk about the acceptance of their families, few seem to have any kind of constant contact with their families. Also, they seem to prefer to give rosy tales about their lives and will talk about negative aspects only indirectly. They say that life on the street is great, but they all have various tales of violence and hassles on the streets. They say that they make more than adequate money as prostitutes, but they are always out of money and trying to borrow more. Also, though they are quite comfortable with their lifestyles, they are aware of the contradictions within the gay community over such lifestyles. All of the above, in fact, is further demonstration of their ordinariness. Like most people, they tell tales that are not always consistent and they offer tales that are contradictory but consistent with their overall values.

Their "politics of pleasure" is another commonality among them. This is expressed in the magical and playful way they approach their makeover from maleness to femaleness. They all talk about how they physically and emotionally feel themselves change as they go through the makeover process each night. Though for us they seemed always to be in drag, for them it is the nightly process of composing their particular "look" that confirms the magic of the transformation. Further, they love playing with all the elements of composing themselves as women: makeup, clothing, hairstyling, and the nightly triumph of the makeover. This also encourages their feelings that they are better-looking and more sexy than "real" women.

Sex and its enjoyment is another aspect of their "politics of pleasure." They all state that they love having sex and that they are quite passionate lovers. Though she is in no way timid, only Iracema expresses that she is moderate in sexual adventures. The rest proclaim themselves to be great lovers and view sex as a domain for play and creativity. In fact, most of them feel that almost no man could resist for long the charms of their sexual skills. Some of them clearly feel that if you have not had sex with them, then you really have not had any good sex yet.

Conversely, for all their joy in how good they are at being women, they all lack any concrete awareness of the daily realities that "real" women deal with. They also lack any kind of feelings about standing in solidarity with women on the issues of sexism and harassment. Though we find Lancaster's argument on the playfulness of transvestic behavior to be insightful and useful in our understanding of the general *onda* of the members of Grupo Unión (Lancaster 1997a), as males the *chicas* do in fact have access to some male privilege, and it is through that access that they can play as women. However, it is that play that can reinforce very traditional and negative assumptions about gender and sex roles.

They also have their own social and personal differences. Vicky, Debra, and Iracema seem to come from Mexican middle-class backgrounds, whereas the rest are from working-class or urban poor backgrounds. Their aspirations for their lives illustrate these differences: Vicky wants to be a lawyer and Susana sees her whole life in terms of being a whore. Though they are all *mestizas,* there are differences in their awareness of colorism and the privileges that come with being light-skinned. Leslie's higher status within the group partially derives from her being the most *güera* among them.

The most obvious differences among them are the ways in which their personalities express their particular forms of personal agency. Leslie is formal and analytical in her presentation of self, Tania is quite bravo and confrontational, Debra and Vicky love verbal games and like to hit on guys to test their resolve, Iracema is funny and witty, and Alejandra is quiet and shy. Their personalities are also reflected in their tastes in lovers and clients, ranging from Leslie's affection for Germans to Iracema's preference for Oaxacans. Their approaches to sexual pleasure and nudity also vary. They all claim that they love sex, but each has a particular approach to sexual enjoyment, and they differ in their pleasure with their own nudity, with Vicky being the most open in her desire to have photos of her and her lover making love. And, as would be expected, they have various differences in their understanding and awareness of social and political issues in Oaxaca and Mexico. They are all concerned with the issues of the rights of sex workers and gays but vary in their understandings of other national and regional issues, with Leslie and Vicky being best informed on wider social and political issues.

In summarizing our findings, we have attempted to keep our "generalizations" grounded in people's everyday lives. We are aware that each of the groups that we are dealing with in this book is representative of the problematic dynamics that can best be referred to as "the politics of representation." We also know that each word in our and Grupo Unión's category of *passive homosexual transvestite street prostitutes* represents separate discursive spaces that are filled with contested discourses on the issues of representation and politics. In the area of male sexuality in Latin America, the works by Carrier (1995), Cornwall (1994), Kulick (1997), Lancaster (1992, 1997a, and 1997b), Lumsden (1991 and 1996), and Prieur (1996) are important and engaging sources that we have drawn upon. Also, the fast-paced debates taking place within the discourses of social postmodernism, queer theory, and postcolonialism have further informed our understandings (Benítez 1992; de Lauretis 1991; Harvey 1989; Muñoz and Barret 1996).

We do not, however, wish to present our material in a pro or con relationship to these arguments, for several reasons. First, we think that our politics and sentiments should be clear from our introduction, and we do not need to keep restating them. What is important for us in terms of these debates is not so much where we stand on these issues but the results of our collabo-

rative efforts with the people we have worked with. Second, given the validity of the sentiments of localization, specification, and social involvement
that various authors and discourses advocate, it would seem more politically
dramatic to leave to the readers themselves the chore of placing this information within larger frameworks. Third, we feel that often in these complex
arguments the debates rather than people's lives get the privileged position.
The issues of fluid identities, personal agency, and transgression of boundaries are not academic debates for these folks but everyday issues about how
they compose and live their lives.

For those readers searching for wider-ranging generalizations about the
social experiences of the *chicas,* we offer the following cautions. First, not all
gay males in Oaxaca define themselves as passive homosexual males. Those
who do seem to view the boundary between passive and active as a boundary that they will not (as of now) cross. We speak of this boundary used by
this particular group of people in describing themselves; we are in no way
stating that this is a fixed boundary for all gays in Oaxaca or throughout
Latin America. Cornwall (1994), in her work with drag queen prostitutes in
Bahia, Brazil, found that they would cross this boundary if clients paid more,
thus adding to the complexity of gender and sexuality in that context.
Lancaster's work in Nicaragua is framed in terms of popular classes, not all
groups (Lancaster 1992). The work of Carrier (1995), Lumsden (1991), and
Prieur (1996) on gays in Mexico deals primarily with gays in the larger cities of Mexico. In Oaxaca itself, this is a contested border within the gay community as its contours are being remapped in terms of international involvements within that community.

Second, not all passive gay men in Oaxaca are transvestites. Again, this is
how they define themselves. We think that Lancaster's work on transvestic
behavior in everyday life as a means to focus on gender boundaries and the
role of play fits with the dynamics of the members of Grupo Unión, and, as
Lancaster suggests, with most people as they compose and play with their
own domains of sexuality (Lancaster 1997a). It is an ordinary reality. Further, going drag or playing with drag is quite popular in the Oaxacan gay
community. There is an annual gay Halloween party, at which there is a drag
costume contest. At the annual Ms. Gay Oaxaca contest the gay community
of Oaxaca comes together in an open public event. Nevertheless, there are
many passive gay men who never go drag, and some who do, do not go to
the extent of being public queens.

Third, not all passive gay men who like to present themselves as transvestites work as prostitutes. The work of prostitution gives the members of Grupo Unión a means to stay in drag, and very few other employment situations would give them that kind of freedom of action. But that is the *onda* of the *chicas,* not of all gays in Oaxaca.

Thus we feel that the ordinariness of the folks in Grupo Unión is best viewed within their local context, rather than trying to make their context the basis for further generalization. We take this position not to be anti-generalization or to show skepticism for the discourses we have talked about, but to make an honest attempt to work within the concerns of these discourses and of the people we are working with. To give a broader view of the fluidity of sexuality and gender in the context of urban Oaxaca, we will look next at older female street prostitutes, other segments of the gay community in Oaxaca, and sexual politics of the intellectual/bohemian sectors of the city.

CHAPTER FOUR

Only the Spoon Knows What's at the Bottom of the Pot!

Other Groups Transgressing
Sexual and Gender Borders
in Urban Oaxaca

INTRODUCTION

In this chapter we want to present a series of ethnographic portraits of other social actors who can also illustrate the fluidity of sexual and gender spaces among the urban popular classes of Oaxaca. How? Well, as the *dicho* in the above title suggests, we can listen to what folks involved in these activities have to say. Through a combination of luck and circumstances, we were able to encounter three different but somewhat connected groups that express these themes. First we will look at a group of older female street prostitutes in terms of their own *onda* and how it compares to the *onda* of the *chicas*. Then we will review aspects of the gay community in Oaxaca and its relation to the AIDS work in the city. Finally, we will discuss the bohemian community of Oaxaca and its presentations of gender and sexuality.

Why these three groups? Female prostitutes seemed a logical group to compare with the folks of Grupo Unión, and clearly they do represent one sector of working women among the popular classes. Further, with the object of constructing a more complex portrait of the entire community, it seemed logical to include the gay community as a point of comparison to the *chicas*. And a presentation of the bohemian community's enactment of gender and sexual roles seemed an appropriate addition to this overall mural of diversity, since this group represents a mixture of artists, political activists, and intellectuals that is ironically not often talked about in the ethnographic discourse on Oaxaca—and certainly not in terms of questions about sexuality and gender. The connections among these groups are both direct, in that many of these social actors know each other through various social and personal contacts, and indirect, in that these groups are separately marking new social spaces in terms of sexual diversity and fluidity within the urban context of Oaxaca.

The structure of this chapter will be somewhat different from that of previous chapters, for we will be including guest essays on the groups under discussion. We will present some of the interview material that Jayne Howell has done with the same female prostitutes that we know, a short ethnographic account by Bruce Trono on gay men of Oaxaca, and an interview and poems by Lupe Ramírez on her views of the bohemian world of urban Oaxaca.

THE KNITTING PROSTITUTES

Only the spoon knows how empty the pot is.

—*Guadalupe Castilla, a female prostitute in her early forties, standing in front of her one-room apartment (basically just a bedroom) and expressing one of her many* dichos, *or insights, about the lives of the poor*

As we started visiting Leslie and Tania on a regular basis, we got to know their neighborhood, and we noticed that on the block down from their apartment there were women in the streets during the afternoons who were working as prostitutes. What was so striking about these women was that as they were waiting for their clients they would lean up against the buildings or parked cars and knit. Thus we came to refer to them as the "knitting prostitutes." There are eight to ten women who work on this block. They start around midday and work until six or seven in the evening. The women tend to be in their late thirties or early forties and are from the city of Oaxaca. Many have children and perceive themselves as working-class women. This was how we found female—in the traditional sense—prostitutes in Oaxaca.

Like the other stories told in this book, the story of female prostitutes is but a partial focus on a small group of female prostitutes who work the streets of Oaxaca. The whole of the elaborate sexual industry in Oaxaca goes far beyond the *chicas* and the knitting prostitutes. Through their story we can illustrate the ordinariness of these women's lives. First, we will provide a short discussion of the sexual politics of female prostitution in Oaxaca, then an ethnographic portrait of Guadalupe Castilla, a woman who has been a prostitute for more than three decades. That part of the discussion will conclude with an essay by Jayne Howell, who has conducted a more detailed ethnographic investigation with this group of women.

On the Street

The street that the knitting prostitutes work is about seven blocks south of the *zócalo* and about two blocks up from the highway on the southern end of the city. They work the full street, but tend to concentrate in the middle of the block. Though these women have no formal organization among themselves, they do know each other from their work on the street and they will cooperate with each other in terms of sharing information about clients or events that are relevant to their work—for instance, when the public health service is having a workshop on AIDS. The block they work has a few inexpensive hotels (where they take their clients), a few residential units, and a variety of small shops and stores. Unlike the *chicas,* the knitters do not openly solicit clients or even call much attention to themselves beyond their knitting. The fact that they are standing around at midday on the street is enough to communicate that they are prostitutes. We were able to talk with eight of these women, and in a short time we identified some other characteristics that distinguish them from the *chicas.* The knitters are older women, generally in their late thirties or early forties, most have been or still are married, most have children, they do not dress up in a strong "whore" look, and they are not particularly "made up" in terms of using makeup or creating a particular "look." They tend to be women who are at the end of their careers as prostitutes, and working this street at midday is a means for them to maintain their involvement in the profession. What they receive for their work is very minimal. They reported that they can make between forty and sixty pesos a trick, and on a good day they would be able to turn two or three tricks. Further, even with such low earnings, this work on the streets still allows them to cover household needs by bringing some extra money into their homes. They are quite ordinary folks in terms of looks, dress, and behavior. Again, we stress that these women are a very small sample of the female prostitutes who work in the city of Oaxaca. In the evening, younger female prostitutes start to come out, working the streets in the same general area. In addition, many of the younger female prostitutes work in cabarets like Casa Blanca, to which we have already referred.

SEXUAL POLITICS OF FEMALE PROSTITUTION IN THE CITY OF OAXACA

Social and political concerns about prostitution have a long and complex history in Oaxaca. At some times there have been red light zones in the city; at others, nonregulation. Currently, city and public health agencies are leaning toward reestablishing a red light zone as a means to provide better working and social conditions for the prostitutes themselves (Mayoral Figueroa 1996). The feminist community in Oaxaca over the last decade has also

aligned itself with female prostitutes on issues of workers' rights and protection for women. They have not raised moral questions about the profession, but have focused on finding ways of encouraging the women to organize themselves for better working conditions and fewer hassles from the
police (Barahona, Garzon-Aragon, and Musalem 1986). Further, with the
advent of the AIDS crisis, the health agencies of the city and the state have
been working with prostitutes on health issues, including use of condoms
for all clients.

We want to present here a brief account of the distinctions between the
knitters and the *chicas*. The first noticeable difference is their respective
reports of their earning power. The women we talked with on the street said
that they can earn 40 to 60 pesos per client, whereas the *chicas* claim they
are able to charge between 80 and 150 pesos per client. The difference has to
do with age, appearance, and access to clients. The knitters are all in their
thirties and forties, and they do not have the means or the time to put much
effort into their "look." Most of them wear rather ordinary-looking clothing—mostly skirts and blouses—that is in good condition but is neither very
stylish nor very provocative. Further, most of the knitters look like many
other working-class women in the city: they are a little on the robust side,
their hairstyles are very common for women their age, and their streetside
presentation of themselves is conservative and demure. Furthermore, with
their level of earning power, they have no surplus funds to put back into the
business for buying new clothing or developing new looks. The *chicas,* on
the other hand, have a great deal of play space in their everyday activities.
One of the explanations for the difference in earning power between these
two groups has to do with their reasons for being on the street in the first
place. To the *chicas,* the street is the location of their autonomy and a means
to maintain their group structure. The street is where they can earn more
money and have better control over what they do with their lives. In addition, the street is where they started to work as prostitutes and it is where
they want to be. To the knitters, working the street, particularly in the afternoon, reflects the fact that they are in the latter stages of their careers. Many
have worked for more money and in different locations in the past. This labor space of the street does give the knitters, like the *chicas*, the autonomy
to arrange their working hours around other obligations, and it frees them
from the necessity of working for a pimp. In addition, many feel that despite
their low earnings, they still do better than the minimum wage, and they
work fewer hours than they would on a regular job. A very strong difference

is apparent in terms of their relationship to their clients. The *chicas'* clients tend to be drawn from the overall middle class and tourist groups within the city. They have more money and have to use condoms in order to obtain sexual services. The knitters' clients are more likely to be working-class or poor rural and urban men. The knitters said that if the choice is between getting a trick for the day or using a condom, they will allow their clients not to use the condom.

Another notable difference in the two groups is their openness about what they do. The knitters are not particularly open when talking about the sexual nature of their work; they do not offer any information on the types of services they provide, nor do they give evaluations of their clients' sexual skills or anything about how they themselves like the sexual encounters. Also, their choices of words and examples are much more timid and genteel than those of the *chicas*. That is, they did not use harsh or strong language with us, nor did they boast about their beauty or sexual prowess. It would seem that these differences, though derived from many factors, underlie the gendering reality of these actors. Though the *chicas* act like women, they are males who have been socialized into the logic of male sexuality, where boasting about one's skills and preferences is part of the process. The knitters, even though they are prostitutes, still live within the logic of being women. They seem to see themselves as stigmatized by their work and feel some level of embarrassment about what they do and feel that what they do is not proper work for women. Being from working-class backgrounds, they do not see themselves as involved in breaking down boundaries or in constructing new social spaces for the expressions of either gender or sexuality. For them, prostitution is what they have *had to do*, not what they have *wanted to do*. Though the *chicas* also suggest that their involvement in prostitution is out of economic necessity, the knitters feel that they have no other alternatives in their lives. Remember that we are talking about only the knitters, and not about all female prostitutes; even among the knitters there are variations in their backgrounds and lifestyles. Whereas it does not take long to get the *chicas* talking about themselves and the sex that is involved in their jobs, the knitters attempt to direct the conversation away from their profession and have not been very forthcoming with details of their work. Though their work has placed them in the situation of transgressing existing gender assumptions, they do not see themselves in that manner.

One major difference in motivation between the knitters and the *chicas* is that the knitters feel that working the streets is the best means to care for their children. In our conversations with them, they strongly stressed that the reason they are in prostitution is that it allows them to care for their children. In contrast, for *chicas* Leslie and Tania, their success in this field is what gave them the economic means to think about adopting and raising a child.

Lupe Castilla

We met Lupe during one of our early visits with the knitters. She was more friendly than some of the others, and she invited us to stop by her apartment to visit with her when she was not working. Luckily, at the time she lived just two blocks away from the street that she worked on, in a small *vecindad* where she rented a one-room apartment. She told us that she was building a house in a new settlement about fifteen miles outside the city. Lupe is a small woman in her early forties. She has been working as a prostitute since her teens, and her work has taken her throughout Mexico. She started in the cabarets, has worked the major resort areas of Mexico (like Cancún), and now is working the streets of Oaxaca in the afternoons. With her limited savings, she has built a little house outside of town. She says she would like to work for only a few more years, then sell her house and return to Huajuapan de León to live near her sister and open a restaurant.

The knitting prostitutes have a more closed style of talking about themselves, which was reflected in the bits and pieces that Lupe gave us of her life history. At first she told us that she was from Mexico City, had been married, and had older children there whom she would visit once in a while. Later, she said that this story was not quite true. She had told us that because she thought we would be upset with her if she said she did not have children. She then told us that she had had a child who had died in infancy and that in Mexico City she had been involved with a man whose children she regarded as her stepchildren, and she would visit them when she went there. She further stated that she was from Oaxaca and that she had been born in Huajuapan de León. Her parents had been *campesinos* in that area, and she had a sister who still lived near Huajuapan. She further said that when she was around eight years old, her mother died, and her father sent her to the city of Oaxaca to live with an aunt. Thus she spent her early teen years growing up in the center city of Oaxaca. In her late teens she entered the profession of prostitution, and except for a short period of time when she lived in the Los Angeles area (six months), she has been working as a prostitute ever since. Though we came to establish a strong and warm friendship with Lupe, she has never been very open with us about her work as a prostitute. She says that she entered into this profession out of economic necessity and has continued working as a prostitute for the same reason. She is proud that she has seen most of Mexico through her work, but she does not express pride per se in being a prostitute, nor does she express shame or guilt about it. She sees herself moving toward the end of this work and hopes to get out of it within the next two years.

It is her *dicho* that we have used for the title to this chapter. When we asked her about particular aspects of her life, she stated that like the spoon, only she can know about that or about what's at the bottom of the pot. Therefore, she is not too forthcoming on some aspects of what's at the bottom. In other areas of her life, though, she is quite communicative and insightful.

LUPE'S WORLDVIEW

Through paraphrasing of several lengthy conversations we had with Lupe, we have developed the following summary of her various outlooks on her life and hard times.

Lupe considers herself to be a religious person with a strong faith—like many others—in the virgins and saints of the Catholic discourse. She considers herself to be a very moral person who has tried to the best of her ability to be fair and honest with people in her life. She does not see that her work makes her any less of a moral person. Prostitution is what she works at, not what she advocates as a way of life. Like María Elena and Victoria, Lupe feels that there is a correct way to live one's life, which for her involves showing civility and respect to others. She stresses that one should not be judgmental about others unless one really knows what the other person has been through, and even then one should show tolerance. She also feels one should have a good time in life, enjoy family and friends, and try not to work too hard because life will be hard enough.

She does not express any particular views on gender and sexuality. She thinks that women, particularly poor women, have a very hard time getting by in life and that men generally make life hard for women. However, she does not have, or at least has not expressed to us, any critique of gender roles per se or any expressions about her sexuality other than that she works as a prostitute. She is aware of the members of Grupo Unión as competitors on the street in terms of clients, though she does not think there is that much competition between them because of the different types of clients who seek them out. She does not have any concerns about the *chicas* being gay or in drag. To her, they are just one more group of street workers and prostitutes. Lupe is aware of the indigenous groups who live in Oaxaca; however, except for her accepting them as part of the general social terrain and having an understanding that living in indigenous villages is much harder than living in other areas, she does not express any concerns about these issues.

POLITICAL VIEWS

Lupe does not express any particular political point of view. Like many others whom we encountered, she has a general popular class outlook on political issues, including the contradictions within this outlook. Though she has been involved with leftist political groups over the land conflicts in her new community, she is not a member of any leftist parties. Like many others in the popular classes, she feels that the PRI's current political system does no one any good. In fact, her *dicho* about the spoon was her response to a question about poverty in Mexico. Her primary concerns are more about the economic crisis than the political. It is economic constraints that she feels most personally, especially as she tries to finish her small house. She thinks that those who are in the popular classes are the ones who have suffered the most and who will continue to suffer. She does not see or envision any type of political solution to these sufferings, other than that you simply have to learn how to get through it all.

She currently hopes to be able to quit working the streets and to live in her little house or sell it so that she can return to live with her sister or her father. Her hopes for the future are bound up with the complex world of gender and sexuality in Oaxaca. Though it is a more diverse and fluid world than many think, there are still many double standards in terms of gender and age that may make it hard for her to execute her plans. For all the transgressive dynamics going on within the domains of gender and sexuality, her desires for the future are for the most part ordinary: to go back home and be with her family (see photos 29 and 30).

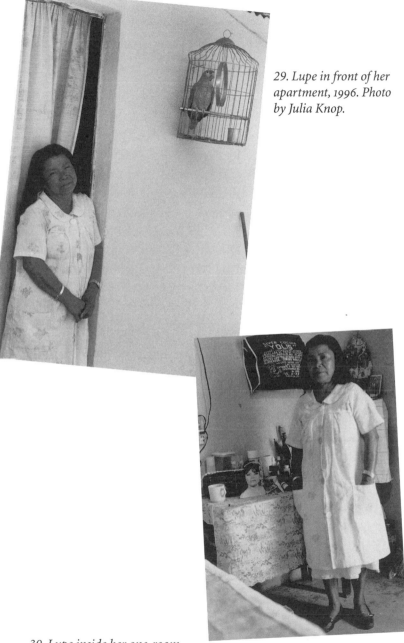

29. Lupe in front of her apartment, 1996. Photo by Julia Knop.

30. Lupe inside her one-room apartment, 1996. Photo by Julia Knop.

"Me Llamo Lupe": Lifestyles of Women Prostitutes in Oaxaca

Jayne Howell

■ ■ ■ ■ ■ ■ ■ ■ ■ ■

Introduction

My interest in the lives of women prostitutes in Oaxaca stems from earlier research into ways that gender factors into educational and employment opportunities in Oaxaca. I had learned earlier that many women who worked as prostitutes had little or no formal education and might previously have worked as domestic servants in the informal labor sector.[1] After I explained my interests to Michael Higgins and Tanya Coen, they introduced me to a group of street prostitutes whom they call "the knitters." In addition to calling these women "the knitters," I also refer to them as "*las Lupes*" because so many have chosen to register with the municipal government using the fictitious name "Lupe," which is the "working name" that appears in their *libretos*.

"Participant" Observation with *las Lupes*

I observed *las Lupes* for a few days a week over the course of three months. Some, like Concha, were friendly with me when I first approached them. Others were more reluctant to talk with me, and I never learned their names or even got them to say hello to me. In time, once they realized I wasn't there to work, most warmed up to me and said hello and asked how I was whenever they saw me. On slow days, a few would spend time with me as they waited for clients to show up. Concha was always friendly to me, and she and I often sat on a stoop outside the hotel where she took clients. At times other prostitutes would join us and talk about working on the street. These women patiently explained what it was like to work on the street.

One of the first things I learned is that the *ambulantes* could immediately distinguish between men who were just passing down the street, those who had come for sex, and members of a group of older men (whom I call "the watchers") who would watch the prostitutes and comment to and about them but never solicit their services. Often I would see a woman make a gesture with her hand or head that I couldn't quite catch, and the next thing I knew she and a man would enter the hotel behind the spot where Concha and I sat. The women normally asked between forty and sixty pesos per trick (five to eight U.S. dollars). Concha said that those women who were willing to do "extras" (such as having sex without a condom or engaging in anal or oral sex) asked more than those who engaged only in vaginal sex with a condom. Regardless of what they asked, the women frequently settled for less, and sometimes they got stiffed after they had negotiated a price. For example, one woman I was observing asked a potential client for fifty pesos. They haggled a bit, then finally agreed on thirty-five. They entered the hotel, and he came out a few minutes before she did. When she came out of the hotel she was frowning. I asked her if everything was okay with her, and she said that he had paid her twenty pesos, although they'd agreed on more. I was puzzled that she was calm about this, because I'd seen her rant in many other situations. She evidently sensed my surprise, and said that she understood that this man was a *campesino* who earned twenty pesos for a day's work. She added that many *obreros* (workers) earn about twenty pesos per day, so she can't expect them to pay her more than that when she's with them for only ten minutes.

The system they had established was that the client paid hotel employees ten pesos to rent the room. For this money, the couple got a room with a full-sized bed, cold water, and a door that they would not lock. Concha told me that although other hotels provided hot water for approximately the same price, some of the rooms were on the upper floors and the prostitute could not be guaranteed that anyone would protect her if she got into trouble. At the hotel Concha frequented, employees looked out for the women and were expected to run to a woman's assistance if she began to bang on a wall, which signaled that there was trouble. If the client was threatening or abusive to the *ambulante*, the employee would forcibly remove him from the room. In these cases, prostitutes would let each other know about *el loco* and identify him if he walked down the street. A prostitute would rarely go with a man who had been identified as dangerous, and if she attempted to do so, another woman or the hotel employees would warn her not to be alone with him.

Concha's Story

Concha has been married for thirty years to an underemployed auto mechanic named Juan, who is now fifty-five years old. They have three children together: the eldest is twenty-seven, and the youngest is twenty-one. Before she met Juan, Concha gave birth to a son, Pedro. She has had no contact with Pedro's father since before her son's birth, and Juan raised Pedro as if he were his own (although he had Concha's surnames). When they first married, Concha, Pedro, and Juan lived with Juan's parents. She had a good relationship with her mother-in-law (since deceased), who accepted Concha's child as her grandson and never distinguished between Pedro and the children Juan later fathered. During the early years of their marriage, Juan worked steadily in one of the few factories in Oaxaca City, and they were able to purchase a small house in INFONAVIT, one of the housing developments the government has constructed for workers. They still live in this house, which is sparsely furnished and reflects their limited economic resources. In the main room are a wooden table, six chairs, a hutch, and a refrigerator. There is one clock on the wall and a picture of each of Concha's grandchildren. The family uses plastic dishes and has mismatched glassware. A small kitchen is off the dining room, as is a closet-size room with a single bed. A staircase leads from this dining area to the two bedrooms upstairs. Only Concha's eldest son has a television or stereo in his room; other family members frequently watch that TV there. Concha has mentioned a number of times that she and Juan do not sleep together any longer: he sleeps on the bed that is off the dining room, whereas she normally sleeps upstairs in her daughter's bedroom.

Although they are no longer physically intimate, Concha considers Juan her best friend. According to her, Juan became a *mujeriego* (womanizer) when their children were still little. He lost his job shortly after their youngest daughter was born. Since that time, he has worked for himself, repairing neighbors' and relatives' cars, but his earnings are not adequate to support the family. Concha realized years ago that she needed to work outside the home in order to pay for her children's studies. Because she had left school after the third grade to sell tortillas with her mother (a *madre soltera*), Concha is barely literate and therefore is not qualified for skilled employment. She and Juan decided that she should work as a prostitute because she would be able to make more money per day than she could make in unskilled jobs such as maid, laundress, or waitress. Concha's involvement in extramarital sexual activities was not an issue for Juan; the couple had stopped having sex years earlier after Concha learned of his womanizing. She has been saving money *en serio* for the past four years, and after accumulating twelve thousand pesos was able in 1996 to construct an addition to her home, where she hopes to eventually run a *miscelania*. She estimates that she will need another seven thousand pesos to pay for the construction of shelving and to purchase goods for the store. She intends to continue working "down there" (her euphemism for being on the street) until she accumulates this start-up money. She had hoped that the money would accumulate more quickly in 1997 than it had during the past five years because her son recently finished university. However, she has just learned that her middle daughter is pregnant. Although her daughter has health insurance, her husband earns a relatively low wage, and Concha and Juan expect that they will have to help her out financially.

Concha's Life in Context

Concha's story is only one of many such stories. My interviews and conversations with prostitutes who went for weekly checkups at the municipal clinic provided a broader perspective on this lifestyle. Most of the women I talked to were from rural communities scattered throughout the state of Oaxaca; a few were from neighboring states, and one was from the lower socioeconomic strata of Oaxaca City. With very few exceptions, the prostitutes had no formal education. In this sense, they were typical of poor Oaxacan girls who are often kept out of school to help around the home or to start contributing to the household budget.[2] For example, thirty-five-year-old Soledad explained that her mother had taken her out of school at the end of third grade to start selling tamales. Others dropped out of school because, as they said, "*no me gustó*" or "*no quise estudiar.*" The facts that they lack formal education and that a majority are functionally illiterate affected their opportunities for employment in their youth and continue to affect their future employment options. I return to this point below.

After leaving school, most of the women worked in menial, dead-end, informal labor-sector jobs, most commonly as maids, waitresses, or shop clerks. Consistently they noted that "*los sueldos que dan no alcanzan*" (you can't support yourself on the salary). It was hard enough for women to support themselves on the wages earned (which in the case of maids may be less than two dollars for a sixteen-hour day—less than half the minimum wage for a ten-hour day!) and impossible to support children on this salary. Given their limited opportunities to work at higher-paying, skilled jobs, it's no surprise that every woman said she worked as a prostitute *por necesidad*.

Furthermore, these prostitutes consistently stated that they worked on the street for the sake of "*los niños.*" Although a handful of women had been legally married at some point in their lives, most had borne children during *uniones libres*. Concha was the only woman living with a man to whom she was legally married. Others had separated because the men were *bien macho*. This term was always used negatively to describe men who could have been womanizers and/or physically violent. Forty-seven-year-old Leti's description of the abuse she suffered is typical: "He hit me. He had many vices: a drunk and womanizer, and he smoked marijuana." The partners of others were *flojos* or *huevones* (lazy men) who did not provide for their children's welfare.

Being single mothers (or, in Concha's case, mothers whose partners don't bring in an income), these women were the primary support of their households. They provided food, shelter (most commonly rented rooms or *casitas de lamina* that they had slowly constructed), clothing, health care, and education for their children. Although prostitution provides a variable income, they perceived it as bringing in more money for the time invested than other jobs available to unskilled women. For example, a *lavandera* (washerwoman) may earn up to forty pesos per day (roughly double the minimum wage). Because so few families have washing machines, *lavanderas* are always in demand. Oaxacans consider this job to be one of the most physically demanding that women hold; not only does the *lavandera* have to scrub clothing, but often she works in cold water and winds up with colds, pneumonia, and arthritis. A few of the prostitutes suggested that they would work at this if they stopped generating any income at all through their current activities, but all made it clear that they would prefer not to.

Once a woman justified (at least to herself) the decision to work as a prostitute, she entered into this lifestyle in various ways. I interviewed and talked with women who had worked as prostitutes on the streets or in cantinas, and some had worked in both settings. The ages at which they started working ranged from twelve to twenty-six. In some instances a friend who worked as a prostitute "*me metío*" (showed the newcomer the ropes), as had happened to the woman who started to prostitute at age twelve. Some friends helped women who were eighteen or older get their *libretos,* while others did so on their own.

A woman who knows employees or owners at a cantina can easily get a job as a *fichera,* a woman who is paid to drink beer with a man and can choose to have sex for money if she so desires. Those without contacts find a job by checking windows for signs that say, WAITRESS WITH PERMIT WANTED. New *ambulantes* who go to work on a street where they don't know anyone are often approached by other women who work the street or by the police, and some may summon the police if a newcomer refuses to show her *libreto.* Whether summoned or arriving on their own, police officers advise a woman without a *libreto* to get one immediately because she is subject to arrest if found working again without it.

Hardships of Hooking

As I spoke with the prostitutes, they discussed the problems that they encountered in their everyday lives. Some of their remarks were not surprising, whereas others were less obvious. Given that finances factored into the reasons for entering prostitution, I'd expected women to identify their greatest problems in this work as the unstable salary and no insurance benefits. Although that was mentioned by most, the more common problems revolved around conditions on the street.

One of the problems I heard about from *ambulantes* at the clinic involved getting established on the street once they'd registered with the government and gotten a *libreto*. First off, *ambulantes* jealously guard their spots on their legally assigned streets. Francisca, a fifty-four-year-old woman who did not work as a prostitute until her husband's death a dozen years ago, remarked, "When I first arrived on the street, one of the women who thinks she's the *lider* wanted to see my *libreto*. I told her that I show my *libreto* to the inspectors and clients if they ask, but that I didn't owe her anything." When I asked Francisca if she had worried that this might cause problems, she replied, "*La calle es libre* (The street is free). I have as much right to be there as they do." I had one unpleasant instance where two women on the street where Concha works evidently did not know why I was there. A woman I had never seen before came up to me and began to aggressively ask me questions as I chatted with Mari, an *ambulante* whom I knew informally. I said to this woman that I was simply trying to carry on a conversation with a friend and meant her no harm. She then began to question Mari about a napkin she was embroidering, and Mari finally turned to me and asked that I meet her at her home someday if I wanted to talk. I started to walk away, and the woman I didn't know approached me again and told me to give her a cigarette. I explained that I don't smoke. She then made a remark about me lying. I chose not to respond to her, and a friend of Concha's yelled over to me, "*Pasa a su casa luego* (Go to [Concha's] house later)." When I next saw Concha, I said that I hoped I had not caused problems for her or Mari by being friendly with them on the street. She laughed and said, "*No hiciste nada, Juanita. Hay puros pleitos alla. Siempre* (You didn't do anything. There are always problems [on the street])." When I mentioned this incident to personnel at the clinic a few days later, they informed me that such situations are common. *Ambulantes* often talk about unpleasant confrontations between them. One member of the medical staff said that she's heard women complaining that when they first arrived as newcomers to a street, the established *ambulantes* would hit them and insult them. In fact, she said, a woman's clothes had been torn off in one fight.

Each woman I spoke with, both the *ficheras* and the *ambulantes*, used some variation of the statement "*Hay que sorportar a los hombres*" (You have to put up with the men)" when asked to identify the worst things about this type of work. Individually, they discussed dealing with drunks, men who agree to pay one price but then renege and pay less once they get to the room, and violence that may erupt at any time, as I mentioned earlier. All of the women knew of prostitutes killed or menaced by men who picked them up. Toni, a mother of two in her mid-forties, told me that she now takes more precautions than she used to because of an incident that happened to a friend of hers. The other *ambulante*'s client tied her up and held a gun to her head as he threatened to do various types of violence, then left after he'd finished reciting his list. Toni's friend eventually managed to free herself enough to make noise and get help. Toni said that this situation really scared her and other *ambulantes* for a couple of reasons. First, her friend could have been killed. Second, Toni says she's met men with many sexual fantasies that they want to act out, but never has she picked up someone who had come to a prostitute for anything other than sex. Nearly everyone I spoke to cited fear of violence as the reason that they prefer to go with clients they've gone with previously, even if it means turning down a stranger's money. Concha would criticize other *ambulantes* who were "so desperate" for money that they would go with *cualquier hombre* (anybody who asked).

Some women specifically spoke about men who insulted them. Ali, a thirty-six-year-old *fichera*, said that she's been asked things such as "*Oyes, puta—¿Por qué te rentas?* (So, slut, why do you rent yourself?)." Women who work on the street can tell verbally abusive men "*a volar*" or "*largate* (get lost)," but *ficheras*' bosses expect them to treat customers politely. This holds true as well when clients begin to grope the *fichera* when dancing or sitting at the table. Ali explained that she tries to wear long skirts so that a man can't get his hands between her legs, but said that younger girls don't yet know how to do this. Many other *ficheras* also cited among the hardships of the job having to drink alcohol in order to get money, and the majority of *ambulantes* said that they prefer working on the street to working in a cantina because they do not have to drink on the street. Clinic personnel indicated that some of the *ficheras* drink as many as thirty beers a day and have corresponding health problems (including diabetes and alcoholism). Ali added that insults and "disrespectful" groping make her "feel bad" about herself, adding that she's ashamed when her children see her drunk and ask her why she's "sick."

In addition to being insulted by the men who contact them, prostitutes may also be subjected to insulting comments from neighbors and relatives who are aware of the prostitute's activities. Some of the women I spoke with, like Concha, tell their children how they earn money and why they do what they do. They stress the hardships of the job and emphasize the lack of pleasure they take from the sexual encounters. Other women do not want their children to know what they do, and tell them that they work as *lavanderas,* cooks, and waitresses. Francisca was angry that her neighbors had seen her on the street and told her three sons what she did. Only the eldest discussed it with her, stating that he personally was shocked and unhappy at this, while her younger sons were in denial. When she explained that she'd been working on the streets for a dozen years to finance her youngest son's studies, he advised her to *cuidese* (protect herself). Other women reported that their relatives had advised them to keep safe, which meant both to beware of abusive men and to use condoms during sexual intercourse. Relatives who were angry about the prostitutes' work—often because they had been embarrassed by the comments of neighbors—criticized the woman behind her back and to her face. These women said that though such remarks often sting they do not result in an immediate lifestyle change because the prostitute has minimal economic resources. Comments made by thirty-six-year-old Pati are typical of the responses I heard in response to criticism from others: "It doesn't matter if they talk to me or not. I say, 'I don't live for you. I work [at this] so that my children can get ahead.'"

THE GAY COMMUNITY AND AIDS ORGANIZATION IN OAXACA

> I think that my landlord wanted to throw us out. Last night I brought home a woman who was in the last stages of AIDS. I put her up in my bedroom, for her family did not want to take care of her and she had no money. Tragically, she died in the night, and we had to go through a lot of hassle to get her into a funeral home, again for lack of money. The landlord was furious because I let a person with AIDS die in his house.
>
> —*José Antonio Peña, a thirty-plus gay male, who is the chair of an AIDS care group (called Renacimiento, "rebirth") in the city of Oaxaca, sitting in his bedroom and talking about his current conflicts with his landlord*

The title of this section is problematic in several ways. First, is there such a thing as a gay community in Oaxaca? Is there in Oaxaca a definable social group that is attempting to compose a public sexual identity around being gay or lesbian while seeking a particular political and social agenda in relation to that position? This is not one of those yes or no questions. In the current social space of male sexuality in Oaxaca, gayness already exists in the category of the passive male homosexual that we talked about in the chapter on the Grupo Unión. The *chicas* certainly represent a group in the process of building a community; however, their concerns are about not just "gayness" but also the issues of sex workers and transvestites. If we mean by "gay community" something like the North American model, the Castro district in San Francisco, for example, then we find that no such community exists as yet in Oaxaca. Through personal contacts and travel, many within the middle-class world of gays and lesbians in Oaxaca are aware of such possibilities as a gay community. Further, many in this Oaxacan group have made connections and alliances with North American and European gay networks. However, many within the Oaxacan middle-class gay world do not view the drag queens as being representative of their gayness per se and they seek a more moderate presentation of personal and public images. Further, in terms of male sexuality, there are numerous *hombre/hombres* floating in and out of these social spaces without a concern for the reality of gayness, since they hold themselves not to be gay. Also, ironically, it is problematic to see male gayness as transgressive in the Oaxaca context, since it is part of existing male sexuality. In these discursive spaces, the passive males who would want to penetrate would be the transgressive actors (Hendriks, Tielman, and van der Veen 1993; Klein and Wolf 1985; Plummer 1992).

As is often the case, external factors are pushing actors within these spaces to think in terms of a community. In Oaxaca such factors include the dual realities of an international gay movement in which Oaxacans are involved and the confrontation with AIDS. Whatever gay males are doing in Oaxaca in terms of the specificity of that social space, that space is connected to international gay activities, if only by the presence of gay tourists in Oaxaca. Further, the whole discourse of AIDS makes sexual orientation or lifestyles a public reality in attempting to address the corresponding health issues. Interestingly enough, in Oaxaca the AIDS discourse is caught in an odd contradiction; some wish to address AIDS as a disease that shows no social boundaries. Thus AIDS is not seen as a gay illness but as an illness that affects everyone. However, what might be seen as an emerging gay community in Oaxaca reads this position on AIDS as one that is attempting to closet the reality of gays and how gays in particular are affected by AIDS. We feel that these external dynamics may be encouraging Oaxacan gays and lesbians to begin thinking in community terms. Before moving on to talk about AIDS organizations in Oaxaca, we will present Bruce Trono's short ethnographic account of the *ambiente* (scene) of gay men in Oaxaca.

La Onda "Gay" in Oaxaca

Bruce Trono

■ ■ ■ ■ ■ ■ ■ ■ ■

My introduction to the "gay subculture" of Oaxaca occurred quite by chance one day as I was window-shopping along the streets near the city center. I was struck by one shop that had several glossy posters of scantily clad, muscular men taped to the front entrance—the kind of photos one finds in the lifestyle magazines targeted for a gay male audience. I went closer to investigate. There was also a poster proclaiming the importance of safe sex for gay men and a page clipped from the personal section of a gay magazine. These posters had nothing whatsoever to do with the commerce of the shop but, as I was to learn later, were simply a way for the shop owner to identify himself to passersby. The message was obvious to gay men and yet not so blatant as to cause scandal among those passersby who were not gay.

I struck up a conversation with Aldo,[3] the owner of the shop, and when I alluded to the posters Aldo did not hesitate to proclaim that he was gay (his word choice), and I reciprocated. We talked about various aspects of gay life in our respective cities. Over the next several weeks I spent a significant amount of time in Aldo's shop, which seemed more like Oaxaca's gay drop-in center than a place of commerce. Aldo had many friends in Oaxaca and seemed to make new ones every day. The afternoons I spent sitting in the shop, I lost count of the number of times some young Oaxacan man would walk by, spot the posters in the doorway, and decide to drop in and find out what this was all about.

It was through conversations with these men that I learned about the who, what, and where of men who have sex with men in Oaxaca. They told me about the various places where they and others with similar interests go and what they do there. Other days I visited some of these places with friends and with their help watched for the signals and meanings behind what these men were doing.

Naturally, I bring to this investigation a particular cultural understanding of what being "gay" or homosexual is and what the meanings of particular sexual acts are. The assessment of homosexuality within middle-class Anglo-Canadian culture tends to focus on desire. A person is homosexual if he/she has the desire to have sexual relations with a person of the same sex. There are ambiguities in this approach, but the important point here is that the identification and consequently the stigma of homosexuality focus on the desires of the participants; issues of gender are subordinate to this focus on desire.

This perception of homosexuality draws a distinct contrast to one particular discourse of sexuality present in Mexico and Latin America that emphasizes gender roles in the defining of sexuality and the production of stigma. This discourse is discussed in the literature on homosexuality in Latin America (see, for example, Carrier 1995 and Lancaster 1992). Within this discourse, a man is "gay" when he takes what is understood to be a woman's role; "effeminate" outward behavior and a "passive" role in homosexual sex acts (i.e., the penetratee in anal and oral sex) are the markers of "gayness." The gender behavior and the "passive" role in sex are presumed to be linked. The "masculine"-behaving man is presumed to be the "active" partner in homosexual sex acts, and his macho "manly" status depends on that—or at least on the appearance of it.

The "gay" man in this discourse bears the brunt of the stigma surrounding homosexuality. By being effeminate and passive, he has violated his "natural" gender role in a very serious manner. Conversely, the *activo*, because he is masculine-behaving and the penetrator in sex acts, has made only a minor breach of his "natural" gender role. So long as he continues to pursue sex with women, his homosexual acts produce little stigma for him. The *activo* man who engages in sex with men is *not* gay within this particular discourse. Of course, these categories are far from rigid, but as an outsider I was struck by the difference between them and the subculture that I knew in another context.

In Oaxaca the two discourses of homosexuality that I have described above exist simultaneously within the "gay subculture." These competing discourses variously influence how gay men in Oaxaca make sense of themselves and their subculture. Questions of social class and community standards of decency and respect for privacy also influence the practices and performances of men who have sex with men in Oaxaca.

Places and Activities

Carlos was the first to point out to me that for men who have sex with men in Oaxaca there are two types of places: *lugares libres* (uninhibited places) and *lugares publicos* (places requiring considerable discretion). These places are distinguished not only by the sorts of activities that are permissible but also by the types of people who frequent them.

Lugares Libres

Lugares libres are a relatively new phenomenon in Oaxaca. These are exclusively gay establishments that are operated specifically to make money by providing gay men with a private place to assemble. In Oaxaca such places of assembly consist of one all-gay disco and one exclusively gay section of a bathhouse. One of the enticements that set these places apart from *lugares publicos* is that here gay men can be open about their sexuality without fear of negative social consequences or physical harm. Furthermore, the problem of identifying other gay men that exists in public places is virtually eliminated in these establishments, as it is assumed that the patrons here are gay.

THE BAR

There was only one exclusively gay bar in Oaxaca at the time of my research in 1995. The disco Club 502 opened about a year before that (but none of my informants seemed to remember exactly when). As far as any of the participants knew, it was Oaxaca's first and only exclusively gay nightclub. A friend at Aldo's shop told me that the club is open only on Friday and Saturday nights from 11:30 p.m. until 4:00 a.m. He seemed to have the days right, but the 11:30 p.m. opening time was slightly optimistic.

After hearing about Club 502 I was eager to investigate as soon as possible. None of my friends at Aldo's shop seemed to be free on the weekend I wanted to go, so I gathered up a fellow anthropology student, along with my courage, and set out late one Saturday night.

From my experience at home I knew that gay bars are never busy until midnight, so we waited until 11:30 p.m. to go, hoping to arrive at a suitably fashionable hour.

The name "502" is also the street address of the bar, so once we were in the 500 block of the street we expected to see some signs of life—flashing lights, loud music, maybe a line outside the door. We saw nothing. In fact, we had to make two passes by the place before we noticed the little numbers "502" on the wall beside the door. They were street numbers like those on any other building on the block— no sign, no lights, and not a sound from within.

Then we noticed the small sign beside the door that read in Spanish, "This is a private party. Only friends of the club are permitted." Did this mean us? Or was there actually a private party in progress? At least we now knew that the place considered itself a "club." Looking closely at the door, we noticed that way up near the top right there was a small plastic doorbell button.

The bell created a stir somewhere inside, and for the first time we heard people talking behind the door. A little hatch at eye level in the steel door opened inward and a pair of eyes peered out at us. Then the hatch snapped shut and there was more discussion from behind the door. The hatch opened again and a voice asked, "Yes?"

"Is this Club 502?" I inquired rather timidly. "Yes," said the eyes. The hatch closed, the door opened, and we stepped inside. We saw little to distinguish the physical environment or activities of 502 from any similar-size gay bar in Canada or the United States (except for the fact that 502 seems to have its peak hours between 2 a.m. and 3:30 a.m.). The bar is actually two rooms connected by an open passage. The front room has some little tables and chairs and a bar at the far end. The second room has the predictable framed black-and-white poster of Madonna, another of a muscular, shirtless man, a small dance floor, tables and chairs, and subdued lighting.

The crowd tends to be young men between the ages of twenty and thirty-five, though many nights I saw a few women there also. The men are generally a stylish crowd, dressed in designer jeans, leather jackets, and brand-name fashions and evidencing attention to detail in grooming. Groups of friends and couples sit together at tables, drink, socialize, and dance. Lovers here can be affectionate with each other, occasionally holding hands, embracing, or kissing. All in all, displays of affection seem subdued in comparison to the straight couples who make out on the benches in the *zócalo*.

The patrons of the bar take advantage of the freedom here by openly expressing themselves in their manner of dress and talk, displays of affection for other men, and of course dancing with other men. This behavior is markedly different from the behavior of the very same men in public. In this place the most important aspect of their identity is "gayness" and they express it.

The experience of gaining entrance to the club, however, was for me the most remarkable aspect of the scene. There are good reasons for such seemingly extreme measures. The subtle entrance and the heavy security at the door do seem to prevent embarrassing incidents in which straight people accidentally stumble into the bar. One bartender also suggested that the local police sometimes find gay men excellent targets for bribes. Consequently, the restricted access at the front doors serves as a minor deterrent for any police who might, on a whim, decide to drop into the club and look for an excuse to shake down clients. The cover charge is prohibitively expensive for many Oaxacan gay men, which contributes to maintaining a mostly middle-class clientele.

The gay bar, like the gay men, is reluctant to announce its existence in Oaxaca. In fact, at the time of my research the only way to find out about the existence of this club was through word of mouth. The attitude of straight Oaxacan society toward the gay bar and the people who patronize it seems to be one of indifference and the low-key profile maintained by the club helps to perpetuate this indifference.

THE BATHS

The other widely known *lugar libre* is the *vapors general* section of the public baths at the Embassy Hotel. Like the gay bar, the gay section of the bathhouse is known to its clientele only through word of mouth. While the activity in the gay disco focuses on conversation and dancing, activity here focuses on sex. In this place men openly make sexual advances toward one another without concern as to who is watching. In many cases sexual acts take place in full view of all who care to be in the vapor room or in the open showers. These sex acts usually involve two men but can on occasion involve three or more. In fact, Oaxaca's gay bath is not significantly different than many of the gay baths that one might find in cities in Canada or the United States.

Lugares Publicos

In theory, *lugares publicos* are all places where one must exercise discretion about one's homosexual interests. And it is true that one could encounter someone who has similar homosexual interests almost anywhere. In Oaxaca, however, certain places have come to be favorites for men who are seeking some form of homosexual companionship. Among the most popular are the *zócalo* and nearby streets, one of the local cinemas, and some of the seemingly straight all-male cantinas.

THE ZÓCALO

Ligando, or cruising, as it is called in North America, can occur at any time in the *zócalo* but is most active in the late afternoon and evening. Located at the very center of the city, this picturesque park is a place where all sorts of people go to see and be seen by others. The cruising activities of men seeking men go on in full view of others in the park without causing scandal. There are two main reasons why these potentially shocking activities go unheeded in the most public space in the city. First, the activities of the cruisers are so discreet and subtle that close observation over time is necessary to detect them. Second, while non-gay Oaxacans may suspect that something is going on here, they seem content to avoid interfering in others' affairs so long as community standards of public conduct are not openly violated.

The primary signifier for *ligando* in the *zócalo* and in the street is eye contact. For the participants, eye contact is an indication that they have been noticed. If both participants look back a second time, this is a significant indicator of interest but will require further effort to verify intentions. A smile, taking a position closer to the other, and finally posing a question of a seemingly innocent nature opens the opportunity for discreet conversation that will eventually "get to the point."

All of this takes place within a complex set of strategic maneuvers—standing, sitting, and walking—with the participants' attention carefully focused on the task at hand. Some walk up and down the paths and change seats frequently, while others sit in one spot and wait for the action to come to them. Once intentions have been established, the participants must find more private spaces for more intimate activity. This frequently presents a problem for men who live with their families and cannot afford the price of a hotel room. The tactics for cruising in the *zócalo* are not significantly different from those for cruising in the nearby streets.

Carlos's demonstration and explanation of *ligando* in the *zócalo* was helpful in establishing *how* this activity was carried out. But my assumptions as to *why* men engage in *ligando* in the *zócalo* were somewhat incomplete at that time. I assumed that all participants were seeking the same thing: a pleasant sexual encounter. Perhaps a bit naive, I was surprised to find that some of these men have more than just sex on their minds.

One afternoon while I was sitting in the *zócalo* reading a newspaper, a man of about twenty-eight sat down beside me on the bench. As most of the other benches were occupied, I thought nothing of it. After a few minutes he asked me for the time. I told him, and he followed up with some small talk that gradually led to a stream of questions about where I was from, what it was like there, what I was doing here, and so on. I too asked him about his life in Oaxaca.

His name was Eduardo, and he actually lived not in Oaxaca but in a small satellite town just twenty minutes away by bus. We talked about all manner of things, and eventually he told me about his numerous girlfriends in town and asked me if I had a girlfriend back in Canada. I told him that I didn't have a girlfriend and would have been satisfied to leave it at that. But Eduardo was determined to find out why I didn't have a girlfriend and why I wasn't terribly concerned that I didn't have one. After evading the issue for a few moments I simply decided to be straightforward and told him that I didn't have a girlfriend because I had a boyfriend. He smiled, nodded, and said, "Oh, I understand . . . I have *amigos* too."

I tried to inquire about his *amigos,* but on this issue it was Eduardo's turn to be evasive. He preferred, instead, to take the conversation in a different direction. What hotel was I staying at, how much does a ticket from Canada to Mexico cost, how much do people make for a living in Canada, and so on. It was painfully evident now that my being gay was somehow connected to his enthusiasm for the topic of money.

Once we had exhausted this subject, he asked me if I would like to spend some time with him. I knew that this was a proposition of some kind, so I simply suggested that perhaps I would run into him some other time and if so perhaps we could chat again. He explained this might be difficult as it was very expensive to get from his house to El Centro by bus and that perhaps I could lend him the twenty pesos necessary (the bus from where he lived to El Centro was in fact less than one peso). I told him that I didn't have that much money with me at the moment but perhaps we would run into each other again some other time.

THE CINE AND CANTINAS

Homosexual cruising in the cinema is generally confined to Oaxaca's one pornography cinema, which ironically screens only heterosexual pornographic movies. Some cruising is also reputed to occur in one other cinema that occasionally plays soft porn. Homosexual activity occurs in the darker areas at the back of the cinema and is generally restricted to touching and oral sex.

Cruising in the *cine* rarely involves discussion, is generally anonymous, and usually offers an opportunity for on-the-spot sexual activity. These marked contrasts with cruising in the *zócalo* make *cine* cruising appealing to some and repugnant to others. Informants claimed that in contrast to other public cruising venues, the porn cinema is practically a sure bet for finding casual, anonymous sex.

It is also possible for men to find male sex partners in some of the all-male cantinas and some otherwise straight bars and restaurants. Cruising in these places requires particular social skills and great care.

The possibility of misunderstandings necessitates great caution. None of the people that I spoke with felt that this was a likely place to meet men, but most claimed to have friends, or friends of friends, who had encountered a partner, or *mayate*, in one of these straight *cantinas*.

People and Identity

ALDO

Aldo is twenty-five years old and the first of the gay men that I met in Oaxaca. He lives at home with his parents, who own some property in Oaxaca and run their own successful business. They subsidize Aldo's shop and much of his leisure activity.

Consequently, Aldo maintains a lifestyle that is the envy of many of his friends. He passes his days selling in his shop, but has ample time to sit and chat with many of his gay and straight friends who drop in throughout the day. He entertains his gay friends with his collection of gay erotica magazines and various other items of interest that he has picked up in his travels to Mexico City and various other places. He runs personal ads in Mexico's gay publications and gets responses by mail from gay men from all over the country. It is not unusual to come into his shop and find Aldo browsing through this correspondence and composing responses.

Unlike many of his friends, Aldo makes no attempt to conceal his sexuality; in fact, he takes a certain perverse pleasure in asserting it. It never fails to bring a smile to his face when the provocative posters in his doorway trigger startled looks from people passing by. Some days he will stand at his doorway and call out in appreciation to the *chavos guapos* (handsome young men) walking by. Reactions range from indifference to angry sneers.

One afternoon a plainclothes policeman entered the shop and had a look around. He then flashed his badge and claimed that he had received complaints about Aldo's posters and pictures from concerned citizens (Aldo had recently placed a naked photo of himself in the doorway). He told Aldo to remove them all or he would be back the next day to take serious action, either to charge Aldo a fine or to close down the shop. Aldo complied but had most of the same posters back up again a few weeks later.

The one exception to his bravado is in regard to his parents. His father seems to make a point of letting Aldo know when they are dropping by the shop for a visit, and Aldo makes certain that all traces of "gayness" are removed before he arrives.

What may be surprising to many Oaxacans who encounter Aldo is the absence of the kind of "effeminate" characteristics that many seem to associate with homosexuality. Aldo is tall, with well-developed musculature from weight lifting, and in dress, speech, and manner-isms, he is indistinguishable from straight men in the city. Like many of his middle-class gay friends, he is contemptuous of overtly effemi-nate males—*obvios*, as they call such men. He feels that these men give gay men like him a bad name and perpetuate stereotypes.

Aldo is very well informed about the gay liberation politics in Mexico City and the United States. The gay nightlife and lifestyles that prevail in Mexico City and various cities in the United States and Canada hold a strong allure for him. He identifies himself as gay and thinks that it is important that gay men be visible and open about their sexual preference. On the issue of gender behavior, however, Aldo feels that effeminate men and transvestites weaken the gay po-litical movement.

Aldo first met other men who have sex with men in the *zócalo*. Though much of his social activity now focuses on *lugares libres* like the gay bar and private gay parties, he still enjoys meeting men in public places for casual encounters. He claims that the men that he meets there are often younger and less affected by the "gay scene." In spite of the fact that he occasionally indulges these *lugares publicos,* he sees them as being a lower form of gay venue. He characterizes the men who exclusively use *lugares publicos* as either desperate—that is, too ugly or too closeted—or too poor to go to a gay bar. In either case, they are not good prospects for anything more than casual sex.

CARLOS

Carlos is a twenty-two-year-old student at the university who lives with his family in a suburb of Oaxaca. His father is a civil servant, and his mother works as a secretary. Their combined income is enough to provide a good life for their family, and because of it Carlos has been able to continue his education. In spite of his parents' support, however, Carlos works part time as a waiter in order to provide himself with a small measure of economic freedom.

Unlike Aldo, Carlos is much more reserved and cautious about revealing his homosexual interests in public, but he opens up considerably when in the exclusive company of other gay men. Around his straight friends at school and work, however, he behaves quite differently because he has no desire for any of these people to find out that he is gay. Though he does not believe that there is anything wrong with being gay, he does not agree with Aldo that being "out" about his sexuality is a good thing. He feels that Aldo's "in your face" attitude about being gay is disrespectful. Though he is almost certain that his parents know that he is gay, he never confronts them with this issue and in fact will go to great lengths to conceal his activities. He does this, he claims, out of respect for them.

Carlos is quite happy to identify himself as a *pasivo* and has no qualms about taking an exclusively "feminine" role in sex or about having a strong attraction for "straight" men. Though he agrees with Aldo that this *activo/passivo* dichotomy is not necessary in gay relationships, he strongly prefers it and wants all of his relationships to be clearly defined along gender lines.

MIGUEL

At the lower end of the middle-class privilege, Miguel, at twenty-three, must make his own opportunities in life. Though both of his parents work, they do not make enough to send Miguel to university. By virtue of his own special talents, Miguel has received a scholarship that provides him with an education and the opportunity to travel from time to time. But he has far greater restrictions on spending than the others and uses his money carefully. Living on his own at the university, however, provides him with a level of sexual freedom not enjoyed by the others.

Miguel identifies himself as gay but rejects the restrictions on sexual activity and gender imposed by the active/passive dichotomy. He doesn't accept that to be gay one must be passive and effeminate, and though his deportment is quite masculine, he confesses that he enjoys both passive and active roles in his sexual encounters. He is not offended by effeminate men or drag queens, though he has no close friends that could be classified as effeminate.

Miguel sees no reason to "out" himself for political reasons and in fact has no interest in the gay identity politics that he encounters in Mexico City and the United States. He has told most of his friends at school that he is gay but not his parents. He is certain that his parents know he is gay and feels that despite the fact that they don't raise the issue with him, they accept it without any great disappointment. If they were to raise the issue with him, Miguel says he would have no trouble discussing it with them.

Miguel enjoys going to gay bars from time to time but finds these exclusively gay venues limiting and often dull. He is truly in his element when cruising in *lugares publicos*. The adventure of public cruising and the variety of people one can encounter are elements that gay bars seem unable to provide for him. He is particularly intrigued by the action that takes place in the metro stations in Mexico City when he goes there on his frequent visits. Even though his sexual encounters are casual and frequently anonymous, he has developed several long-lasting, close friendships as a result of some of these encounters.

Though these men all identify themselves as "gay," they differ in their understanding of what it means to be "gay" and in their approaches to dealing with their own homosexuality.

Some Closing Thoughts

While it is tempting to look for something "exotic" in the practices and understandings of gay men in Oaxaca, I would be misleading the reader if I did not acknowledge that much of what goes on in Oaxaca's "gay subculture" is entirely recognizable to me based only upon my experiences as a gay man in Canada. Those homosexual practices that I have associated with Oaxaca's working-class men, the widespread use of public cruising, or the focus on gender roles in the production of identity and stigma, for example, certainly exist within the gay subculture in Canada, though their prevalence within and influence on "mainstream" gay culture in Canada or the United States is open to some debate. Yet in the context of my study, such practices struck me as being worthy of note.

Also notable are those practices and behaviors that I have associated with the gay middle class of Oaxaca. *Lugares libres* and notions of sexual identity that focus on desire, for example, might easily be attributed to the growing influences of the gay subcultures of the United States. What may be most interesting here is how these two competing discourses of homosexuality have been incorporated and merged by various individuals to create a truly unique notion of who they are and what it is to be gay. A more thorough study might ask more specific questions about this process of incorporation in identity formation.

In looking at those practices and notions that I have found to be remarkable in Oaxaca's gay subculture, I cannot but wonder what a gay outsider might find remarkable about Toronto's gay subculture. What would Aldo and Miguel find interesting, boring, distasteful, shocking, intriguing if they were to pass a month in my home city?

AIDS ORGANIZATIONS IN THE CITY OF OAXACA

Currently in Oaxaca there are three agencies or groups that are openly working on the issues of AIDS: El Frente Comunal, an AIDS educational group; CoeSIDA, which is the government health service focusing on AIDS; and Renacimiento, an AIDS care group. This section begins with some qualifications on our part. We will explore some of the social connections between the presence of several AIDS organizations in Oaxaca and what might be seen as an emerging gay community. We are not suggesting that some automatic connection exists between gayness and AIDS, but we do think that not to recognize or talk about what effect AIDS is having on gay realities in Oaxaca would be irresponsible on our part. We are not saying that AIDS is a gay illness, nor are we denying that it can affect everyone; what we are saying is that the AIDS epidemic has affected the way *everyone* confronts sexuality (Singer 1993). Further, in the case of gayness, this epidemic has affected how gays are perceived and how they perceive themselves. Ironically, the tragedy of AIDS has opened up space for gay voices that were in the past silenced in Oaxaca. The material reality of the passive/active male sex discourse clearly makes AIDS an illness that does affect everyone, but in order to understand how that is so in the context of Oaxaca, it will be necessary to understand what that discourse means or has meant in terms of being gay in that social context.

The second qualification is that when we talk about the dynamics among the various groups in the AIDS world we are not attempting to evaluate or judge their programs. We are quite aware of the complex and important medical and political debates that have been part of the AIDS world for more than a decade. Another irony here is that in North America and Europe this debate is currently centered around new forms of treatment and access to these treatments. One example is the concern over the "cocktail" drug therapies now being used for folks who are HIV-positive and the suggestion that these cocktails might be the first step in the control of AIDS. These debates have a limited effect on the reality of AIDS in Oaxaca, for neither the medical structure nor many of the local actors have the financial means to participate in such "experiments." When we asked about the use of AZT for people with AIDS in Oaxaca, most folks stated that it was not an issue yet, since no one could afford to use the drug anyway. We encourage our readers to familiarize themselves with this critical debate, but it is far beyond the scope of what we are addressing here. Our friendly criticism of the AIDS organizations and the gay community in Oaxaca will concern the social dynamics between them, not strategies of intervention or treatment.

Our third qualification is in terms of the number of people who have AIDS, who are HIV-positive, or who are seeking treatment in the city and state of Oaxaca. In Oaxaca, no one has very good data about this. Estimates run from several hundred to several thousand. What is "perceived" is that AIDS is present, people are dying from it, and people need information about the issues. All of the AIDS agencies in Oaxaca are working within these parameters, and the differences among them are in terms of style and organization, rather than recognition of the problem. They all realize the need for something to be done.[4]

El Frente Comunal

El Frente Comunal is a nongovernmental AIDS education and services agency. It is chartered to educate the Oaxacan community in general on the issues of AIDS, to argue for safe sex for all, and to provide advice to people with AIDS. It does not do testing or offer any medical advice or treatment services. Its central activities are organized around giving talks or offering workshops on what AIDS is and how it is thought to be transmitted. It vigorously advocates practices of safe sex, with a primary focus on the use of condoms for any kind of sexual activity, as well as stressing monogamous relationships. At the Frente Comunal office in the center of the city one can obtain informational materials, get free condoms, and request a speaker to come give a presentation to a group. El Frente sends sex educators to schools, workplaces, or anywhere they are invited. The trained volunteer staff of about ten persons are competent to give talks or workshops on the issues of AIDS. Only the administrative staff receive wages for their work. The organization has an advisory board made up of prominent Oaxacans who advise on various issues and concerns. Again, El Frente is not an activist agency but an educational group.

We went along with Julia Cortez, a psychologist who is one of the Frente volunteers, when she gave the standard AIDS talk at one of the public high schools in town. It was in the format of a slide show that introduced the issues of AIDS as a sexually transmitted disease that can be prevented through the practices of safe sex and monogamous relations. The show was informative, as current as such talks can be, accessible to the students, and, within its own framework, nonjudgmental. When Julia spoke about sex between couples and the need for safe sex even for couples, she used slides that always had three pairs of stick figures for couples: male to female, male to male, and female to female. She did not talk about gayness as having anything to do with AIDS, nor was there any discussion about the male sexuality of active/passive actors. Julia was a good presenter and she kept the attention of the students, who were in their last years of secondary school. They asked questions, and they seemed to be neither shy nor embarrassed by the topic. For what it attempted to do, Julia's presentation of the Frente talk seemed to be a reasonable presentation.

CoeSIDA

CoeSIDA is a state health agency funded by both state and federal funds. It provides testing for HIV-positive/negative, information on AIDS to sex workers—male and female, the health books they need to work the streets, health outreach programs through the state, and some limited counseling for people with AIDS. It also gives workshops to other health workers on how to deal with AIDS and people with AIDS. CoeSIDA does not do the direct educational work that El Frente does. It has a staff of doctors, public health workers, and psychologists. This agency is by far the most formal and structured, and since it is part of the general health service of the state, it does not have to rely on donations or grants for its maintenance.

Renacimiento

Renacimiento is the only organization dealing with AIDS in Oaxaca that is openly gay and works directly with people who have AIDS or are HIV-positive. It is also the group with the least funding and organizational skills. The story of Renacimiento is also the story of José Antonio, its chairperson and its primary activist. Thus, to tell the story of this group we have to enter the "gossip" networks between these AIDS agencies.

On paper, Renacimiento is a group that attempts to find people with AIDS and help them directly. This can and has involved informing people with AIDS about what their options are in terms of medical help, telling them how they can obtain medications, housing, and work, and also providing a place where they can die. José Antonio has been evicted several times for allowing people with AIDS to die in his apartment. Renacimiento's board of directors has organized the programs of direct involvement with people with AIDS, and like El Frente, they also do educational work on AIDS and safe sex. José thinks that Renacimiento's educational workshops are more direct than El Frente's are; for example, in the workshop that he does, he uses a cucumber to show how to put a condom on. José feels that his messages are a little less moralistic than those of El Frente. The organization also provides direct material aid to people with AIDS in terms of food, clothing, or housing. It is these activities that have resulted in some negative evaluations of the group, not for helping people but for how they have gotten the money to these people. Some have suggested that Renacimiento has taken the free condoms from El Frente and sold them to prostitutes in the streets. It also has been suggested that it elicited funds for its work for which it has never accounted or that it is using people with AIDS to raise funds for its own use. We found these claims not to be true but rather to be reflections on José Antonio's limited organizational skills. One night a week José Antonio walks the streets of the center of the city, contacting male and female prostitutes to give them condoms that he has gotten free. Though he asks if they will make some kind of donation to Renacimiento, he always tells them that the condoms are free. Also, Renacimiento set up interviews for us with people who have AIDS but asked us to donate either money or materials directly to the person who was interviewed. Renacimiento gets no money for itself but only direct donations for people with AIDS. José also sells national gay magazines as a way to raise money. One of Renacimiento's problems is that the organization has not been able to attain the status of a nongovernment organization (NGO).

José Antonio

José Antonio is in his mid-thirties and was born in Oaxaca, in the central part of the city, where most of the prostitutes work and live. He comes from a large working-class family, and he still lives with his mother and grandmother. He has always felt gay and like the *chicas*, he became sexually active as a young teenager. He also defines himself as a passive gay man. However, he has only been "out" as a gay activist for the last five years. In fact, he is the only gay person we dealt with in this study who has a story framed in a discourse of crisis and victimization. He says that he always felt gay, and in his youth he would see queens hanging around the cantinas near where he lived and where his father used to drink. He said that he never explored any of these feelings until his mid-teens, when an older man invited him to a secret place, where he attacked and sexually abused José. José did not mind the sex, it was the abusive attack that bothered him. He does not think that this experience made him gay, only that it was uncontestably the wrong way to be initiated into one's gayness.

José went on to get a teaching degree, and he spent most of his twenties out in the rural areas of the state teaching and exploring his own sexuality. He said that he would find himself involved with teenage boys in the place where he worked and that a few times these affairs caused his transfers. Though this story could be read as a tale of an older man "hitting on" young boys, it is not quite that. In the short life histories that the *chicas* gave us, they all said that it was in secondary school that they encountered their first lovers and that these lovers tended to be older boys or in some cases—like Vicky—their teachers. We think that, as in many social settings, adolescence is a time of sexual experimentation, and secondary school is one of the arenas in which such experimentation takes place. Further, we think that there is perhaps a socialization pattern of rural to urban going on. If you are a young gay out in the rural areas, then teachers are a means of finding out what is going on in the bigger world. Further, since we are dealing with the passive/active sexual separation, young males could have sex with José as a means of becoming sexually active without being gay, and teachers could have sex with someone like Vicky and not be gay. We are in no way attempting to downplay what can be and no doubt at times is sexual abuse; we are only pointing out that these activities are taking place in a sexual context that is different from what we might typically expect about schooling and sex. José would meet his lovers in the late afternoons for sex or just being together. He worked in several villages over the years and returned to Oaxaca in the summers.

About five years ago, José took a leave of absence from his teaching job to begin working on the issues of gay rights and AIDS education. At this time he was involved with Raúl, an interesting young man who grew up on the streets in Oaxaca. A short portrait of Raúl will appear later in this section. Currently Raúl is HIV-positive, and many of José's critics suggested that he came out of the closet and got involved with AIDS because Raúl contracted the virus. Neither Raúl nor José has said this to us. José does talk about going to Mexico City with Raúl, where they were both tested and found that José was negative and Raúl positive. It was after this that they both got involved with the various issues surrounding AIDS. Raúl is not gay—that is, he has always been the active one and currently he is married and hopes to have children.

José defines himself as a passive gay man, in that he does not penetrate. He does feel that even though many *hombre/hombres* say they are not gay, he thinks they are, but they just do not want to accept that about themselves. Also, though José likes drag queens and thinks they show a great deal of creativity in how they make themselves up, he has only gone drag once and has no plans to try it again. Like the *chicas,* he does not at this point in his sexuality seek any kind of genital stimulation. He told us that, in fact, when he was young and he had his first ejaculation, he thought he was menstruating. Now he likes gentle and caring sex with his partners, and he is attempting to get a little more assertive with his lovers. He says that he has now tried *beso negro* and likes it. His whole family knows that he is gay, which is no big mystery since his mother and grandmother live with him and his apartment is the general meeting place for Renacimiento.

Renacimiento's board of directors is filled by volunteers. José is the president; Joel, who is studying to be a teacher, is vice president; Ida, a dancer, is the treasurer; Francisco, a janitor in a school, is the administrator of the group; Blanca, a social worker, runs the educational work; Armando, a jeweler, is in charge of humanitarian aid; and Carmen, who is an *ama de la casa* (housewife), and Enrique, a restaurant worker, are in charge of organizing volunteers for the group. As stated earlier, though these folks are listed as officers of the organization, it primarily runs on José's energy, with the aid of anyone he can get to help him. All the members of Renacimiento are supposed to work directly with people who have AIDS. They try to provide psychological and therapeutic help to all people affected by AIDS—that is, to those who have AIDS and to their families. Both of the two people with AIDS that José works with still live at home with their families. He has worked with one woman for more than five years; he thinks that she is in the second stage of the illness, though he states that currently she has no symptoms. The other person he works with is a male who has been HIV-positive for two years. The whole group currently is involved with some twenty-three persons who are HIV-positive, six women and seventeen men. They range in age from nineteen to thirty-two. The volunteers meet weekly with these people, visiting, talking to their friends and family, taking them for walks, and helping with errands like shopping or taking them to the doctor. José says that these folks are all poor, though six of the group are still working and thus do not need as much help as the others. Of the twenty-three, eight are in the final stages of AIDS and eight are in the second stage. Most can receive limited help at the Civil Hospital, but like many people among Oaxaca's popular classes, they are distrustful of the services from the Civil Hospital (Higgins 1974). José has personally contacted several doctors in the city who will help people with AIDS, particularly in getting them medication at low cost or for free.

Rightly or wrongly, José feels that his organization has been marginalized by the AIDS mainstream groups because of personality conflicts and because he has been openly gay in his approach. There is little or no cooperation or contact among these groups. Both because of time and because of our own particular involvements, we are not able to sort out all the conflicting factors here. We can say, from what we have seen, that José has a heart of gold, working full time for the last five years with the various projects of Renacimiento. It is the only group that is directly reaching out to people with AIDS. We are also aware, however, that José's skills do not lie in either organization or management. The group has been trying for several years to get together the money to file as an NGO, but it never seems to have enough money to do this. In the chapter on the Grupo Unión, we discussed the great fund-raiser in Etla, which is typical of José's endeavors. However, it is also clear to us that those in the mainstream use the evidence of José's limitations to curtail his involvement in general AIDS work in the city, which seems to us very shortsighted. Unfortunately, in a very ordinary way, AIDS organizations are not exempt from conflicts involving personalities, turf, and political games.

José's position is that he and other local gay men were responsible for bringing the AIDS question into the public discourse of Oaxaca and it was their actions that moved the city powers to put together El Frente, but local politics among health workers and the middle class of the city took over their idea and excluded them because they were too openly gay and wanted the discussion of AIDS also to address the issues of gays in Oaxaca. Bill, a North American resident of Oaxaca and chair of El Frente, and the people at CoeSIDA tell a different story. Bill agrees that José and his friend were part of the original group that began working on the development of AIDS services for Oaxaca but suggests that José was not central to how things developed and, further, that he was more of a hindrance than a help. Bill thinks that José's style is too strident and that it tends to anger people more than to enlist them in the fight against AIDS. Though Bill is gay himself, he seems to suggest that José's approach is a little too gay for Oaxaca—or, more accurately, a little too gay for the middle-class sectors of the city that AIDS workers need for their financial and political support. Further, people at El Frente and CoeSIDA suggested some kind of financial improprieties during José's early involvement in this process, which is why they are not eager to work with José or his group. José says that as the interest grew about organizing an AIDS service in Oaxaca, he was pushed out of the group because he was too vocal about his gayness. He says that he used some of the early funds of the primary group to take some folks to Mexico City to get tested for HIV, a test that at the time was not available in Oaxaca. He does not view that as a misuse of funds; instead he thinks that that is what the funds are for.[5]

We now present two short portraits of HIV-positive males who work with and have been helped by Renacimiento: Raúl and Primativo (see photo 31).

31. *José, Raúl, and Primativo, 1995. Photo by Tanya Coen.*

Raul

Raúl is a man in his early thirties who has lived a difficult and challenging life, with his greatest challenge yet to come—how to live with being HIV-positive. In the past he was José's lover, but he is now married and hopes to have children. Here is a summary of his story as he told it to us.

I was born in Mexico City and came to Oaxaca when I was very young. I can say that my life has been somewhat hard, but I do not regret it. My father abandoned my mother when I was only a year old, and she, with her new husband and his kids, moved us to Oaxaca. They did not get along and life at home was very hard, so when I was about eight years old I left home and went to live in the streets. A funny thing is that when I was about sixteen I met my real father while I was working on the streets. It was no big deal.

What did I do when I was eight years old and living on the street? I was part of a group of small boys living on the street. We would sell candy or gum during the day or night, and we would try to go to school. We would sleep in abandoned buildings or in the parks. It was dangerous, but it was also like a big adventure each day. In fact, most of those boys that I hung out with are now all dead because of crime and drugs. I took an easier route, I became a prostitute for gay men, but I was always the active one, never the passive one. It was during this time that I met a *gringo* family in Oaxaca and they took me back with them; they lived in San Antonio, Texas. I was about twelve at the time and I stayed with them until I was fourteen. The thing I remember the most is that my foster father turned me on to *mota* (pot).

I returned to the city of Oaxaca when I was fourteen and began living the street scene pretty heavy. I would work the bars and get people or my lovers to let me stay with them. This is when I met José, and we have been friends and lovers off and on since then. Now we are just friends and I do not think we will ever be lovers again— my wife does not like that part of my past. When I was nineteen, I moved to Tijuana, and that was a wild time. I pimped in bars and also worked as a prostitute again and dealt some drugs. Also, I got into drugs very heavy; I was even doing heroin. I do not know for sure how, but I kicked that habit on my own. I left Tijuana when I was twenty-two and went back to Oaxaca to get my life back together somewhat. I joined up with José Antonio again and it was about this time we began thinking about putting together a group to deal with AIDS.

Yes, this was an issue that was important to us at that time because we found out that I was HIV-positive. Renacimiento was the first gay activist group in Oaxaca to deal with this question of AIDS, but because we were so open about the gays in the group, we got a lot of shit from people around here. Frankly, it was our actions and protests that got people in the city and state government to start thinking about AIDS and what to do about it. At first we had a lot of support for our plans, especially among the artists of the city. But to be honest, we were not very good at organization and managing our funds, and people felt we were using the funds that we collected for ourselves. We were not, but because of poor management skills we were not able to defend ourselves very well and we began to lose the support we had. Many of the ideas that El Frente and CoeSIDA use came from us. I am glad that these issues are being addressed, but I feel that they have stolen their plans of action from us.

Now I am married and I plan to beat this AIDS stuff. Given what I have lived through, I know I can do it! My wife does not like me to work with Renacimiento now; for her it brings up my past that she would prefer to forget, but you cannot do that. So now I work at odd jobs, and when I have time I help José. What I would like to do is work with the kids who are now living in the streets and give them advice on how to live and how to get off the streets, not the way I did it, but through staying in school and getting a good job. I think they would respond to me because I came from the streets.

Primativo

Primativo is a short man in his mid-forties; he was born on the coast of Oaxaca and has lived most of his adult life away from the state of Oaxaca. Several years ago he came back to Oaxaca, got married, and has been working as a cook and herbal curer. He and his wife have three children. In May 1995 he learned that he was HIV-positive. Below is a summary of the story of his life as he told it to us.

I was born out near Huatulco, but when I was eight years old, my parents died and I was orphaned. I came to the city of Oaxaca and found jobs in the streets, selling candies or other things. When I was a little older, I started hanging around some of the cantinas in the center of the city and got introduced into the Oaxacan gay world. It was in this context that I met many *locas vestidas* (drag queens) who were working as strippers in some of these cantinas. I was invited to join them as an assistant, and for the next twenty years I traveled all over Mexico working with these drag queen strippers. I would help make their costumes, help them with their makeup, and in fact I started dressing in drag myself and would perform in their shows. Also I started taking shots to get breasts and make my hips rounder. I think that's where I might have gotten this AIDS thing. I also got into prostitution, which is also where I might have contracted this illness.

Several years back I got tired of this lifestyle; and I was worried that I would never have a family. So I moved back to Oaxaca and got a job as a cook in a local restaurant. There I met the woman who was to become my wife. We got married and we have three children. One child died at birth, but we think the doctor did something wrong, like drop him or something. After that I started to study how to cure people with herbs and other things, and I have used that to help my family.

Last year I learned that I was HIV-positive; it was devastating at first, mainly because I had to tell my wife about my past, which she did not know about. By the grace of God she has stayed with me. I am afraid that my boss at the restaurant will find out that I am HIV-positive and I will lose my job. This AIDS thing is very strong, and my curing knowledge cannot fight it. I have no choice but to attempt to keep going and hope that I can beat this thing, but who knows?

SUMMARY

In talking about the relationships between these AIDS agencies and the gay community in Oaxaca, we are in a formal sense dealing with remembered history (very short-term) or, more informally, with gossip. Depending on whom you talk to, you get different stories. Bill, who chairs the Frente Comunal, feels that Oaxaca needs a community-run AIDS educational group that could benefit the whole community; however, reaching the "whole" community in Oaxaca and qualifying for public and private grants means making the messages as noncontroversial as possible. Bill, drawing from his North American and San Francisco experiences, thinks Oaxaca is a context in which the debate about AIDS would not have to focus on it as a gay illness, given the sexual realities of Oaxaca's gay community. Some of the gays, however, see the issues differently; specifically, this was not how José Antonio and his group see the issues.

What is the relationship between an emerging gay community and the different AIDS organizations in Oaxaca? To explore that question we will first make some friendly interpretive comments. First and foremost, we respect all the various actors who are involved in attempting to bring the issues of AIDS and its consequences to the social world of Oaxaca. It is a profoundly important struggle, and we do not wish to assume that we understand the

whole situation or that we have better insight than the actors who are involved in the effort. We would like to offer, though, some suggestions. In
fact, we suggest that an understanding of the ethnography of small-group
dynamics is a useful tool with which to approach what we have been talking
about in this section.

There is a political economy to the AIDS struggle in Oaxaca. It involves
the cultural capital of turf, professionalism, class position, and prestige.
Those working within the AIDS agency world seem to take the position that
what they are doing is more important than what the other groups are doing and that the other groups should change to the way they are doing their
work. Our view, as outsiders, is that all the actors could work on being a little
more tolerant toward each other, rather than just defending their own turf.
It seems clear to us that one of the differences between El Frente and Renacimiento is a difference in class style that is talked about in terms of "professionalism." El Frente's directors assume that they are working to educate all
of Oaxaca, and in their view that struggle requires a type of professionalism
that is missing from Renacimiento—or more specifically, from the *onda* of
José. José and the other members of Renacimiento are neither very slick in
their approach nor neutral in their use of the language of professionalism
found in the presentations of either El Frente or CoeSIDA; unlike those
groups, however, they are working directly with people who have AIDS and
doing critical work that is not offered anywhere else. For us, it is not a question of professionalism but a division of labor for an attack on the problem.
Since El Frente desires to bring the mainstream of Oaxaca into this struggle,
its choice of style of presentation is valid and reasonable, as is that of Renacimiento in terms of its audience. Also, there seems to be a contest of sorts
among these groups over who has the best approach to these issues or who
will have the prestige of being the best fighters against AIDS in Oaxaca. We
suggest, however, that it is not a contest between groups but the struggle
against AIDS that needs everyone's involvement.

There is nothing wrong with the different approaches that these various
groups are using, but there should be more cooperation and a lot less competition. These differences can be seen in how the two groups—El Frente
and Renacimiento—approach their public fund-raising drives. El Frente
uses events like the walkathon for raising money. This involves folks meeting at El Llano (a large park and plaza several blocks above the *zócalo*), where
they walk laps around the park, having signed up people to sponsor their
walking with pledges of money. This is a nice event; those involved enjoy

participating, and it is a safe and respectful way of involving the mainstream of Oaxaca. Renacimiento gets most of its limited funds from the Ms. Gay Oaxaca contest, a drag queen contest with an interesting regional flavor. The contest is open to all who wish to go in drag. There are three different competitions: formal evening wear, bathing suits, and regional dress. The last event is a playing out of the Guelaguetza. The straight Guelaguetza is a folkloric dance celebration each year in Oaxaca in which dances from the eight different ethnic regions of Oaxaca are presented. At the Ms. Gay Oaxaca contest these dances are performed in drag. The person with the highest scores from all three events is crowned Ms. Gay Oaxaca. This well-attended event is a big show that attempts to bring the gay community together to camp it up and enjoy themselves while doing something to fight against AIDS. It is a combination of gay pride and the fight against AIDS. However, it is not an event that Frente folks like to be part of, just as Renacimiento does not like the idea of the walkathon. Both groups could support and participate in each other's events or at least advertise each other's events, which is more than they are doing now. In our view, in terms of the ordinariness of diversity, both approaches and both events are necessary, but more important is that all the actors in this struggle cooperate with each other to achieve the overall goals of combating AIDS.

LOS BOHEMIOS

The Intellectual and Artistic Sectors of the Popular Cultures of Oaxaca

> I think women here in Oaxaca are a little sexually conservative, especially about asking for oral sex. However, I think they say they are conservative, but in private I think more is going on.
>
> —*Lupe Ramírez, a young bohemian woman, talking about contemporary sexual mores in Oaxaca during lunch on the patio of her house*

Here we wish to talk about the world of *los bohemios* (the bohemians) in Oaxaca. We choose this term—*los bohemios*—to capture the *onda* of a mixture of actors in the popular sectors of Oaxaca who are connected by a shared progressive outlook on social and personal issues and by the assumption that as artists, intellectuals, and social activists they live some kind of unconventional lifestyle. This is a mixed group in terms of age, sexual orientation, ethnicity, origin—both national and international—and income (though the majority of their families are clearly in the middle class). *Los bohemios* represent one of the scenes within the middle-income sectors of the urban popular cultures of Oaxaca. This is the crowd at the street cafes in the *zócalo;* they hang at the hipper salsa clubs, and they are a part of the group that shows up for art openings and Zapatista solidarity events. *Los bohemios* are assumed to be part of Oaxaca's cultural world; however, they are curiously absent from the ethnographic discourse on Oaxaca. One reason for their absence from this discourse is that they are so close to the general social networks of anthropologists. (In fact, many of them *are* anthropologists.) It has been assumed that they are too similar or ordinary to those composing this discourse to be thought of as part of these stories. We do not think so; if for nothing else, the way in which *los bohemios* themselves are trying to deal with the areas of gender and sexuality is the kind of ordinariness in which we are interested.

If you are in Oaxaca looking for this group, the easiest way to find them is to go down to the *zócalo,* wander over to the Bar Jardín—which is on the northern end of the *zócalo*—and take a seat at one of the outside tables. More than likely, a third of the patrons there will fit into the bohemian category. Oaxaca is one of few cities in Mexico that still observes siesta time, from two to four in the afternoon. Years ago, only the bars and restaurants on the *zócalo* were open during siesta; now with changes in public and private working hours, that tradition is not as strong as it used to be, but Oaxacans still like to have a drink, something to eat, and meet friends during these hours. And they like to go to the *zócalo*. The group we are talking about would not call themselves bohemians per se; perhaps they would say they are cosmopolitan or just middle-class Oaxacans. We use this term for lack of a better one, and it seems to fit the *onda* of this group. Because of their interest in politics, art, intellectual issues, and partying, they tend to have overlapping social networks. This group can expand or contract depending on what's going on in the city. When new research agencies or university programs are developed, there are more folks in this social milieu; when these kinds of programs are closed or when grants for projects are limited, then some of these folks move on. There is an age range within the group as well; those who came to Oaxaca in the sixties are now the elder *bohemios,* whereas those just entering the scene are the neophytes. There are certainly differences in status and reputation within this group. The plastic art world of Oaxaca is currently dominated by the works and presence of Francisco Toledo. He does not hang out in the *zócalo* very often, nor does he run with this group. As in any general collection of people, there are people within this group who will talk about hanging out with Toledo (and they may have in fact done so), while others will suggest that he is now passé and that their own work is much more interesting than his. If any of them had a chance to work with Toledo, however, they would be there without fail. This is also true of those in the academic world, particularly in anthropology. Those who hung out in the *zócalo* in the 1960s and 1970s now tend to be the senior researchers at various agencies in the city, or they are running programs in the university or in the state government; younger scholars, who are often working for these veterans, will go to the Bar Jardín to talk about the old guard's outdated methods. (However, when given a chance to work with any of this old guard, they do not hesitate to do so.) There is an interesting crossing over of actors who work in the government, schools, or public institutions like museums, which means, in fact, that most of these folks work for the government in some fashion. The overall political orientation of this group is a mixture of popular and progressive politics that still draws from the Marxist tradition in Latin America, which means they actually know something about José Martí, Frida Kahlo, Rigoberta Menchú, José Carlos Mariateguí, and Ernesto "Che" Guevara. This does not mean that those within this group share a singular point of view, but most of their debates do take place within a progressive discourse. For example, they argue about the relevance of Marxism in postmodern Mexico or about whether or not North American feminism can address the realities of rural women in Mexico. We intend nothing in this account to sound mean-spirited because there are various actors in this group whom we know very well, and they are a fun group; they like to party and dance.

La Onda de los Bohemios

Who are some of the people that we are loosely defining as *los bohemios*? They are people like the group of women—Julia, Lupe, Margarita, and many more—who for the last decade have maintained the Rosario Castellanos Casa de la Mujer, a women's resources center in Oaxaca. There is the artistic crowd centered around the Rufino Tamayo Graphic Arts Workshop, who are attempting to find artistic space beyond the acclaim of Toledo. There is a large anthropological community that spans several age groups: the elders, such as Alicia Barabas, Miguel Bartolomé, Margarita Dalton, Victor de la Cruz, Salomón Nahmad, and Stefano Varese, who through their fieldwork and their dedication have given the anthropological discourses of Oaxaca international stature. There is a next generation of anthropologists and social scientists who are continuing this tradition—Jaime Luna, Pedro Lewin, Teri Pardo, and many more; and there is an ascending generation of younger anthropologists who rightfully complain about their elders and are looking for ways to move up in the hierarchy. There is also another group of folks— Ilhui, Lupe, Angeles, and others—who are involved with international education and language training at the university. We must reiterate here that we are arranging these actors into a group for our narrative purpose; *los bohemios* is not a united group where all are in agreement. It is full of different factions and social groups whose only contact with each other is in the context of various gossip networks.

Worldviews among *los Bohemios*

What gives some general boundaries to this group is their attempt at trying to compose and recompose their various identities with some kind of political awareness and an expression of libertarian sensitivities. They talk a great deal about the contradictions of gender differences, sexism, sexual orientation, class, and race in terms of their own personal lives and how that helps or limits what they understand to be the political issues that they profess to believe. This is not meant as a cynical statement nor as a suggestion that they are doing more than the other groups in the popular sectors. Because of *los bohemios*'s middle-class positions in Oaxaca, they have access to the international discourse on many of these issues and actions; that is, they know the language and, as the *dicho* goes, they also attempt to walk the walk. How successfully? No more or less than most of us or most of the other groups in this volume. This group has many problems centered around the issues of gossip, sexual affairs, assumed political differences, and personality conflicts. There are clear differences in terms of sexual orientation. Interestingly enough, within this group the reality of lesbians is more apparent and open to a degree than in Mexico and Oaxaca in general. There are many women within these boundaries who are openly gay inside and draw upon support within the group if their sexuality becomes a public concern. However, openly gay men are less present, though this statement applies more to older peer groups, not younger ones. The reality of the passive/ active male sexual discourse frames the expression of gayness within this group also. There is tension about conflicting gender realities within the group. Most of the women within *los bohemios* express solidarity with feminism, but they have different ideas about what feminism can mean politically and personally. Because this is not a large social group per se, there is much—for lack of a better term—couple switching. This is not something kinky, but persons who were a couple last year may not be so anymore; often each person will find a new *compañero/a,* who will also be a part of the group and who more than likely has been involved with someone else in the group. Such a combination of people and emotions makes putting parties together interesting, but everyone tends to be fairly civil about all these fluid arrangements. It is interesting that this switching of partners does take place independent of sexual orientation. The majority of *los bohemios* are middle class and the Oaxacan segments are generally mestizo, with some indigenous persons involved. The international sectors are drawn from other Latin American countries, Europe, and the United States and Canada. This, too, is a mostly mestizo group, with some African and Asian actors.

To give more ethnographic texture to *los bohemios,* we will present a short narrative about a new youth group—Los del Sótano—followed by an interview with Lupe Ramírez (one of *los bohemios*) about how she relates to and lives within this social group.

Los del Sótano

Los del Sótano—those from the basement or from below—is a loose collection of young students, artists, writers, and activists who have a dream of creating a new alliance of the youth of Oaxaca—punks, anarchists, students, and workers—that can be mobilized for political action. Though their dream is of a broad-based alliance of youth, those in Los del Sótano are middle-income students from the various universities in Oaxaca. Some of the core members of Los del Sótano had been involved in national student organizations that focused on issues of indigenous peoples and women, and they wanted to organize themselves to address these issues in Oaxaca. In addition, the Zapatista movement was for them a powerful expression of hope and of the need to get involved in critical political actions. In the spring of 1995, Los del Sótano was able to put on a day-long solidarity rally for peace in Chiapas.

When we met this group, about nine persons formed its core, three women and six men; three of them were studying law, four were in civil engineering, one was studying public administration, and the other was studying communications. They had gotten together the year before and had been able to put out a newsletter, *Los del Sótano,* that was a collection of short stories, feature news, poems, drawings, and cartoons that attempted to place national issues in the local context of Oaxaca. They envision their newsletter as a nonsectarian publication that stays culturally and politically hip by bringing in as many voices as possible, voices that have not been heard before: punks, anarchists, rockers, and gays. The members of this group are aware of and accept the fact that they are middle class; they do not pretend to be revolutionaries or urban Zapatistas. They see themselves as social actors who wanted to be involved in the struggle for a more democratic civil society in Mexico and Oaxaca. They think it would be false on their part to act like armed revolutionaries when they can use their location within the middle class to fight battles there. They have a loose affiliation with students in the art schools and with some of the musical and writing *tallers* in the city. They see themselves as children of the countercultural urban social movements of Mexico City from the late eighties, which were also combinations of *bohemios* and *politicos* looking for a new political *onda.* They attempt to have open and tolerant views and actions on gender and sexuality. They think that the Oaxacan community is very conservative in the area of gender and sexual issues and that just by being pro-feminist and open to gays, they will be making political statements.

We did not get a chance to work with this group for very long. When we returned the next year, the group was smaller, and a monthly supplement that was part of another weekly progressive newspaper in the city had replaced their newsletter. We do not know, in terms of their everyday actions, how well they can walk the walk and talk the talk. However, for us, the reality that new configurations continue to emerge within the boundaries of *los bohemios* illustrates both the attraction of their *onda* and the commitment of some folks to keep pushing the boundaries of social action and change.

The following is a short narrative that Ms. Ramírez offers about her life, concluded by some of her poems. Ms. Ramírez, we believe, provides a good example of what we call *los bohemios.* She and her generation are clearly interested in gender and sexuality as part of the politics of everyday life. We were at a brunch gathering at Lupe's house when the conversation quoted at the beginning of this section took place, about women's involvement in oral sex. Several of Lupe's friends also suggested that it was something that men wanted done to them, but they did not know how to do it in return for women. The consensus among them was that they were not sure about what other women were up to, but clearly they felt it was time for the guys to learn how to get down. Lupe and her friends represent for us the young and emerging sectors of the bohemian world of Oaxaca. Lupe is in her late twenties, has command of several languages, is politically aware and active, and is quite reflective about how she can compose herself within the constraints of contemporary Mexico.

A Few Things about My Life

Lupe Angel Ramírez

■ ■ ■ ■ ■ ■ ■ ■ ■ ■

To begin with, I need to say that I grew up in a traditional middle-class Oaxacan family; my father is a gun repairman and hunter and my mother is an *ama de la casa* (a housewife). I grew up in a middle-class atmosphere with all its prejudices and sexism. Something that greatly influenced my life was that when I was twelve years old and my brother Lazaro was fourteen years old, we took a course in parapsychology that was recommended by one of our neighbors. In this class we learned for the first time many things that were different from our household. For the first time we learned something about vegetarian eating and cooking, we were taught how to meditate, and we learned exercises to improve our memory and to help us concentrate when studying or reading. These were some of the benefits that we attained from this class.

The workshop in parapsychology was one of the most important studies that I have done in my life. It was like a totally different world than I had ever known about or seen before. Along with learning to meditate, I developed a belief in energy and nature that became for me a new religion. I was raised within the Catholic tradition, but suddenly I replaced that with the adoration of nature and the sun, which my beliefs now revolve around. I left my Catholicism behind when I was around eighteen, which made my friends happy. Now I think about the energy of nature, I see the power of it all the time, in the mountains, or in the ocean, which is like a brother to me because it has the power of energy.

From these experiences, then, I began to read more and to submerge myself in books about other cultures so that I could learn about other options in life. This provoked in me the interest to know other countries and the people from those countries. Thus, later I learned my second language, English, which gave me the opportunity to know about other ways of thinking other than those in Oaxaca. From these experiences there began in me the knowledge that there existed other alternatives in the lives of women—and for me.

Thus I decided to make my "culture" a mixture of many different ideas. I chose things from other cultures that I liked; however, I still believed in my own culture—*como oaxaqueña*—because without a doubt it is necessary that one be from a specific culture. One of the things that I learned from other cultures was the manner in which women live, independently, economically, and emotionally. One of the things I like about *gringas* is that they seem to have a better style of personal communication. For example, it seems that *gringas* are very direct in telling someone what they like about that person or also are very direct in telling a person what about them is irritating. However, here in Mexico, this style is seen as somewhat rude, thus often here you never know or rarely know why a person may be upset with you. When I look at, or better yet, when I encounter alternative ways of life from other cultures I try to make them part of me if I like them. For example, it is curious that in Spanish there is no exact word for "roommate" because this does not happen here that frequently; thus, we tend to use English for this *onda* when I could just as well say "*compañero de cuarto*"—roommate. I think that my Oaxacan culture is dynamic and always changing; I do not identify with or accept that there is some kind of singular Mexican identity. We are a mosaic of various cultures; thus my own cultural style is a mosaic. I do not close off the influences of other cultures in my life.

I have elected, then, to be a new *mexicana* woman, free of prejudices of all kinds. This is hard to do at times because Oaxaca has a lot of very socially conservative people. If you decide to be different you will have fewer friends than if you are conservative. It takes more time to meet people, and when you do meet people, it is about the quality of their being, not about the number of friends you can have. My family has had to very painfully accept the *onda* of me and my brother and out of necessity they have adapted to this. It was hard at first because we have lived in the same city; I am single and live by myself.

How do I define the new Mexican woman? Well, she is a woman who is critical of her culture, who does not think that she must have a man to be part of Mexican culture, one who knows the good and the bad of this culture, and further can identify those things that do not help in the emancipation of woman. The new Mexican woman is a woman who has discovered a new manner of living in the Mexican context without having to flee her place or destroy her family; it is a woman who lives in harmony and can teach other women that there are ways of being that are more humane and free. As Rosario Castellano said, "There have to be other ways of being that are humane and free."

I consider myself a feminist because I have always persisted in my belief that women certainly do not have any limitations simply because they are women. I have not been too involved with some of the feminist groups in Oaxaca, like the Casa de la Mujer. I have attended some of their conferences, however, and I think that in terms of things I know—through reading and lived experiences—their approach does not offer me that much. I think for women who have not been exposed to any kind of feminism, what they do there is very good, like for housewives or young women. I think that they should deal with more contemporary issues, like they hardly ever talk about homosexuality or domestic violence, strong themes!

In terms of dealing with men, it is a difficult thing for me to be in a relationship with someone. I am a feminist, and the number of men who can accept this viewpoint are very few. There exist in

Mexico great numbers of men who abuse women. One out of three women here [is] domestically abused; for this reason alone I wish to stay single forever. Like the *dicho* says, "It is much better to be single than have a bad companion." For this reason, most of my romances have been with internationalists who have a different outlook on these issues. I have been sexually active since I was eighteen. I am now twenty-eight, and I always have my partners use condoms, which is the right thing to do. I do not like to have casual sex without some sort of romance also.

In terms of my short romances, they were the consequences of my going off to other cities and not having to endure those *macho* Mexicans for very much time. I had *novios* who were more emancipated about these issues because they were from other countries. I like being free or liberated in terms of these issues, and I enjoy my friends who think this way too. However, I think that many of my friends are still thinking of having some kind of stable or long-term relationship, which I understand perfectly, but it is not for me. I do not know for sure if I really like short romances or if I am demented, or if it is really nothing but the circumstances of my life, but for me it is better to be single than to be involved with *macho* Mexican men. This is what that *dicho* "It's better to be alone than to have a bad companion" means to me. I never think much about having kids. It is something very far away in my life now. I have three nephews; that's more than enough. I saw all of them this weekend, and though it was great, I was very happy when I left with the reality that I will never want to have kids!

I want to be a teacher of literature; at times I cannot believe that you can get paid to read books and then talk about them; that would be so wonderful. To write makes me happy, and I hope that my stories and poems can demonstrate that there are Mexicans who wish alternatives to the established way things are done.

You could consider my youth or teen years very interesting, looking at them from the outside, but within myself I had many conflicts or problems with all of the racial, sexual, and social prejudices that

one had to fight against. For example, there is the concept of beauty
here that both manages you and your attempt to manage it, that says
you should be *güera*, thin, and very refined, all of which I am not. I
have had to learn to have other self-concepts than these, which I have
learned from people in other countries and by reading. There was
one time when I thought about getting plastic surgery on my nose
since many of my friends were going to get their nose changed from
looking Zapoteca to one that was more European-looking. Luckily
at the time I had a friend from Canada who told me that he was en-
chanted with my nose, so I ended that idea. I learned a great deal from
him; he was the person in my life at that time who helped open up the
world for me.

My parents have had to accept me and my brother as we are. This
they have done with the fear of shame from society and the pain of
their assumptions because my brother is gay and I am a single, liberal
woman. Now, with my mother, I have a good relationship; there are
things about her that are very good and other things that bother me,
but that is because I always have a critical look on all things, where
some Mexicans think that their parents could do no wrong. In terms
of my father, there is animosity that I would like to get beyond, but he
is an example of the typical Mexican *macho* male.

When we learned in my family that my brother was gay we were in
disarray; my mother was very angry, especially because all she thought
about was what was going to be said about all this in "society." My
father, surprisingly, was much calmer; he thought my brother had an
illness. Me, I was confused; I was only seventeen or eighteen at the
time and was very ignorant about all this; later we talked a lot about
all this. I got to know his lover at the time, who had a good *onda* and
was a wonderful guy. I do not have any problems with this now; in
fact, I feel super open to all this. My parents have had to accept this
even though they have never wanted to understand it. My brother is
now very comfortable with himself; soon we will meet his new lover;
they are thinking about coming from Chicago to visit in June.

32. Lupe Ramírez, 1997.
Photo by Joni Kubana.

Racism in Oaxaca or Mexico? Let me see. I think that here in Mexico now, racism is still very pernicious—very marked. Like Marcos says, "To be Indian is to be synonymous with being poor." Every day I see in the *zócalo* many indigenous people protesting, and it is curious that none of these folks are *güeros*. Also there are still many racist expressions that people use, like you smell like an Indian or you look like an Indian, or you have a face like an Aztec, which is synonymous with saying that you are ugly. The model for attractiveness is Euro-Americancentric, like you see in the magazines.

About the Zapatistas, I am very happy that this movement exists during my time or during this epoch that I am part of. I have a very special grand admiration for Marcos, he is a man who has renounced the conformity of his social class and left the city so that he could be with the indigenous peoples of Chiapas, people of the mountains. It is said that he has taught many to read and write and they in turn have taught him about how to live in the mountains. The Zapatistas have [awakened] Mexico; as they have said, "We are here, we are not going away, we are present." Some of the articles that Marcos has written I assigned in my class.

The kind of films that I like are what you would call art films, those that take existential or social themes. My students think that I only like sarcastic types of films. Who knows, but those are the kind of films I like. Of current films my favorites are *Il Postino, Cinema Paradiso, Once Were Warriors, Leaving Las Vegas,* and many others. All of these have left me crying because they touch parts of my life.

Poems by Angel Ramírez

Note: When she writes her poems and stories she uses the name Angel Ramírez

MOVEMENT

Your eyes dissolved
into the chairs on the patio
while I moved the orange of the walls.

We shared the drops of rain.

The belt of a father
the extension of the arm.
We hid the pain in the earth.

With the tongue of another
you left.
Far from the house
your desires opened the windows.

I found a new solitude
and the pages filled with mosaics
in a city of angels.

An encounter, two
within the years
looking at the separation
sitting in my patio chairs.

BUNK BED

Far from the confusion
of the loving couple,
a refugee,
the stairs divide
parallel dreams.

Hits in the hollows of the tubes,
laments in the welds.
In the closed eyelids, the patio.
Endless games
in the pleats of the sheets.
A bunk bed that sways softly.

CONCLUSIONS

What do the realities of these various groups—female prostitutes, the gay "community," and *los bohemios*—presented in this chapter say about the fluidity of gender and sexual *ondas* among the popular cultures of Oaxaca? We hope that their realities provide some other interesting ethnographic portraits of what we mean by the ordinariness of diversity in terms of gender and sexuality in urban Oaxaca. Also, we are attempting to use the ideas of fluid social identities to give some ethnographic texture to the concepts of transgression and personal agency. As we stated in the introduction, first and foremost, all of these dynamics of ordinariness are taking place in the overall material context of postmodern existing consumer capitalism. Concurrently, it is these sites of contestation where the various gender and sexual *ondas* are composed in the material reality of everyday life. These contested sites or hegemonic terrains are navigated by the dynamics of how the actors presented here can or may use their personal agency to transgress assumed role exceptions. We feel that the use of ethnographic portraits offers a means to capture these dynamics. We do not see the actions of personal agency as some means to introduce idealistic assumptions about human behavior;

these portraits are not about romantic bourgeois individuals in drag, but are efforts to place the voices of these people and their understanding of their realities in a broader context. We understand that the issues of gender and sexuality that we have presented in the form of the everyday lives of these folks contain many complex debates in the postmodern world of politics and argumentation. We are not attempting to solve any of these debates, but only suggesting that the voices of the "knitter/Lupes," José, Aldo, and Lupe need to be added to these debates.

CHAPTER FIVE

Thanks to God for Giving Me Polio, for I Have Been Able to See the World

Los Discapacitados of the City of Oaxaca

I did not do much in my youth. In fact, I spent most of the time in bed. I did not go to primary school until I was about sixteen.

—*Rocío Matos, a twenty-four-year-old woman who has had polio since infancy, sitting in front of her bedroom at her parents' house and talking about her life*

INTRODUCTION

Rocío is a member of a new popular cultural group that is emerging in the city of Oaxaca, a cosmopolitan advocacy group called Los Discapacitados. They are seeking new rights and opportunities for people with disabilities in the city and region of Oaxaca. They are organized into a grassroots association named Acceso Libre (free access), which is seeking access to public space for those with disabilities, attempting to develop education and employment opportunities for *los discapacitados,* and encouraging people with disabilities to be more open and public about their social needs. Coming from different sectors of the popular cultures in urban Oaxaca, the leaders of Acceso Libre have been wheeling and dealing to build both local and international alliances to attain these goals, with an emphasis on culturally appropriate and community-controlled programs. Through their struggles they are demanding from the other popular urban cultures of Oaxaca a new form of social tolerance: the symbolic and literal recognition of their presence within the city.

This chapter will focus on three corresponding processes: (1) illustrating ethnographically the context of everyday life for *discapacitados* in terms of living in the city of Oaxaca; (2) presenting short life histories of various members of this community to show the diversity of these actors in terms of the social process of race, gender, sexuality, ethnicity, and class; and (3) analyzing how these patterns of everyday life and personal concerns have been woven into a means to build a community based not upon identity but upon affinity. Their success in these endeavors may provide insights into the postmodern concern to understand the social construction of fluid identities (Haraway 1991 and 1997).

Acceso Libre was formed about nine years ago to begin working on the issues of *discapacitados* in the city of Oaxaca. In the past, people with disabilities were represented either through rehabilitation agencies or through sporting events like the Special Olympics. More often than not, they were stereotyped into either being charity cases or street beggars. However, many people with disabilities were openly seeking to change these images. Germán López and his friend Pedro Flores (both contracted polio in their infancy) felt that it was time for the voices of the disabled to be heard. Though they had both been active in wheelchair sports, they identified other issues that they thought needed to be addressed, including accessibility of public spaces for people with disabilities, access to public transportation, employment, or school opportunities for people with disabilities, and most important, outreach to people with disabilities across the whole state of Oaxaca.

HOW WE MET THE FOLKS AT ACCESO LIBRE

As is often the case in fieldwork, our encountering the folks at Acceso Libre was a matter of luck. After we had begun working with the drag queen prostitutes, we thought that we should make some contacts with female prostitutes so as to develop a comparison between the two groups. We went to the office of El Frente Comunal to seek information about female prostitutes and to look into the activities of groups working on the AIDS issue, and we met Lourdes and Gabriela, two sisters who were the staff persons running this office. Besides their charm and friendliness, what was obvious about them was that they were people with disabilities: Lourdes had some problems walking and had a slight speech impediment, and Gabriela was in a wheelchair. Lourdes had been born with her disabilities, whereas Gabriela was in a wheelchair because of an accident several years before. As we were talking with them about information on prostitutes and AIDS, we had an ethnographic flash—here was another sector of the urban popular culture in Oaxaca that few people were aware of or that had not been dealt with from an ethnographic perspective.

Lourdes and Gabriela informed us that they were part of a group in the city called Acceso Libre, which was an organization working on the concerns and hopes of people with disabilities (*discapacitados*). They helped us set up a meeting with Germán and Pedro, the two coordinators of this group. What was the relationship between Acceso Libre and the AIDS office? About two years before this time, groups concerned with AIDS and the *discapacitados* lobbied the city to address their issues. These activities were separate requests; however, the city government had a creative response. They agreed to help fund and set up an AIDS education service—which was to become

El Frente Comunal—and since one of the concerns of those seeking programs for the *discapacitados* was finding work for them, the city also agreed to help Acceso Libre and suggested that the first project could be to organize an office staff to run the AIDS education office. That is how we came to encounter Lourdes and Gabriela in this office.

When we started asking them about their background and whether they belonged to a group or organization, they told us about Acceso Libre, and they set up the appointment with Germán and Pedro. A few days later, we met with them in the office of Acceso Libre. At that time, the group was about two years old and had some office space in the city offices for public health. The primary achievement so far has been putting an access ramp into the city hall. Also at this time, because of lack of funds and time, they were only working with people with problems of locomotion but were hoping that in the future they could encompass the concerns of those with seeing or hearing problems. That future is now, for in 1996 they received a Kellogg grant to form their center for *discapacitados* in Oaxaca.[1]

The following summary of the social and political context of *los discapacitados* in Oaxaca is based upon our various discussions with Lourdes, Gabriela, Pedro, Germán, and others in Acceso Libre.[2]

SOCIAL CONTEXT

Events

SPORTS

For more than twenty years, there have been organized sporting activities in the city of Oaxaca for people with disabilities. Sports programs for *discapacitados* are organized and housed within the DIF agency (Sistema Para el Desarrollo Integral de la Familia—System for the Development of the Whole Family). It is through these programs that local and regional *discapacitados* teams have competed in national and international tournaments of basketball, tennis, track, and swimming. We spent numerous afternoons watching both the male and the female basketball teams practice. This was quite an amazing experience for us. We knew a little about wheelchair basketball before this, but neither of us had actually seen a game "up close and personal," as they say in the sports world. The overall sports program is run by Cornelio, a world-class athlete who has won several gold medals at Special Olympics games around the world. His basic practice routine (because his main sport is track) involves wheeling/running up to Monte Albán each morning.[3]

The basketball teams practice several afternoons a week and on Saturday mornings. They play on an outdoor cement court that is now part of the new sports center. The coach, who is not disabled himself, works with both the men's and the women's teams. Like most basketball teams, they divide the practice time between drills, exercises, and intersquad games. Generally, the men have enough players to be able to field two complete teams, whereas the women often have few players; thus, they will have intersquad games of three on three. The rules are the same as for regular basketball except that the rule for dribbling is stated in terms of the number of times that a player can push his/her chair while dribbling the ball. The style of play on both the male and the female teams was quite rough-and-tumble. In fact, when one watches them play, it is a little intimidating. For example, all the players will be at the other end of the court, but as soon as a shot is made or missed, they all quickly turn in their chairs and start wheeling toward the other basket. It is quite a sight—ten speeding wheelchairs with the players hollering as they push their chairs at full speed. Also, after a layup is made, the shooter, who is going full speed toward the metal basketball pole, must either stop or quickly turn to avoid running into the pole. They move fast and they brake very fast in their chairs. It is impressive.

Like most basketball teams, they have a set of plays they try to run—screens, blocks, and set-up shots—which are countered by defensive plays. These intersquad games are aggressively played, and often players will get quite angry. Some will even go after each other, ramming each other with their chairs, knocking each other out of the chairs, and falling onto the court floor, where fights will continue until someone pulls them apart. This is true of both the male and the female teams. This behavior is not encouraged, and fouls are called during the intersquad games. If a player is too aggressive, the team will attempt to "chill" that person. Pedro told us that basketball or other sports activities are an arena in which *discapacitados* can express many of their frustrations through anger and aggression. This is all right if it is channeled into developing as a strong athlete, but not if it becomes disruptive to the team. As would be expected, there is a great deal of verbal exchange during the games. Cutting comments about one's style of playing and behavior

33. Women's wheelchair basketball game, 1996. Photo by Julia Knop.

go on constantly. Many of the plays involve either long shots from the outside or layups under the baskets. These activities are quite impressive given that they have to shoot using only upper-body strength. It is clearly a shooter's game (see photo 33).

PARTYING

Like anyone else, the *discapacitados* like to party and have a good time. We spent numerous hours partying with these folks. The biggest party we went to was for the raising of the Christ child. On the Day of the Three Kings (January 6), the custom in Oaxaca (and other parts of Mexico) is that during the day people serve a circular cake at home or in their workplace; inside the cake a small plastic doll is hidden. The person who gets the piece of cake with the doll in it has to give a party on February 2, the day that the Christ child stands up. We went to such a party, organized by some of the folks from Acceso Libre. We went with Pedro; his wife, Patty; and their daughter, who is also named Patty. The party was held in the barrio of San Martín, on the western side of the city, in the home of a young woman, María.

She was quite small and could not walk, but she was a very energetic person nevertheless. She wheeled around during the party greeting everyone and making sure the guests were getting food and drink. She lived with her sister and mother, and they ran a little store. The party was out on their patio. Before the party, we paraded through the barrio, carrying the image of the Christ child and announcing that the party was about to begin. The parade was similar to the ones that folks have for the *posadas* during Christmas (reenactments of Joseph and Mary's search for a place to rest). After the parade we returned to María's patio, and the party began. Those in attendance were a mixture of folks, and everyone was eating, talking, drinking, and, when they got around to putting the music on, dancing. Everyone danced, including our host. Some of the *discapacitados* who can walk, like Pedro, would use their crutches to support them while they danced, while those who needed to stay in their chairs simply danced in their chairs. What most of them did was to move up to the front of their chairs and lean forward to move their bodies to the music. They would hold their partners' hands and turn and dip within the confines of their spaces, and they would "get down." It was a great time. And like most parties given by Oaxacans, it went on until the early hours of the morning. When we left, our host, María, was still out there dancing.

Social Spaces

As part of this social context, we need to explain where the word *discapacitados* comes from. As far as we can tell, this is a word that people with disabilities in Oaxaca and Mexico have composed for themselves. Like many other emerging groups within the popular sectors, how they name themselves is personally and politically important. The most commonly used words for people with disabilities in Mexico have very negative connotations. One of the more commonly used words was *minusvalido*—which literally means someone of less value, like "invalid" in English. Thus people with disabilities in Mexico and Oaxaca have coined *los discapacitados* to convey the concept of people with disabilities.

Before the formation of Acceso Libre, there was no grassroots organization for *discapacitados* run for and by themselves in Oaxaca and very few throughout the rest of Mexico. Their issues and concerns in the past were addressed within two general contexts, either families or institutions. Traditionally, families cared for *discapacitados,* using their own resources. Clearly, this meant that the forms of services or rehabilitation sought were class-based—those with funds could find the services they needed, whereas those with limited funds used what services they could find and afford. For the poor, this often led to a life of seeking charity or, for many, begging in the streets. Many people in Oaxaca had no contact with disabled people except their experiences with beggars or those seeking charity on the streets, for those *discapacitados* who had the financial means to seek help or services tended to withdraw from the public eye; that is, they would avoid contact or keep it to a minimum. The exception to this is the sports world of *discapacitados* in Oaxaca, which has been active for more than twenty years and has produced several world-class athletes. The separation between those *discapacitados* who must resort to public begging and those who can afford private maintenance remains. There are many reasons for the limited understanding of the situation among the public. Two factors stand out: first, the stigma of being disabled, which is reinforced for the general public through the image of street beggars, and second, the lack of physical accessibility throughout the city. Over the last decade these patterns have begun to change, and the primary goals of Acceso Libre are to completely alter these conditions and assumptions.

There have been many programs for people with disabilities at both the national and the state levels, but only recently have city governments become involved. This involvement has been in the areas of general health care, rehabilitation, and very limited programs of social services. However, the majority of these programs are institutional programs that are set up to provide what someone else identifies are the needs of the *discapacitados,* not programs run by and for *discapacitados.* The institutional programs range from surgical reconstruction operations covered by public health to schools for children who are either physically or emotionally challenged. Over the last decade, many of the outpatient services for *discapacitados* have been organized under the general authority of DIF, a national program charged with addressing the overall needs and services of marginalized families, women and children who are not covered by existing state or federal programs per se, and new areas within these boundaries. It is also a political machine that is run symbolically by the spouses of the heads of government—on the national level, the president of DIF is the Mexican president's spouse, whereas at the state level it is the spouse of the state governor who is the director of the DIF programs. Whatever the effectiveness of these programs might be, the heading up of them within this system does fall within the world of the political patronage system. The problem with this is that many of the people with disabilities are not included in this patronage system. Since Acceso Libre has become a funded organization, it now is a "player" in this world, and it is able to affect the current programs attempting to mobilize the *discapacitados*.

ACCESO LIBRE

About five years ago, various members of the *discapacitados* community in Oaxaca began brainstorming about areas of concern to them that were not being addressed in Oaxaca. At the time several organizations did exist to respond to the needs of *discapacitados*—sports groups, associations for the blind and the deaf, and the Council for People with Disabilities. These groups, however, dealt with those *discapacitados* who had in one way or another come out into the abled world of Oaxaca. Many began to feel that there were more issues to be addressed. Germán and Pedro took the initiative to begin working on a new organization—one to be run by the *discapacitados* themselves, one that would publicly and politically address a variety of issues. It was from these ideas that Acceso Libre emerged. The organization had three goals at the beginning: access, mobilization, and education. Because the group was started with limited funds, by folks who had problems of locomotion, they decided to make public access the first goal. This project was related to the other goals; that is, publicly pressing for physical access to buildings, especially government offices, gave them a means both to mobilize the disabled community and to begin educating the general community about the concerns and desires of the *discapacitados*. This campaign proved to be very successful in terms of actually getting ramps and access routes installed throughout the city—the ramp into city hall was the major victory in gaining public awareness of the issues that this group faces.

Mobilization was organized on two levels: within the community of *discapacitados* themselves and within the general community. The mobilization of the *discapacitados* included various outreach programs to identify the kinds and degrees of disabilities present within the general population of Oaxaca and to find out where these people lived and worked. The outreach programs went directly to the homes of persons with mobility problems to persuade them to get out of their homes and to encourage them to confront their disabilities by reentering public and social life. Reentry could range from getting into sports programs to coming to work for or organizing for Acceso Libre. These outreach activities were also ways to mobilize the general public about their concerns. The more the general public could see the *discapacitados* pursuing their own programs and goals, the less they might generalize and view these people as either beggars in the streets or those dependent upon public institutions. Thus, Acceso Libre began to organize workshops that would train *discapacitados* for employment in both the private and the public sectors.

Further, Acceso Libre wanted to increase awareness among the general public of the diversity of gender, class, and ethnicity in the world of *discapacitados*. For example, the group wanted to inform the public that women with disabilities had to deal with problems different from those of men and they needed their own spaces for this. Clearly the limited economic resources of particular *discapacitados* would dictate the degree of their involvement in the programs. Acceso Libre wanted to learn how to develop programs that did not limit access on the basis of social class. Further, the group hoped to collaborate with the indigenous communities of Oaxaca to learn about their own particular means of addressing the concerns of the *discapacitados* in their communities.

In terms of women's issues, the women in Acceso Libre organized a space for themselves to meet and address their own issues and concerns. From these meetings emerged a committee of disabled women within the overall group who have been in charge of organizing workshops for women, with the subject matter ranging from computer classes to cooking lessons. For the last two years this women's group has maintained a sewing collective, in which they put designs on T-shirts and sell them in the local community. Acceso Libre has also organized special groups and programs that do reach out to the *discapacitados* living in the poorer barrios of the city and to the indigenous communities throughout the state. In fact, Acceso Libre is involved in a collaborative project with the Rehabilitation and Training Center for American Indians at the University of Northern Arizona (Marshall et al. 1996).

What is the general social context for *los discapacitados* of Oaxaca? To start with, there is the distinction within the community between those whose disabilities are accidents that happened during or shortly after birth or accidents that occurred in the course of their "normal lifetimes." Both Pedro and

Germán have had polio since early infancy. Thus, they have had to deal with the hassle and opportunities of this type of *onda* on a constant and daily basis. This is what Pedro and Germán have known as ordinary life. They do not have images of themselves as something other than what they are. On the other hand, those who have become part of the world of *los discapaci-tados* through accidents of life have a harder time accepting that reality because they have to transform both their physical and their emotional worlds into a new context that is very daunting and humiliating to them at first. In fact, such feelings can remain for a very long time, sometimes forever.

Let us illustrate this difference with the example of the wheelchair. For those *discapacitados* who have had problems of locomotion from birth, the reality of the wheelchair has a different set of meanings than it has for those who have suffered accidents. For Pedro and Germán, wheelchairs were a means for increasing their personal autonomy. Like many others in Oaxaca who have had polio, they have spent literally years either in hospital beds or in their own bedrooms going through and recuperating from various operations on their legs that would give them some kind of mobility, though generally only with the aid of leg braces and crutches. For them, access to a wheelchair opened up their worlds and gave them the physical means to move about on their own without the help of others. For others, like Gabriela, the wheelchair at first was both a symbolic and an actual reminder of the dramatic changes that had taken place in their lives and a physical representation of the new limitations now present in their lives, often involving being dependent on other people. The wheelchair, for Gabriela, was at first not a means of personal autonomy but a confirmation of her confinement and lack of mobility.

Another *tope,* or barrier, for *discapacitados* is the reality of coming out, both emotionally and physically. There was (and continues to be for some) a feeling of public embarrassment at being disabled, which involves both the person with the disabilities and his or her families or guardians. Some *discapacitados* and their families blame themselves for their problems, are embarrassed by their disabilities, and do not want to be seen in public. This is one of the issues that Acceso Libre seeks to address.

However, even when *discapacitados* are able to cross the personal and emotional barriers, they come up against the real physical barriers present in Oaxaca. If you are a *discapacitado* who lives out in the rural areas of Oaxaca, you will have very little in the form of access within the community and little or no accessible transportation. If you are a *discapacitado* living in one of the poorer *colonias* surrounding the city on the hillsides, getting yourself in and out of the *colonia* would be hard enough if you were more or less able; to maneuver the steep, rocky dirt paths in a wheelchair or on crutches would be difficult and dangerous, to say the least. And once you got out of your village or *colonia,* it would not be easy to navigate the city streets of Oaxaca. None of the buses are equipped with loading ramps for wheelchairs, nor is the public style of bus use very sensitive to the needs of such travelers. If you have a wheelchair, you can attempt to navigate the streets on your own; if not, your transportation options are either a taxi or some form of personal vehicle. If you have limited funds, you just stay at home more often than not.

As the *discapacitados* navigate these *topes* of Oaxaca, they are also dealing with their own personal concerns of gender, sexuality, class, and ethnicity. In terms of gender, women with disabilities have learned that, besides facing the problems of disabilities, they also confront gender bias both within and outside their community. For example, when attempting to find work—which for women may mean accepting a lower salary, and often in marginalized work—women *discapacitados* also find they are perceived as being somehow even more disabled because they are women. Men are stigmatized because of the assumption that because they are disabled, they are not sexual and thus are not quite fully men. There are also certain patterns of *macho* behavior in evidence among male *discapacitados* who assume that they can have easy sexual relations with women *discapacitados* because they are the only options that the women will have. Women report that male *discapacitados,* like "normal" males, seem to maintain several relationships without being either very honest or very civil about the situation. Further, for both men and women within this group, it is as difficult to establish and to maintain important intimate relationships as it is for any other group to do so. Social-class position strongly affects *discapacitados,* for even if they are middle class, the overall cost of medical and social programs eats into any family's monetary resources, and those on the lower end of the economic scale obviously confront *topes* that are even higher and often impossible to get over. If you are an indigenous person with disabilities, then ethnicity is yet another element in the puzzle. That is, one has to confront the social dynamics of racism in Oaxaca as well as one's disability.[4]

ETHNOGRAPHIC PORTRAITS

Gabriela and Lourdes: Two Sisters, Two Different Realities

The stories of Gabriela and Lourdes are powerful tales of strength, creativity, and triumph in very difficult and austere conditions. Now it is also a tale of sadness. In August 1996 Gabriela died from complications of a kidney infection. Because of her spirit and hopes we will present this portrait in present tense as our tribute to her. Gabriela García Juárez: *Presente.*

■ ■ ■ ■ ■ ■ ■ ■ ■ ■

Gabriela and Lourdes are sisters; Gabriela is thirty-two and Lourdes is thirty-one. Though separated by one year in age, their lives were in stark contrast to each other until 1990, when Gabriela fell through the roof of her house, resulting in severe paralysis of her lower body. Until that point, Gabriela had been living the regular life of an "abled" person. She was married, had two children, had gone to college, and ran a small business. She was also dealing with an unfaithful husband who had gone off to the United States. Lourdes was born with a severe birth defect that affected her ability to walk, talk, and stand straight (see photos 34 and 35).

Both Gabriela and Lourdes were born in the city of Oaxaca, and luckily for them, they were born into a middle-class household that would be able to use its adequate material base to help both of them through their life crises. Their father, Feliciano (age seventy-one), was a local merchant who had made a reasonable income. Their mother, Josefina (age sixty-three), was a trained accountant, but she was not working at the time of our research. They have one older sister, two younger sisters, and one younger brother. All their siblings have gone to college and have professional jobs. The "ordinariness" of this middle-class family has been strongly tested by the drama of the two sisters' lives.

Gabriela had been married for about twelve years when she had her accident. She and her husband, Umberto, had a house out in Xoxo (a city that had been incorporated into the city of Oaxaca through urban growth) and, as is the case with most folks, they were adding to the house as they were living in it. One day, Gabriela was working on the roof of her bathroom, putting on tiles. It was raining; she slipped, went through the roof, and fell to the first floor. She hit the floor standing and collapsed. Her spine had been

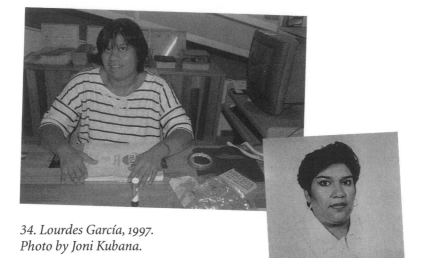

34. *Lourdes García, 1997.*
Photo by Joni Kubana.

35. *Gabriela García.*
Photo by Joni Kubana.

crushed in the fall. She was taken to the Civil Hospital, where she was operated on. The operation saved her life, but it was not done correctly (a story
told by many *discapacitados*). Soon after this operation she was taken to
Mexico City, where the family sought more appropriate and adequate medical care. Thus, Gabriela began a journey—like many others—of long delays,
numerous operations, long and painful periods of recuperation, and even
longer periods of rehabilitation.

She was in Mexico City for more than a year. She stayed in the hospital
for three months after a series of operations and then spent three months in
bed at her aunt's house, attempting to recuperate. During this time, she was
also going to the military hospital for physical therapy. She remembers going for three months without being moved, including not even bathing. For
more than six months she could not sit up, and it was more than nine months
before she could sit up and move her upper body a little. During the time
she was in Mexico City, her children were back in Oaxaca, living with her
family, and Lourdes was left in charge of them. One of the ironies of their
lives was that Gabriela's accident provided the means for Lourdes to develop
an autonomous lifestyle for herself.

Lourdes was born two months premature and had to stay in an incuba-
tor for the first two months. She had severe developmental problems. She did

not learn to talk or walk correctly, and there were concerns about her mental and emotional development. She did not enter primary school until she was twelve years old. The family tried to put her in kindergarten when she was younger, but she did not do well. She would fall frequently, so the family kept her at home. She too went through various operations that allowed her to walk with the aid of braces. She became the household concern, and everyone in the family would do everything for her. They even made pathways through the house with the furniture arranged so she could hold on to it and thus walk through the house. Since Gabriela and Lourdes were close in age, they did many things together, like going to the movies or to parks. After Gabriela married, however, they didn't get to see as much of each other.

With Gabriela's accident, all of this changed. The crisis threw the household into turmoil. Because her siblings were either married themselves, working, or going to school, they could not take care of Gabriela's children. Josefina, the mother, was going back and forth to Mexico City to be with Gabriela, so she could not care for the children, and their father had to keep working to bring in the funds to pay for all their newfound expenses. Gabriela's husband had left for the United States to find work to help out, which he never did. Lourdes was the only one left who could care for the children, and that was a tricky situation since Lourdes had always been the one being cared for, not the one who knew how to care for others. She had never learned how to cook, do laundry, or keep house. She had been exempted from the chores because she was special.

During that year, Lourdes, with the help of her nephew and niece, learned how to do all those things and more. She started cooking, shopping, and doing general child care. She had to learn to walk without the help of others or the things placed strategically around the house. She had to learn to walk around the city, use the bus and taxis to go shopping, and get the kids to school. She began to envision that she could live a somewhat normal life and that she could, in fact, take care of herself.

Lourdes had been moving somewhat in this direction of autonomy for a few years. She had gone through six different operations on her spine, but at nineteen she still could not walk right. Finally, a doctor told her she could walk if she wanted to. It would take courage and willpower, but it was possible. It was Gabriela's accident that provided the final push to get her to walk on her own. Since she was the only one who could help out during this time, she had no choice but to push herself—and she did. She has never gone back to her dependent ways. She now considers herself an independent young woman and does not ask permission from anyone about how to run her life. Before Gabriela's accident, she never left the house on her own; she went out with Gabriela or not at all. The horror of Gabriela's accident became the avenue for Lourdes's movement toward independence and self-assurance. It affected the other members of the family, however, in less positive ways.

Their younger brother, José, felt slighted because of this ordeal; first it had been Lourdes who got all the attention, and now it was Gabriela. From his point of view, no one ever paid much attention to him, and now it was Gabriela's kids everyone worried about, not him. He began to drink very heavily and eventually sought counseling. The oldest sister found the whole situation too tense and confusing; she left home and moved to Salina Cruz, where she got married. The younger sister, Josefina, was the most understanding, and struggled to get the family to recognize its overall problems and talk about them. She urged everyone to work together so that they could stay together. At this time, both parents were quite dispirited and worried about how to cover these new expenses.

After more than a year in Mexico City, Gabriela returned to the family home in the center of the city and began to try to put her life back together. Her primary concern now was not herself but her children. She sold her house and all the things in it to raise some money. Her husband had more or less abandoned them. Once in a great while he would send the kids cards or call, but after a time even that had stopped. Gabriela never asked if she would be able to walk again; she knew the answer. She was grateful to be alive. She was glad that at least her children had someone to care for them. In addition, now she was facing the new challenge of learning to use a wheelchair. She had become like Lourdes had been: she did not want to leave the house, and she did not want people to see her crippled. Then Pedro and Germán began coming by to visit. Lourdes had begun working with them as they were developing Acceso Libre, so they knew about Gabriela's fear of going out in public and of trying to use a wheelchair.

Germán and Pedro gradually coaxed her out of the house, and took her on small trips around her block. Once they took her across the city and left her, and she had to get back on her own. It scared her, but she did it. Now she was able to go out and about, and now she, like Lourdes, was hardly ever at home. Both Gabriela and Lourdes got involved with Acceso Libre, and through that connection got their jobs at El Frente Comunal. Gabriela also was the one behind getting a women's group organized as part of the overall structure of Acceso Libre. She had encountered various forms of gender and sexual harassment when she was ambulatory, but now she found she was also being discriminated against because of her disability. She wanted to fight this, and she did. She had a strong ally in this fight, too. Lourdes, the little sister who could never do anything for herself, was now right behind her, literally pushing Gabriela in her wheelchair.

Gabriela and Lourdes are quite contemporary young women in terms of their lifestyles and viewpoints. They gave us insight into the gender and sexual dynamics within the *discapacitados* community. They had observed several patterns in these social dynamics. One was the question of self-esteem in relation to sexuality. They feel that most *discapacitados,* especially young women, are timid and shy in these areas because of the norms of ableness in defining attractiveness. Their bodies, in their various shapes, do not exhibit the body shapes that are coded as attractive, and since they are not included within those boundaries, it is assumed that these people are not sexual, or if they are sexual, they are grateful for any attention they receive from "normal" bodies. Gabriela and Lourdes do not take this point of view; they feel that such representations put pressure on them to seek to satisfy their intimate and erotic needs within their own community. However, as Gabriela and Lourdes point out, male *discapacitados* do not hesitate to express patterns of male privilege or *machismo* within their group. Here Gabriela and Lourdes are referring to their own immediate peer group, which is involved in sports programs and with the workshops and projects of Acceso Libre. These groups are primarily young (in their teens or early twenties), and there are more females than males. Because the domain of intimacy and dating among these young *discapacitados* is expressed within patterns of timidness and shyness, there is not much open talk about who is dating whom or who is involved with whom. They feel that the men within the group take advantage of this by having several *novias* at the same time and justifying their behavior with the negative logic of "Well, who else are you going to go out with?"

Gabriela and Lourdes stress that as young women they have sexual and intimate desires, and they wish to pursue these desires without playing such mind games, but they are aware that these dynamics are quite ordinary outside of their own community as well. Lourdes hopes to have an important intimate relationship sometime in her life. She sees herself as heterosexual and as attractive. She has her doubts about how sexually free she should be and how that would affect her wish to marry someday. She does not like the idea of abortion, but is unclear on what should be done in terms of making it legally available. She understands how childbearing is a burden upon women, especially poor women. Since she began working at the Frente Comunal office, she has clearly advocated that, no matter what you're doing, it should be done safely. Gabriela's views on sexuality and intimate relationships had been traditional before her accident. She was married with two children. However, since the accident, her husband has left to go to the States, and she has moved to divorce him. She has recognized that her accident did not make her an asexual person, and she feels that as she becomes more competent with her new lifestyle, she will also deal with sexual and intimate desires and needs as they develop.

Both Lourdes and Gabriela are aware that the middle-income earning base of their family gave them the material means to seek the lifestyles that they are now entering. They are aware of the effects of class differences on the lives of women, particularly women with disabilities. This is why they both are concerned about developing workshops for women with disabilities that will give them some economic means to be independent. They also recognize how hard this is to attain. In addition, they are working to ensure that indigenous people with disabilities will be able to find space within their projects at Acceso Libre.

Lourdes and Gabriela, when they have time, like to go to movies, listen to music, or go dancing. Their politics are liberal within the Mexican context. Like many others, they think the PRI's time is up, but they do not know what will come after the PRI. They know about the corruption in the Mexican political system and they favor changes in that system but do not think that such changes are going to come very fast. They are aware of and intrigued by the Zapatistas' cause and other armed struggles taking place in Mexico, though they do not envision brigades of *discapacitados* joining up until there is better access into the mountains for them. Their work with El Frente Comunal on AIDS has encouraged in both of them a very cosmopolitan view on sexual tolerance in terms of diversity.

The lives of these two sisters have taken them on new and difficult paths. Before her accident, Gabriela thought her life was set. She was an energetic young career woman who was going to make a life for herself and her children. Outside of her concern and love for her sister, she was not interested in the concerns or needs of *discapacitados,* nor was she particularly interested in women's issues. The fall through the bathroom roof changed all that. Through the trauma of that accident, she has emerged as a strong young woman who is now organizing women with disabilities with a feminist perspective that she did not have before. Lourdes, the formerly dependent sister and companion, has become an autonomous young woman seeking her own life on her own terms. Gabriela's trauma became the avenue of Lourdes's new hopes and accomplishments. Although each sister would have preferred a different route to these outcomes, each sister is proud of the other's accomplishments.

Gabriela passed away in the summer of 1996. Her family handled this shock and new trauma with great dignity and are proud of what Gabriela accomplished in her short life. Though Lourdes grieved deeply, she exhibited a high level of courage and the determination that Gabriela's death would not derail her new *onda,* for to fall back into older patterns of dependency would negate the courage her sister Gabriela had shown in her life.

The following is a summary of the lecture that Gabriela gave at a conference on women with disabilities in the United States. In this lecture she is explaining how their group developed its women's clothing workshop and how that artistic experience helped them to redefine themselves.[5]

Mujers Discapacitados de Oaxaca
(Women with Disabilities of Oaxaca)

Gabriela Garcia

■　■　■　■　■　■　■　■　■　■

Upon founding our textile design workshop in Oaxaca, we know that we began from nothing and we have discovered how to at first copy and then to create our own designs and establish ourselves in a parameter no different from any other business on the level of those who fight for themselves, and with a society that does not understand our needs, against a deplorable economic status and in a country of crisis.

We must establish that all women with disabilities have the rights to freely choose a job, accept nothing less than fair working conditions, favorable salaries, work hours, and training that will better our chances of advancement.

Women must demand these things because the government and private industry have the perception that when a disabled woman is given a job, she is not qualified but receives the job as a favor for her disability. Due to these factors they may expect very little of her, and in turn perpetuate a situation in which they are reluctant to promote her. They may also feel that an increased responsibility may worsen the disability—due to the popular belief that the disabled are weak and sick. Consequently, the jobs that disabled women usually receive are monotonous and servile ones with low salaries.

Therefore, self-employment should be considered a more effective way for disabled people to reach favorable economic development, where they don't have to work a double load, prove that they are apt for the job, or demonstrate that their disabilities do not obstruct their competence.

Disabled women who already have a job must avoid being hidden away from the public view or out of the sight of the clients, but instead they should seek to integrate themselves into the everyday image of business. Only if this is done will they be judged for the quality of work that they do and be taken into account so that opportunities to develop will not be denied them and that prejudice will be diminished to assure that both disabled and non-disabled workers can feel good working together and can interact freely.

In the fight to produce sufficient income to live on, a notable expression of creativity is exhibited by disabled persons trying to generate income. This economic situation for disabled women is difficult in all countries, particularly in the poorest ones, like Oaxaca. In many countries disabled women are the poorest of the poor. It is calculated that two-thirds of disabled people do not have work. Exclusion and social isolation form part of the daily experience of disabled people. Due to this isolation many are dependent on their families. We cannot continue under these conditions. Disabled persons must be included in decisions about their own development in order to attain equal opportunity. The government itself should be a better example. It could employ many disabled persons; it could offer better access to its meetings. It can transcribe documents into Braille or make tapes and recognize sign language as one of its official languages. Only as equals can we, the disabled persons, continue our social development to its fullest potential.

Equal opportunity will only become a reality if society adapts to the diversity of its members. Creating our own fountain of resources is important, especially for those in Third World countries, where unemployment is high and we lack resources to initiate and sustain projects. Along these lines we can learn skills that will increase our self-help and social and economic independence. In addition to the textile techniques, we learn about the administrative context: hopefully incorporating a plan that will permit general profits to be used, once salaries have been paid, for the hiring of more apprentices. The apprentices will work from their homes, which is easier. Also, we would want to perfect the techniques of marketing, handling finances, and client relations. Further, to achieve self-employment we would want to consider looking for resources in the form of loans instead of donations, and develop strategies for low-income workers to save money.

In addition, to accommodate environmental demands, products that are inherent to the region and from the earth could be searched for and used, such as in the case of clay, stone, palm leaf, and waste products, among other things.

The community must be taken into account if one wants to receive effective backing and true acceptance. When we speak of the self-betterment of disabled women we find that it is these factors that have not received real attention for all women:

- The heavy load of poverty that women carry
- The inequality of treatment and the few opportunities for adequate education
- The inequality of access to health care and its benefits
- Violence against women
- The little opportunity that is given to women to participate in structural and political economic changes
- The scarcity of opportunity to participate in the productive process
- The difference in opportunity between men and women to make decisions at all levels
- The lack of promotion in the advancement of women

> As women with disabilities, who earn a great deal less than non-disabled men, we are ever reminded of our lack of privileges and the obstacles ahead of us. Perhaps through art we are going to take control of our lives and participate fully.
>
> Art does not differentiate between people who participate; an artist can be the person who paints a picture or the one who sells it, the one who creates a play, the artist who performs, or even the woman at the box office who sells the ticket. We may begin copying a figure, but along the way we develop our own style in which our own creativity takes part.
>
> It is our chance to erase with a clean sweep the part that always has been given to us to play a submissive part without making our talents stand out. We can create a quality of life without anyone questioning our values or determining the steps we must follow to rule our existence. [We must restate the true role that we] as disabled women in a chauvinistic country . . . have in this society . . . : we will rescue our own existence without radicalism or shame, to drive a future that is our own. This is the art in which I believe, in which I have educated myself, and in which I have established my values, but above all it is my employment—and it is my employment that gives me the means of living.

Rocío and Iris: Two Different Stories of Polio

Rocío and Iris are two young women who have been affiliated with each other through both Acceso Libre and sports programs. They are about the same age and are friends. Each in her own way has triumphed over polio and is pursuing her own independent life as best she can. However, social class and ethnicity have affected how their lives and triumphs have developed. Rocío is twenty-three years old, has finished primary school, and has hopes of either becoming a seamstress or working in the computer field somewhere. Her family has very limited funds and has maintained itself over the years through her brothers' sending money back from the United States. Rocío's mother and father come from the Zapotec community in the southern end of the valley of Oaxaca. Her father is an alcoholic who does some construction work when he is sober, and her mother runs a small store in their house with Rocío's help. Her mother also prepares food for sale in their barrio. Iris is from Tuxtepec, and her family has always had middle-class monetary resources, which greatly helped Iris work through and beyond her polio. She has a university degree in business administration from the University of Sinaloa (in coastal central Mexico), and she currently works for the state rehabilitation agency in Oaxaca. Following are short ethnographic portraits of these two women.

ROCÍO'S REFLECTIONS UPON HER LIFE

What was my youth like? I was twenty-two before I began to walk. When I was about a year old, I was hit by polio. I was born in Chiapas, but my mother felt that there were not adequate doctors or medical services there to deal with polio, so we moved back to Oaxaca. However, when we returned to Oaxaca, things were not that good because my father started drinking. Thus, I was not attended to very well; my mother on her own could not do very much because she also had my younger siblings to take care of. Neither the time nor the funds were available to attend to my problems. It was not until I was five that my mother consulted a doctor here in Oaxaca about my problem. He was a doctor in the village, and he did help my mother. Through him we went to the Civil Hospital, and they wanted to operate on me so that I might be able to walk. So when I was five years old, I had my first operation; it was on my right knee. They told my mother that, with orthopedic braces, I could walk. Well, that was okay, but when we returned to the village and when they finally took off the cast, my mother had no money for the braces. My father was drinking heavily. Once in a while he would work, but often he did not. Thus, the money my mother had did not last to cover all my expenses. We did not have enough to pay for the braces, which then cost five thousand pesos, a lot of money for us. One of my uncles wanted to lend the money to my mother, but we had no way to pay it back. No matter, there was not anything to do, so we just accepted it. Much later, when I was seven or eight, I started to go to CREE [El Centro de Rehabilitación Integral: a rehabilitation center in the city], and there I started a rehabilitation program that was all exercises, but still we could not afford the braces, so it got hard to continue going. We were living in my mother's village and sometimes she could take me. Other times she did not have the money for the bus fare. It was just hard, so I stopping going for the rehabilitation. It just got too difficult to keep going.

So the doctors at CREE made me some braces out of plaster, and with crutches—I was about nine then—and the plaster braces, I could walk a little. My mother was glad that I could walk about, but since these were only plaster braces they did not work that well or last long, and the doctors said that I needed regular braces. They told my mother that she needed to find the money somehow, for the longer we waited, the more the knees would calcify, and then it would be harder to repair them and allow me to walk. But my mother could not do anything. We did not have the money. Thus, I just went back to the way I was, not doing anything and not walking. Several years later, my older brother told my mother that he wanted to help out, and he told her that he would buy me a wheelchair. With this chair I could get around the house, and go out a little bit around the house. But I just stayed in the house; I never left for anything. My mother went to see the schoolteachers in a school near here, and they told my mother that I could enter this school and study; but I was sixteen years old, and I was entering primary school. I was in the first grade for a few months; then I passed on to second. I continued through primary school, and I was finished when I was about eighteen. I wanted to go to secondary school, but it was too much work for my mother be- cause it was quite a bit farther away. Thus, I stayed again around the house and did not leave much. Once in a while my younger brother would take me around the barrio—not very far—like going to the church or something.

In 1991, I got bored being in the wheelchair; I did not want to use it anymore. I wanted to be able to walk, to be able to leave on my own. So I asked my younger brother to accompany me to the Civil Hospital. He said, "Sure, let's go," and we went to the Civil Hospital. I talked with the doctors about new chances to have an operation to help me walk. They told me that there was a chance, and that I needed to wait for these specialists to come from Mexico City, and maybe they could help me. They said that they could take me back to Mexico City, and everything like transportation et cetera would be covered; even the operation would not cost me anything. So I waited. When they finally arrived, it was in December, and I went, they talked with me, did new studies, and said they could do the operation here in Oaxaca. I said okay, and they set up an operation for the fifteenth of December. But there was some kind of disagreement between the specialist and the local doctors so that I could not have the operation. The doctors at the Civil Hospital said that they did not have the facilities or the right kind of equipment to do this kind of operation and that it would be hard and dangerous to do it here. There were to be five operations on my legs. Because I had been sitting so long in the wheelchair my bones were very calcified.

So they did not operate, and they told me to wait. On the sixteenth of December the doctors began the paperwork to get me these operations in Mexico City. They were requesting that I get these operations without having to pay. The specialist said that they would leave all the papers that I needed and that I should come to Mexico City in a few days and all the paperwork would be completed. When I returned and talked with the doctors at the hospital, they said that the specialist had not left anything or done anything about getting me these operations. Now they said that they could do the operations here. I said that it was not possible here, and that I needed to have them done in Mexico. They said, no, they could do it. I was very doubtful, and in fact a nurse there warned me that the doctors here were only students, and they wanted to do the operation so that they could learn how to do it. She said if the doctors suggested Mexico, you should go there, but I asked her how—I did not have any money. She told me we should get it somehow, for it would be better.

I talked all this over with my mother, and she said somehow she would find the money. My older brother loaned us some money, so we went to Mexico City. When we arrived, we found the doctor who had been attending to me here in Oaxaca. He asked me how I got there, and I told him I had to pay my own way, even though we thought that we were going to get these costs covered. He thought that the folks in Oaxaca would cover the cost, and we said that they had not and that my mother got the money for the trip and the visit. He said that he could get the cost of the operation waived but that we would have to cover our expenses while we were there. We had a relative in Mexico City whose house we could use. It took several months of consultations before they did the operation. It was not until sometime in April of that year that they operated on me. After the operation, I was in a cast and had to stay in bed for more than two months. It was very painful. I was in a cast from the waist down to my feet. They had done five operations on me and had not told me the details of all of it. It was very painful, and we were staying quite a distance from the hospital. It was expensive to get back and forth; we had to use taxis to get back and forth and they were quite expensive. Sometimes the pain was so strong, especially at night, that I could not sleep. It was expensive, but my papa arranged for a *carro de rescate* (ambulance) to take me back and forth between the hospital, but they wanted more than twenty-five thousand old pesos, which was more than we had. No matter. We had to pay it, and for a while they would take me to the orthopedic hospital.

They took the cast off on the sixteenth of July, and then I had to do almost three months of rehabilitation. We did not get back to Oaxaca until August of that year. Then the doctors told me that I would need braces that went from my waist down so that I could learn to walk and that a shorter brace would not work. Thus, my mother had to talk to my brother again to see if she could borrow more money for these braces, for they too cost several thousands of pesos. He did not have the money, but he felt that he could get it somehow. He did send the money to my mother. It took a year or so before we could buy these braces. When we bought them and got them to Oaxaca, I began to try to use them and it was very hard. It took a long time to learn how to use them. It was hard to walk, and I had to start another rehabilitation program to learn how to use these braces. So I went back to CREE for the rehabilitation. During the rehabilitation program, the doctors at CREE told me that I needed more operations, and then I would only need to have a brace on the lower part of my left leg, but this would take four or five more operations. Then I could walk well, they said. But my mother said that there was simply no way that we could find the money to do more operations. I would have to learn to walk as best I could with what I had now. She said we have done what is possible; there is no more that we can do. I wanted to get these other operations.

When I started to walk more or less, I still had a lot of fear of going out by myself. My mother told me not to be fearful, but I was scared. I would fall over little things, like the steps in front of the door, for example, so she helped me and took me places. After [she helped] for a while, the doctor at CREE told her not to help me and to let me do it on my own. He said that if I fell or tripped or got dizzy, it would not hurt me, and that I had to learn how to do this on my own. If I did it on my own, even if I fell, I would learn how to do it and would get over my fear. I told my mother that this was true, and that she should let me do it on my own and we would see what happened. So I began doing these things on my own. [Rocío's mother made a comment that this was very hard on her, and that when Rocío was out and about, she was always worried.] Little by little, I started going to the rehab program by myself.

Thus, I lost my fear of going out after a while. I told one of my friends at DIF that I wanted to change the braces, I did not want to use those that were from the waist down but wanted one only on one leg. I told the folks at DIF what the doctors in Mexico said I could do, so we made the changes in the braces, and I started to use crutches with only a brace on one leg. It was hard work to learn how to walk with the crutches, but finally I was able to do it and get out and about on my own. But the doctors at CREE said that I still needed some more operations for my legs because my legs would get used to how I was walking now, which would cause problems later because I was only using my right leg, not my left, and that would make any further operation later in my life very hard to do. But to go to Mexico City for another time would be too hard. She (the doctor) said hopefully we could correct these problems through rehabilitation.

However, you know what? The rehab was not doing all that I needed. I could walk around the house and do a few things, but it was still hard work. I went on this way for a few years. A doctor told me that if I had started with braces when I was young I could have walked better, but since that was not so, I would always have to use braces. Not all folks with polio have as many operations as I have had. For example, Iris did not have very many, but that was because they attended to her when she was very young. I still hope somehow to attain this other operation so that I do not have to use braces, but who knows, maybe I can get a job in Mexico City, live there and save my money. My mother says that if I do this, it would have to be on my own, that she cannot do that again. I can do it. I could work to get the money to go, and I could live with a family relative in Mexico while I get the operation. I would get a job there also, and I could cover my costs for taxis to get the rehab and all. This is what I think I could do.

Rocío is now living in the Los Angeles area with her brothers, working in a clothing factory, and learning English. She says that she likes it there and hopes to return to Oaxaca in a few years.

IRIS

I am twenty-six and moved to Oaxaca in 1996. I am from Tuxtepec, which is on the border between Oaxaca and Veracruz. When I was very young—early infancy—I contracted polio. I was the only one in my family to be afflicted. I have a big family, with lots of brothers and sisters. My parents confronted this trauma honestly and directly. They said that they would seek and attain the best medical care possible for me; however, I was to be treated as normal by my brothers and sister. I was not to get any special treatment from them, nor were they supposed to feel sorry for me. This was a great thing for me. Though I knew that I was different and thus had to do some things differently than others, it did not mean that I could not do them. I was never pampered nor told that I could not go to school or do sports. It was up to me to struggle with how to do these things.

My family was a great help. First of all, we had the money to seek health care, and like many others with polio, I have had numerous operations so that I can walk. I had my operations early in my life so that my bones were not as brittle or calcified as happens to many who do not have the means to seek medical care early. Secondly, since they did not pamper me or make me the special child of the family, I learned to be myself and how to fight and struggle for the things I wanted to do, and I still do.

I went to the University of Sinaloa to work on a degree in business administration. I wanted to be able to work in programs for people with disabilities, not as a counselor or rehab person but as an administrator so that I would be in a position to develop programs that were more relevant to folks with disabilities. I decided to come to Oaxaca City to look for work because it was close to home but far enough away that I could live my own life. My parents did not pamper me because of my disabilities, but they are still parents. I love them, but I like being on my own.

I am very excited right now, for I just got my own apartment. I had been living with a family, but it's going to be great to have my own place. I like different kinds of popular music, especially music from Cuba. I have just broken up with a *novio,* and I think that I will stay single for a while. I have always dated, both "normal" guys and *discapacitados.* I did not know about gays here among the *discapacitados.* I haven't known too many gay folks. Also, I do not like that word—*discapacitados*—but I do not like any of the other words like that either. I have not been involved with Acceso Libre too much, and I do not get along with some of the folks there. I mainly have been involved with sports and basketball, which I love to play. That's where I met Rocío. She is such a great person, and I think it is tremendous what she has accomplished in such a short time.

UN TRÍO DE DOS QUE SE LLAMA UNO Y MEDIO

A Trio of Two Called One and a Half— Germán Pérez and Pedro Flores

Work together for a world where the greater value is to be human, rather than to be "normal," and a world where war, poverty, and despair do not contribute to disability. A world where we are all equal, with the same opportunities, with the same responsibilities, the same rights—where we are struggling together for a world more just, more equitable, and more accessible, but above all, more humane.

—*Germán Pérez*

Germán Pérez and Pedro Flores have been the major forces in the development of the grassroots movement of Los Discapacitados in the city and region of Oaxaca. Germán studied physical education and worked for a period of time as a schoolteacher. Pedro went to art school to study music and singing. For many years the two of them have sung together, performing in the classic trio style of Mexico, mainly romantic ballads. However, since there are only two of them and they both have polio, they refer to themselves as a trio of two, called one and a half. This is an example of the kind of humor they like to use. Both have been active in attempting to find ways to address the issues of *discapacitados,* especially in the area of sports and community involvement. It was within this context that they began dreaming and thinking about a new kind of organization that would become Acceso Libre. They felt that more than just sports activities and general community awareness was needed for the *discapacitados* of Oaxaca; there needed to be an organization that was run by and for the *discapacitados* themselves. Also, since they were both urban Oaxacans who had grown up in the city, they knew that in their efforts to create such an organization they would find themselves involved in the turf battles of local political and institutional structures that claimed already to address such issues. Their level of sophistication is seen in how they lobbied to link the concerns of AIDS groups and *discapacitados* in the setting up of El Frente Comunal. Instead of competing for limited city funding, they lobbied to find a way to combine the two interests, resulting in gains for both groups. This involved, as stated earlier, the setting up of the AIDS office staffed with folks from Acceso Libre (see photo 36).

German's quote above is the prologue to a monograph on the conditions of indigenous *discapacitados* in the state of Oaxaca that Germán, Pedro, and Gabriela coedited with Catherine Marshall and George Gotto from the American Indian Rehabilitation Research and Training Center in Flagstaff, Arizona (Marshall et al. 1996). As Germán and Pedro were beginning to move their dreams into action, Catherine was visiting Oaxaca in search of research possibilities that linked North American indigenous peoples with disabilities to other indigenous peoples with disabilities in Mexico. The joining of their respective forces provided the energy and financial means for the emergence of Acceso Libre and the placement of the *discapacitados* as vocal and visible actors within the urban popular culture of Oaxaca. Part of the success of these efforts lies in the dynamic personalities of Germán and Pedro. Here we will provide a summary of their backgrounds, current lives, and future hopes. This information comes from various discussions in their homes and offices, and in cafes around the city.

GERMÁN

Germán is thirty-six years old and currently lives with his family (mother and brothers) in the central part of the city. His father and mother are from San Pablo Huixtepec, which is in the southern end of the Oaxaca valley in the area of Zimatlán and is predominantly Zapotec. His mother's grandparents and other family members were involved in numerous political disputes over land that often got violent. Germán's mother married his father, left the village and moved to the city, where his father owned a small store and some real estate that is now worth quite a bit. He still lives in the family home with his mother and one of his brothers. He has seven surviving brothers, though one of his brothers has died. His father died more than a decade ago, and Germán says that he died from his drinking, though he does not

36. Germán singing
and Pedro playing for a
friend, 1996. Photo by
Tanya Coen.

37. Germán Pérez
and Pedro Flores
singing, 1996. Photo
by Tanya Coen.

suggest that his father was abusive or hostile—just that he drank too much
(see photo 37).

Germán is quite a complex person. He has been afflicted with polio since
early infancy, and like the majority of people in Mexico with polio, he has
gone through numerous operations and rehabilitation programs during his
youth. He has also had the experience of spending months at a time recuperating in his bed. He used that time to read, think, and write. He writes
poems, short stories, and songs. He is quite articulate, strongly opinionated,
and very bright. He is also an excellent organizer and motivator. He has a
cutting sense of humor, a charming mode of self-presentation, and a zest for
life that has moved him beyond any limitations that polio has offered up
to him.

Germán does not contend that being disabled is a form of identity in the
sense that all *discapacitados* share common views or approaches to their lives.

This view, from Germán's standpoint, is that because the general "able" community does not understand or fails to be responsive to various concerns of people with disabilities, the collective efforts of *los discapacitados* are necessary. He is aware that they have to create a representation of themselves as a collective group so that they can effectively organize and lobby for their shared and particular needs. For example, all *los discapacitados* require access to public and social space, though that access will be different for those with locomotion problems than for those who have hearing or vision limitations. Though these would not quite be his words, Germán does understand that what unites this community is the necessity to affiliate in a collective struggle to attain their goals. For him, this is not an attempt to share a common identity that derives from being disabled. He also understands that because there is not a shared identity per se among themselves, there are differing factions within this community as it attempts to place itself within the larger popular culture of Oaxaca. As stated in his quote above, it is more important to be humane than to be normal.

Germán went through the Oaxacan educational system to earn his degree in physical education. Before organizing Acceso Libre, he did work as a teacher in the rural zones of the state of Oaxaca, was a youth organizer in the Mitla area, and also worked on programs for *discapacitados* for DIF. He also states that he and Pedro used to lead a pretty wild life of partying and drinking. Now neither of them drinks. Germán feels that often many *discapacitados* will turn to heavy drinking as one way of dealing with the hassles of everyday life. Germán tells tales of being in one of the *colonias* on the Cerros del Fortín, being very drunk, and trying to figure out how to get down the dirt paths in his wheelchair. The combination of the history of his father's drinking and seeing how many other *discapacitados* hid their fears in drinking has moved Germán to seek sobriety. He still likes to party, but he now chooses not to drink.

Germán is somewhat of a cynical romantic. He has had several important relationships with different women in his life but none that involved marriage. He is not sure about marriage. He feels that in the context of contemporary life it is very hard to be in a marriage that is assumed to be forever. He is not sure that is something he would want or would be able to do, though he likes romance and having romantic interludes in his life. His lovers have been from both the "normal" and the *discapacitados* communities. He is aware of the diverse sexual world of Oaxaca. He knows, through his work at El Frente Comunal, the world of prostitutes, both male and female. He knows of the *chicas* and was familiar with Casa Blanca, the cabaret that Leslie and Tania were so fond of. He has not expressed whether he has known prostitutes in a more personal sense. He is aware of the sexual lexicon of males in terms of dealing with straight women and gay men. He understands the idea of passive and active gays and says that it is their *onda* and who is he to judge.

He sees his immediate future as tied to the development and maintenance of Acceso Libre so that it becomes a permanent structure. Certainly the grant that the organization currently has makes such a future quite concrete. Germán has a very active mind and likes to argue political and philosophical issues that affect both the world of the *discapacitados* and others. He enjoys contemporary music and literature. He is keenly aware of both international and national political issues that affect him and affect how Acceso Libre can position itself. He knows that Mexico is mired in a continuous economic crisis that has pushed many people into harsher living conditions and that the concerns of the disabled have to be addressed within that context. He is impressed with how much they have attained in a short time, and as yet he is not overwhelmed by how much more they need to do. He does not see himself or other *discapacitados* as victims seeking handouts but as assertive and creative people confronting like everyone else *la vida dura*—the hard life. Life is hard not because of his or others' disabilities but because the current world is politically and economically a very harsh reality that affects everyone.

He hopes someday that he will have the time and the means to travel the world. He would like to spend time in Europe, to roam the streets of Paris, Madrid, or Rome. He feels that he knows Mexico fairly well, is getting some exposure to the United States in his collaborative work with the folks in Flagstaff, and would like to take on the rest of the world. As he says, "Thanks to polio, I have done more than many others; there's no reason to stop now." You can capture a sense of his hopes and desires in his April 1994 poem for Gabriela.[6]

FROM EVER SINCE TO YOU, . . . GABY

Yesterday, ever since yesterday
everything became clear, sober,
your presence was reflected by every object
every material object of light color
the wind brought your smile, your anger,
your simple and plain way of loving.
Yesterday, yesterday the bitterness
which I felt changed. It became a
residue of courage which we both need
to overcome the great determination
to separate the pure and warm union of
our bodies which consequently means the separation
of our souls, that which ignites men (mankind)
of weak spirit and lacking grace.
Yesterday I took the situation apart
piece by piece and let flow
the clear liquid oxidize deep in my soul
which leaves a sweet bitterness of dissatisfaction.
Yesterday, only yesterday!
I was only remembering you
I remembered your kisses and hugs
I remembered your way of making love to me
I remembered you and as I perspired
I received inspiration and burning passion to see you
yesterday and only yesterday I confirmed
how much I love you.[7]

PEDRO DAVID FLORES REY

Pedro is thirty-seven years old, and he and his family are from the city of Oaxaca. His father worked in various commercial activities that provided the family with an adequate middle-income lifestyle. Pedro has ten brothers and sisters. He currently lives on land that is part of the family compound. His father bought land that once was on the outskirts of town; thus they have a very large tract of land that is now almost in the center of this growing city. Pedro is married to a school psychologist—Patty—and they have one daughter, also named Patty, who is ten. Pedro and Patty have been having their house built over the last couple of years, and they now have a very nice two-bedroom home that is the upstairs part of a commercial building. They rent out the lower part of the building. Currently these spaces are used as a restaurant and a variety store. Pedro went to Escuela de Belles Artes, where his focus was supposed to be on music, but he spent more time partying and never received his degree. His work history reflects his constant involvement with the concerns of the *discapacitados.* Before Acceso Libre, he worked as a coordinator for both the national social security and DIF in their programs for *discapacitados.*

Pedro grew up with strong support from his family. He was encouraged to do what he wanted and not to feel limited by his disability. Polio put limits on his life, but it did not limit him. Like many others with polio, his childhood and adolescence were filled with operations and rehabilitation. It is quite amazing to us that people like Pedro emerge from such trials and tribulations without bitterness and in fact envision their lives as positive. An example of this attitude is the acquisition of a wheelchair. Those of us who are able to walk without assistance would view having to live life in a wheelchair as a form of imprisonment. For Pedro, getting access to a wheelchair was a form of freedom and mobility; it expanded his world. With a wheelchair he was mobile and could go places on his own where he could not go before. In sports, for example, without a wheelchair he is excluded. He cannot play basketball or other sports because of his limited mobility, but in a wheelchair he is an active and assertive ballplayer who has gotten to tour throughout Mexico (see photo 38).

Pedro is a very cosmopolitan young man. Since he is a guitarist and singer, he is very interested in contemporary musical trends, both Mexican and international. Though his playing and singing styles are traditional, his overall musical tastes are eclectic, ranging from rock to classical. His politics are

38. *Pedro Flores, 1996.*
Photo by Tanya Coen.

progressive in terms of showing concern for such struggles as that of the
Zapatistas, but he is pragmatic in knowing that to develop programs like
Acceso Libre, one must work with conflicting factions of local politics independent of any political position. He is well informed about local and national politics, and baffled by the conflicting messages coming from the
United States in relation to immigrants, especially Mexicans. Pedro admires
many aspects of what the disabled communities in the United States have
been able to attain, especially in terms of community living, but he is offended by how often some people in the United States exhibit no real understanding of Mexican lifestyles and concerns, let alone any concern for
those who are disabled.

Pedro and Patty have been married for about ten years. They met through
mutual friends. They are both from the same *colonia*—San Juanito. They
never seem to talk about how his disability limits their relationship; they simply act like most contemporary couples, struggling to combine professional
careers and family life. Patty is a school psychologist and works five days a
week, whereas Pedro's work, formally also five days a week, often extends into
evenings and weekends, depending on current projects of Acceso Libre. They
attempt to create a fair division of labor in terms of child care and household chores. Patty, their daughter, is a very bright and active ten-year-old
who keeps both of her parents busy. Pedro and Patty have an affectionate
relationship that involves spending a lot of time together. Patty (the mother)
is an articulate person who is also quite cosmopolitan in her style and be-

havior. They both like to have animated conversations about contemporary issues of politics and lifestyles. They enjoyed the project that we were working on, especially the *chicas*. Like many, they were intrigued to learn more about the everyday life aspects of them. It was interesting that both Pedro and Patty were surprised by the complexities of the *chicas'* lives and how the *chicas* played with the categories of gender and sexuality.

Pedro and Patty are quite an engaging couple, struggling with all the joys and frustrations of middle-income lifestyles in urban Oaxaca. Though they have two incomes, these incomes go toward general maintenance, particularly the cost of the construction of their house. They have competing social demands coming from their respective families, work, and friends. Like many other couples, they attempt to juggle these demands and somehow find time for their own concerns, which range from dealing with their daughter to finding time for their own intimate desires. Pretty ordinary stuff.

Pedro has a very positive outlook in terms of his life. He is proud of what he has been able to do through Acceso Libre and what Acceso Libre has been able to do to help build a community for *discapacitados*. Pedro spends a great deal of time visiting with *discapacitados* who have not come out of their closets yet. He mixes empathy with toughness that seems to encourage those who are shy and embarrassed about their disabilities to move on with life. Like Germán, he does not see people with disabilities as having a common identity but common histories that allow for affinities that can become the basis for collective struggles and achievement. Because of this, he is a passionate advocate for the idea that people with disabilities have to be in charge of their own programs and those programs have to be directed toward increasing their autonomy and self-esteem through concrete and basic programs. However, he confronts even these passionate positions and concerns with a combination of determination and humor.[8]

CONCLUSION: THE POLITICS OF AFFILIATION

Here we will explore what the daily realities of *los discapacitados* can tell us about the ordinariness of diversity in urban Oaxaca. First, they do have a worldview of ordinariness that gives them hope, and they are hopeful that others can come to understand this viewpoint. Like the members of Grupo Unión, they seek neither special rights nor privileges, but they do seek that others understand them as real people who make up a sector of contemporary society, and they have particular interests that they lobby for, as any other sector of the urban scene would do. Ironically, with the combination of local politics, the national economic crisis, and their own endeavors, they are becoming "players" in the social/political context of the city of Oaxaca. Over the past decade a combined economic and political crisis has been going on in Mexico. How these forces have framed the concerns of *los discapacitados* is an interesting story.

In the municipal elections of 1995 in the city of Oaxaca, a set of opposition candidates organized by the PAN won the local elections. What the long-term effects of that change will be remain to be determined, but one of the immediate effects was the alteration of the middle-class political patronage network of Oaxaca. Many who had cultivated long-term connections with the PRI had to develop some new *palanca* with the new political forces very rapidly or start looking for new sources of patronage within the city. The world of the *discapacitados* before Acceso Libre had been safely contained within the state and federal domains of DIF. Acceso Libre was opening new political space with its organizational skills but not attracting too much attention because it was not a source of funds that could generate jobs or work for others. However, the organization received its $300,000 (USA) Kellogg grant at the same time that the old PRI guard was looking for new networks. All of those who had not been too interested in their programs were now seeking out Acceso Libre to offer aid to its new programs, and for that aid they would want paid consulting jobs. You cannot get any more ordinary in the political economy of Oaxaca than to be a source of patronage jobs. What is ironic here is that this was what Acceso Libre hoped to avoid in building its organization. It may not be that easy.

In the political infighting between the new political forces—the new city government, the PAN, and the older established forces of the PRI dominated by the governor of the state—the social space of the *discapacitados* is being affected. With its new funds, Acceso Libre has opened a center that is run by and for the *discapacitados*, who through it are struggling to demonstrate the effectiveness of grassroots organizations that are not connected to political parties. However, both the PRI and the PAN argue for grassroots development as proof of the strength of their political concerns. Thus, to these different political groups, Acceso Libre is a gem sitting out there as proof of their particular positions. The problem is that Acceso Libre does not want to be claimed by anyone—that is what the organization is fighting against. This discord is splitting the community of *discapacitados,* who find themselves being courted through political favors offered by the PRI. It has also affected the plans of the inauguration of the Acceso Libre center. The organization wants to do this with the governor and his wife in attendance, but since the current governor's spouse is the official coordinator of the state DIF agency, the governor's office has been stalling on attending until it can figure out where in the new political context these independent *discapacitados* fit—another very ordinary political reality in Oaxaca.

We also think that the ordinariness of the everyday life of the *discapacitados* offers insights into numerous issues that have been engendered by debates within the postmodern discourse. We would like to suggest that they offer some very profound insights in terms of the issues of identity, body imagery, and sexuality. Donna Haraway has been a forceful advocate for moving away from identity-based politics and toward the construction of coalitions of affinities. She wonders if the "epistemologies" of Western peoples will "fail us in the task to build effective affinities" (Haraway 1991:157). We would suggest that perhaps there is one "Western" epistemology that is already grounded in the constructions of affinities: *los discapacitados*. Germán, Pedro, Iris, Rocío, Gaby, Lourdes, and many other *discapacitados* do not feel that they have a common identity but that they have a social and historical affinity through their particular disabilities. Clearly they have used their affinities to create a political and social space that did not exist before—a grassroots and community-based agency that has altered the political landscape of Oaxaca. Because their actions were based upon affinity rather than identity, they have no perceptual or emotional investment in the idea that all *discapacitados* can be united or that they even get along with each other all the time. They do feel compelled to defend the realities of *discapacitados*, but they compose defenses that are about the common issues that affect them through the existing social conditions of Oaxaca, not a supposed shared identity. We do not wish to belabor this point, but it is important to understand the realities of these people not only so we will be more tolerant about people with disabilities but also so we can learn something that might be useful to us through our affiliation with them (Charlton 1998). Let us illustrate this with two other postmodern concerns—body imagery and sexuality.

The politics of postmodernism has forcefully confronted the issues of body imagery and sexuality in existing capitalism (Cornwall and Lindisfarne 1994; García Canclini 1995; Haraway 1991; Lowe 1995; Nicholson and Seidman 1995; Richardson 1996; Rubin 1994; Singer 1993). There are far too many arguments and authors in this debate to review them here or to explain in detail. However, these arguments have forcefully shown the heterosexist nature of body imagery in existing capitalism and have called into question whether the cyberspace world of tomorrow will be any different (Balsamo 1996; Springer 1996). The crux of these arguments centers on how a particular type of female body has been and seems to continue to be used as the code for appropriate body images and behaviors in our everyday lives. From the cinematic male gaze to the gendered bodies of cyborgs, a hegemonic pattern continues to enforce a form of male privilege and attempts to deny that privilege to females. This debate calls for the reimaging of the body and for political struggles against the hegemony of heterosexism. It is a complex debate that is often too Eurocentric in its flavor for our taste, but nevertheless it addresses several important issues that we would encourage our readers to become familiar with. However, we think that perhaps the everyday lives of the *discapacitados* can offer us some insights. Clearly the high level of self-esteem expressed by so many in Acceso Libre cannot come from assuming that their bodies fit into "normal" images of beautiful bodies. The arguments on body images are centered on "normal" bodies that may be made less normal through resisting the hegemony of heterosexism, but they rarely talk about the kinds of bodies that Germán and Gaby have (Barbach and Levine 1980). Clearly, if we want to learn how to envision and develop body imagery that is free from this kind of commodity capitalist logic, an exchange of ideas with the *discapacitados* would be valuable. Again, they have rethought or reconfigured their body imagery not in response to these postmodern debates but because it is the context of their personal agency and intimate everyday lives. Their answers may not be the answers for others, but their logic of discovery might be useful to everyone. However, we will not know until we so-called "able" folks start asking.

We would suggest that this could be true also in the area of sexuality. Actors in the post-epidemic world of sexuality are actively seeking to construct new forms of sexuality that would be neither genitalcentric or even bodycentric (Singer 1993). The world of virtual sexuality is here now, not in the future. Like the debate over body imagery, this debate sees the contrast of contemporary sexuality as linked to political economy of consumer capitalism and argues for a recomposing of our sexuality as a form of political struggle (Rubin 1994). This debate is about the need to recapture forms of pleasure and desire that are not exploitive nor centered on body assumptions of classic capitalist beauty. Though the sexuality of people with disabilities is sometimes talked about, the discussions center around in what sense people with disabilities can approximate "normal" sexuality. Maybe we should open a different type of conversation. Again, the sexuality of *los discapacitados* is already not framed in terms of normal sexual or classic images of beauty. They have had to recompose their styles of sexuality to map out their own domains of sexual pleasure and desire; maybe that is something, again, that we can all learn from.

Are such dialogues possible? Certainly, we have found that Germán, Lourdes, and Rocío were more than willing to talk about such things if somebody asked them. Do they have more profound or insightful answers than we "normal folks"? Not particularly, for they have to weave through their other domains of situated knowledges in seeking their own ordinary sexuality and body images. But what we can learn is that, for them, these are not postmodern debates; they are the actions of their everyday lives.[9]

CHAPTER SIX

A Conclusion
of Sorts

HOW DO WE end this book about the ordinariness of diversity without falling into the trap of overgeneralization? What we think these actors have in common is the ordinariness of their diversity. We fully recognize that for the last decade the debates in the social sciences and areas of cultural studies have been dominated by how to deal with difference and at what level difference or diversity is to be prioritized over other realities. With respect and admiration for those who have been fighting these battles, we believe that these debates may have moved us into a reality of double binds à la Bateson; that is, you are "damned if you do or damned if you don't." How to unravel and understand all the intersections of the situated knowledges of race, class, gender, sexuality, ethnicity, ableness, and others is a daunting endeavor. We think the way out of the double bind is also as Bateson suggests. Since one cannot obey either message, one has to step outside of the message network (Bateson 1972). We suggest that to read diversity as the ordinary reality of everyday life is one way out of such double binds. Further, we would encourage others to take this idea or concept into directions other than the ones we have chosen. Thus, in this conclusion of sorts we would like to explore where this concept has taken us in understanding the *ondas* of various urban popular cultures of Oaxaca.

Urban Popular Cultures of Oaxaca

We have presented various ethnographic portraits and sketches of persons from the popular cultures and classes of urban Oaxaca and have suggested that this panoramic look at these groups gives a stronger impression of what constitutes the *ondas* of the city. We have tried to move beyond just residential-based ethnographic research to see how these actors navigate their way through the hegemonic terrains of urban Oaxaca. We view the cultural and personal expressions of these folks as representative of the ways hybrid social spaces are composed and recomposed (García Canclini 1995; Pieterse 1995). That is, the people in this study, within their own ordinary social space, move back and forth through social zones of the traditional (such as the beliefs in the Virgen de Juquila) to the popular (such as the *chicas'* protest march on the city hall) and mass-based communication networks (like Víctor, María Elena's son, who is trying to figure out how to get into the international tourist trade network to sell his carved figures). For García Canclini such movements back and forth represent the hybrid social spaces of postmodernism, and it is these movements through socially contested sites that provide the material base for the fluid identities that these actors have composed. This is why we have stressed throughout our presentation that the abstract debates about identities and social action within various postmodern discourses are the everyday realities for these people. Further, because such activities are framed in the context of their everyday lives, such *ondas* can be captured through ethnographic narration.

We are aware of the problematic issues of representation that we are dealing with in this presentation (Gilroy 1993). Thus, we have kept our presentations framed in the context of these people's everyday lives in urban Oaxaca. We have also placed that context within the overall context of postmodern consumer capitalism and how Mexico and the region of Oaxaca are articulated to those dynamics (Coen and Higgins 1994; Lowe 1995). Further, though we have presented these people's lives as ordinary, we have attempted to keep in focus that such ordinariness does not negate the reality of inequality and violence that is also tragically part of this ordinariness (James 1997; Scheper-Hughes 1992). In no way are we suggesting that we have solved or could solve the complexities of these profound debates over representation, identities, and difference in relation to the realities of racism, sexism, and classism that also remain as part of the ordinariness of existing consumer capitalism (Bartolomé 1997; Fraser 1997; Haraway 1997). We feel that by understanding aspects of how these actors, in the context of urban Oaxaca, have used their personal agency (often in a transgressive manner), we can give partial understandings to the material processes that have engendered these complex realities. We encourage readers to use this information to form their own understanding of these issues rather than depending upon our providing such announcements. We want the stories of the people from the urban cultures of Oaxaca and our collaboration in these stories to provide ethnographic texture to these issues. We do not want to use these stories as a means for us to return to the position of the "knowing subject," providing either objective accounts or sagely theoretical insights.[1]

We are also aware that the accounts we have presented here are only partial stories about these people's lives. The folks in Colonia Linda Vista are people that we have known for some thirty years, yet each time we return we learn more about them. For example, we never knew that my (MJH) comadre Victoria had relatives in Mixteca Alta, where my doctoral adviser, Douglas Butterworth, did his research (Butterworth 1962) or that my compadre Arnulfo's nephew ran the biggest whorehouse in Oaxaca. Certainly the people in Grupo Unión, Acceso Libre, the knitting prostitute group, Renacimiento, and *los bohemios* have many more stories to tell and each group's *onda* merits individual study. We wanted to present a panorama of the urban popular sectors, and we think that these partial presentations do capture the texture of the ethnographic realities of the city, framed in our use of the ordinariness of diversity. We have plans to continue working with these various people over the coming years, but we would encourage others to meet and work with these groups as well.

Given the partialness of these portraits, we were surprised that these people from their different locations within the urban popular cultures of Oaxaca did not use the voices of victims to tell their stories and that they would often use voices with the radical accent of the "politics of pleasure" (Viegener 1993). Most of these actors certainly saw many things in their lives that had been harsh, and they felt that they had come through some very hard times; such perceptions were not composed in terms of being victims, however, but in terms of being folks who had survived such challenges in the process of just being and living. Doñas María Elena and Victoria see the patterns of their gender and sexual histories as being framed in terms of male authority, but through different circumstances each emerged with a life that was better than she had envisioned. Also, each has prioritized the emotional and material support of her adult offspring over the problematic advantages of bringing a new male into their lives. They have denied themselves the possible pleasure of a sexual life in favor of the real pleasure of their own personal freedoms and continuous close contact with their adult offspring. Juan is a little defensive about the changes in his life, but he finds solace with his young lover, whereas Lucía, like María Elena and Victoria, somewhat enjoys her new demands (now taking care of her grandchildren) but revels in her newly attained personal freedom. Though the children have gone through some very harsh times, especially Alma and Cristy, they still see their lives as positive and open to new opportunities. Francisca and Arnulfo proudly claim that they have not been victims of racism, not because they naively assume that racism does not exist but because they have transcended any constraints that others have attempted to place on them. For them the politics of pleasure involves their being free from the daily hassles of work and having free time to do what they want. Again, none of these actors are naive, and all have dealt with the various horrors and tragedies present in the context of their social histories.

The members of Grupo Unión were also quite positive in the ways they composed their stories. As we got to know them better, we were quite aware that they often liked to give rather rosy accounts and would frequently avoid giving many details about the harsh aspects of their lives in terms of their backgrounds or current situations. Much of their presentation of self in their everyday lives can be represented by the zest of their pursuit of the politics of pleasure. They see themselves not only as sex workers but as workers who are quite good at sex. At times they seem to feel that no man can resist their charm and skills of persuasion. One of Leslie's favorite phrases was how their lifestyle as drag queens was one of breaking through old assumptions, yet she also sought the most ordinary of desires in terms of marriage and children. Most of the *chicas* entertained the hybrid heterosexual fantasy of living with the man of their dreams; yet the very fact that they are drag queens seeking to fulfill such desires acts to subvert the assumption about what heterosexuality is (Cornwall 1994; Richardson 1996). In addition, the current sentiments of Tania and Iracema not to seek a permanent lover or husband further question gender assumptions in terms of who is being sexually assertive, themselves as women or themselves as men who are women. There is a great deal about their everyday behavior that is derived from male privilege; here we are talking about how, in the ordinary pursuit of their own various desires for pleasure, assumptions about gendered forms of sexual pleasure become problematic and behaviorally quite fluid.

In ways different from the *chicas* but still similar to them, *los discapacitados* present a very strong expression of their style of the politics of pleasure. They often talked about the consequences of accidents of birth or life that they had experienced but not about themselves as victims. It was also clear that many of those coming to this emerging community of *discapacitados,* especially those who had recently suffered serious accidents, had difficulty getting beyond victimization. Germán and Pedro focused on using Acceso Libre as a means to move people away from such negative mind-sets. Those who had moved beyond that level often seemed to revel in all the things that they found they *could* do. They were very proud of what they had all accomplished in such a short time. For many in this community (such as Marta, the host of the party) life was a celebration of possibilities, not a lament of limitations. Again, this is not some naive worldview; the untimely death of Gabriela was a harsh reminder of the persistent danger they have to face. The desire among *los discapacitados* for the reality of ordinariness to include them challenges those in the so-called "able" world (including us) to rethink assumptions of body and sexual imagery and move away from the heterosexual canon with its idealized norm of perfection that none of us can affirm (Singer 1993).

The knitting prostitutes approach their work in a pragmatic way, as the means to meet the conflicting demands of child care, household obligations, and control over their own working conditions. They sought to express their politics of pleasure more in terms of work autonomy than in sexual adventures. Like the "*chicas,*" however, they voiced no moral concerns about their jobs, saying only that this kind of work gave them the means to control their working hours and style of work. José Antonio and his friends in Renacimiento would seem to have the most grounds for using the trope of victimization, given the history of their group in relation to other AIDS agencies in the city, their various personal conflicts with folks in those agencies, and the fact that some of them are HIV-positive. José Antonio does talk about his introduction to sex as part of an abusive relationship that he had with an older man, but he does not suggest that that's what made him gay—only that it's not the way for young people to be introduced to sex. Despite all the trials and tribulations in keeping Renacimiento going, he maintains an amazingly positive outlook on his life and the work he is doing. Both Raúl and Primativo are attempting to stay hopeful about their lives while they try to understand and struggle with the reality of being HIV-positive. And our representative of *los bohemios* in Oaxaca, Lupe Ramírez, expresses various creative and insightful views on how she hopes to compose herself as a *nueva mexicana*.

Why do we want to stress the absence of the voice of victim among these actors and emphasize expressions of what can be viewed as forms of the politics of pleasure? There is clearly no absence of harshness and struggle in these people's lives, and in fact their stories could easily be positioned in that framework. Since they themselves were composing stories from different vantage points, we felt that we should honor that. That these various actors frame their lives from such positive perspectives is encouraging, for if anyone would have the right to be pessimistic and fatalistic, it would be some of these folks. We, in fact, find people in more affluent social positions, especially middle-class Anglo actors from the United States, to be much more pessimistic and fatalistic than any of the people we have dealt with in this study. Though it is often assumed that groups designated as "marginal" will view the world through the lens of either pessimism or fatalism (Hunt, Valenzuela, and Pugh 1997), it has been our experience that middle-class actors are more likely than those in the popular sectors of Oaxaca to do so. It may be that such tropes of despair are another form of class privilege (McLaren 1997).

A difference of cultural and political economies is also being expressed here. The social and political terrains of Mexico's economy offer a variety of spaces where people can compose themselves differently from what is offered in the context of United States and European affluence. In the political context of the United States the trope of victim can make more social sense than it does in Mexico. We are suggesting, like Scheper-Hughes (1992), that there is a political economy of emotions that is part of these processes we are talking about. Thus we are not suggesting that the lives of these actors in Mexico be used to criticize those in the United States or other places that do use the voice of the victim; instead we are recognizing that either style of presentation requires that analysis of such stories be contextualized to the political economy of the actors doing the telling.

Another point stressed by Viegener about the politics of pleasure was the quest for utopian visions (Viegener 1993). Like many other writers, he suggests that utopian visions are the space where social hope and transformation can be cultivated and protected. For many of the people presented here, just surviving and getting by has utopian aspects. For others, like the *chicas* or the *discapacitados,* arriving in a social context of valid social tolerance would seem utopian, whereas for José Antonio, a real utopian achievement would be to get Renacimiento funded and well organized.

The Politics of the Ordinariness of Diversity

The work we have presented here expresses what we refer to as ethnographic praxis (Higgins and Coen 1992; Coen and Higgins 1994). In Managua, Nicaragua, we were able to link the Barrio de William Díaz Romero to the Chicano community of Greeley, Colorado, through our ethnographic work that was part of a solidarity project (Higgins and Coen 1992). Helping that community build its own community center was a materially visible achievement that affirmed the connection between the two communities. However, such work had little or no effect on the macro relations of Nicaragua's social and political quest nor the attacks on those hopes by the United States government. For us, the praxis involved in this project has involved the collaborative work with these various folks to search for ways to present their "ordinary" stories as a means for opening and creating new social spaces of tolerance. What our approach lacks in a utopian sense, however, is a way to move this praxis from an ethnographic process to a political one that is beyond the "text." Here we wish to state that we have no better ideas or answers than many other people who are exploring these themes; what we offer are suggestions for debate and dialogue.

We think that those in positions of affluence need to renew their (our) commitments to offer unconditional support for the struggles of actors in the popular cultures for affirmation, liberation, and transformation. No matter how the "new world order" is justified, it means poverty and death for the majority of people in the world so that a minority can maintain its own well-being. For there to be a world in which the ordinariness of diversity is the "normative" reality, the vast inequalities in the material wealth of the postmodern world must be addressed and changed. It does not take a rocket scientist to figure out that most of the struggles of people in the popular cultures for liberation and transformation are rooted in their attempts to address the quest for material fairness in the world. Such struggles, we contend, should be supported unconditionally; that does not mean, however, that they should be supported uncritically. We of the affluent world need to understand the ethical basis of such concerns and join in the struggles or find ways to address the root causes of these concerns in our own various contexts. We should not be so cynical as to belittle the quest for material fairness, nor should we be so critical of how difficult such a quest can be. We need to renew our skills at utopian visions and recognize the necessity of working toward some kind of redistribution of the wealth in the existing world. How? There are thousands of models and plans that need critical debate and testing. We think a *dicho* we learned in Nicaragua might be suggestive here: "Those who work get to criticize!" One can affirm one's solidarity through involvement, and that involvement will provide the space for critical input. But how does one get involved?

Where one gets involved is at the local or grassroots level. It seems to us that one of the confusions encountered in postmodern argumentation is about the value of political action. If there are no grand narratives or universal truths, then how does one struggle for such issues as social justice or material fairness? This has never seemed to be much of a paradox for us, since we view these issues as being composed through social construction, as their affirmation would be. A fair and just world will arise not from universal truths but through the hard work of ordinary people organizing, mobilizing, and acting upon their shared values for such social conditions. This view is not particularly original or novel, but it is worth restating. It would seem that the question of where to begin was answered by the Queen's comments to Alice when she said that you begin at the beginning. The type of political action required to compose the social spaces needed for the ordinariness of diversity begins at the local level, around local issues. One is not using the media's assumption of political correctness when one seeks to build broad-based alliances for social action; one is expressing the basic ordinariness of politics. If you are organizing to gain a local tax to support a creative arts center, there would be no reason to assume that drag queens or *discapacitados* might not be interested in such an issue—perhaps even more so if those particular groups knew that their support was being sought because they had requested similar support from the arts groups on issues of primary concern to them. Alliance building through shared affinities over issues is the way to move through hegemonic terrains of existing consumer capitalism; in that context, linking diverse ethnic, sexual, gender, and class groups together is not just politically correct (in the older leftist sense), but it is also politically smart. If we can read difference and diversity as our ordinary reality, we find that there are not any single-issue groups per se, but numerous frontiers where links of affinity can be constructed.[2]

The question arises of how to forge such alliances. We feel that in the current context of postmodernity, institutional politics seems to be ineffective in addressing most people's everyday political and economic concerns. This is certainly true for the people that we have presented in this volume, and it seems to describe the situation in our respective social worlds here in the United States. It seems to us that many people identify their most important political issues as concerns about identity or emotions (Fraser 1997). In the United States such issues are referred to as cultural politics, in which gender, sexuality, and ethnicity engender much more interest among everyday people than do issues about free trade or communications regulation. In Mexico, it is not so much any detailed criticism of the PRI's economic logic that fuels the distrust of the popular classes as it is emotional feelings of unfairness. We are suggesting that if that's where people's attention is being focused, we all need to find politically meaningful ways to address such concerns in an open and effective manner, with ideas that do not suggest that those whose frames of reference are either emotional or identity-based need to be brought to more insightful understandings. Within the ordinariness of diversity there are no positions that a priori are more insightful; instead there exists a range of insights to be listened to and recomposed through struggles of affinity building.[3]

Utopian Desires within the Ordinariness of Diversity

Continuing in this speculative style, we suggest that the politics of the ordinariness of diversity is in fact pretty ordinary, which is what it should be. Here we will explore briefly what we think can be the utopian desires present within this "discourse."

If we could enter into a world beyond that of existing consumer capitalism, a world where the ordinariness of diversity was the normative reality, what would the dynamics of everyday life look like? We think that it would be a social context in which it would be possible to compose one's everyday life by accessing various equivalent sites of knowledges and experiences. It would be a world in which Lancaster's ideas about the performative qualities of gender (Lancaster 1997a), Foucault's activity-identified sexuality (Foucault 1978), Marx's arena of freely associated producers (Marx 1967), and Marley's visions of a community in which the color of people's skin was no more important than the color of their eyes (Marley 1978) would be daily possibilities, not utopian dreams. Differences would be performative; that is, since differences would be composed in social spaces of equivalent value, then differences would represent various bodies of knowledges that could be freely accessed if desired. Remembering that we are speaking here of utopian desires, we would see this world as one in which material difference would be minor, determined more by regional location and lifestyle choices than by class domination so that groups could maintain and cultivate their ways of life. Others could access these sites of identity either through direct participation or by composing corresponding or hybrid equivalents. The politics of such a world focuses on producing a context for the material well-being of all and maintaining vigilance against the reappearance of hegemonies that would prefer such realities to be ranked in terms of privilege instead of equivalence. This could be the world that Martin Luther King dreamed of when he asked us to "join hands and sing in the words of that old Negro spiritual, 'Free at last! Free at last! Thank God almighty, we are free at last!'" (King 1963).

Ethnographic Praxis and the Politics of Responsibility

In closing this exploration of the urban popular cultures of Oaxaca we need to leave the "hoped-for world" of utopian desires and return to the real world of the streets, bedrooms, and patios of urban Oaxaca. These utopian visions are what we hope will come to pass through the attainment of a world in which the ordinariness of diversity is normative. The folks we have introduced here may or may not share such hopes. What they are most concerned about is the context and quality of their existing everyday lives, which could be less stressful if they were viewed and interacted with on the basis of their ordinariness instead of on the basis of some assumed status as "other." Correspondingly, we have suggested that the abstract arguments being explored in the discursive spaces of postmodernity about identities, representation, and political action would be well informed by listening to the stories being told in the streets, bedrooms, and patios of the urban popular cultures of Oaxaca. For in that social context such concerns are not abstractions but the substance of everyday life, and we can all learn from such understandings. It is our contention that the most radical expression of ethnographic praxis is the acceptance and celebration of the ordinariness of diversity. With such a praxis we can all learn together how to construct a more reasonable and fair world.

We have posited throughout this presentation that there is no common or core humanity that we all share, that the content we have in common is our differences; difference or diversity is our most ordinary social reality. In terms of our understanding about the debates on the politics of representation and responsibility, we will close with a further clarification of what we mean by these claims.

We understand that a wide range of common behaviors and feelings exists. We all have the capacities of feeling happy, angry, sad, joyful, and much more, but the affirmation of such feelings takes place within the intersections of the existing political economies of consumer capitalism and through the avenues of personal agency. The social representations of such actions are the discursive and behavioral components of gender, sexuality, class, ethnicity/race, ableness, and other hegemonic terrains. We find these hegemonic configurations to be wonderfully fluid and diverse. Unlike many writers and critics who engage in these debates, however, we do not view the existence of difference as a barrier to either communication or collaboration (Marchand and Parpart 1995). As we have been saying, we are all operating in the overall material context of existing consumer capitalism that has been creatively and critically represented by various postmodern styles of interpretation. Since the material context of this political economy is framed in fragmented allocations of time and space (Harvey 1989), the various counterlogics of social action, alternative social formations, curious modes of accommodation, carnivalistic social parodies, creative modes of personal or collective resistance, and the brash hope in armed struggle are all sources of insight and important information on how the system looks and operates from different positions. Further, such a panoramic view would help us locate ourselves in these processes. What we are saying is that we want to add our voices and those from the streets, bedrooms, and patios of urban Oaxaca to the debates on difference and diversity and the quest for social justice. The various voices that make up the complex expression of diversity offer more material from which we can construct a future. For us, this would encourage that our politics of action move away from offering invitations of inclusion (since everyone is already present) and focus on dismantling the hegemonies of privilege that prevent access to material well-being for so many ordinary actors in the postmodern world.

We have to the best of our ability addressed very complex and well-thought-out debates and issues in the areas of social sciences, cultural studies, and the various discourses of identity and class-based political organizing. In these debates questions often arise as to who gets to do theory and whose versions of which theories get read and used (James 1997). These debates are what has fueled our passions for the kind of ethnographic work we have done. We are not attempting to debunk or refute any of the various positions; we simply want to present some stories from folks who have not often been heard from and suggest that there might be a simpler way to confront these issues—that is, through the ordinariness of diversity. Further, such a point of view eliminates any need to prioritize anyone's particular locations over someone else's and allows us to seek creative and radical means to struggle for a context in which the ordinariness of diversity has enough social spaces to provide justice and fairness for all those engaged in navigating through these various locations.

NOTES

NOTES TO CHAPTER ONE

1. *Onda* in Mexico has several different meanings. Its dictionary definition is "wave," like an ocean wave. It can also be used to mean "what's happening"—*que onda*, to indicate that you like someone—*que buena onda*, or to indicate a lifestyle—*ellos tienen una buen onda*. We use it here to mean "lifestyles" and "happenings."

2. The following brief review of the current political economy of Mexico should be helpful to the reader: Structurally, Mexico is organized around a market economy and democratic institutions. The democratic institutions are modeled after those of the United States, with executive, legislative, and judiciary structures. The president serves a six-year term and cannot be re-elected. There is a bicameral legislature, with a house of representatives and a senate, and an autonomous judicial system. These features, along with many other fine principles of liberal democracy, are codified in the Mexican Constitution of 1917. But no matter how refined these legal concepts are, they remain in the constitution and not in people's everyday lives. For the last seven decades, the whole system has been run through the authoritarian power of the presidency, backed by the organizational strength of the PRI (Party of the Institutional Revolution), the business elites, and the military (Cockcroft 1996). Those who have governed Mexico for the last two decades are a combination of the economic and political elite articulated through the political and governmental structures of the PRI. They have been attempting to move the country from a political economy that was a

form of protectionist capitalism to an unfettered form of neoliberal capitalism (Castañeda 1993).

At the national political level, Mexicans are being presented with at least three types of trickle-down or free market alternatives. For the last two decades, the PRI at the national level has been dominated by technocrats trained in the United States, who have been looking for ways to push Mexico further into the global economy through what they view as policies of national development and modernization that required a move away from protectionist policies to a supposedly open market and less government regulation. The PRI promises that, if it is kept in power, it will keep the country on course to get through this current economic crisis. That is, even though the economic gains that have trickled down for a decade have been almost nonexistent, the PRI suggests that it will find ways to increase the flow. Many think that the PRI is not to be believed anymore and that profound changes are on the way for Mexico (Castañeda 1995; Fuentes 1995).

The PRD (Party of the Democratic Revolution) was formed after the contested presidential elections of 1988. It began as a loose coalition of progressives and leftists in support of Cuauhtémoc Cárdenas (the son of Lázaro Cárdenas and the president of Mexico in the 1930s) as both the man and the image to build a progressive national opposition to the PRI. The PRD supports the need to expand and create new and more effective social service programs in all areas; however, this party maintains that until civil society is reformed through democratic structural changes, other changes will be ineffective and hard to support financially. The PRD has grudgingly accepted the reality of the "free market," but the hope is that the party can guide that market through democratic changes that should positively affect economic growth among Mexicans (Castañeda 1993).

The PAN (Party of National Action) has traditionally been viewed as the conservative, pro-business party that wants to correct the "leftist" programs of the government. Its strong focus on ending government corruption has effectively made it a champion of democratic reform. It has presented a convincing argument that the economic problems of Mexico resulted from the corrupt way the PRI has run the show rather than from deficiencies of the free market approach (Krauze 1997).

This review of the political economies and histories comes from works by Marjorie Becker (1994), Jorge Castañeda (1993), James Cockcroft (1996), Margarita Dalton (1990), Gilbert Joseph and Daniel Nugent (1994), and our own understandings of these processes from both the national and the local media of Mexico and Oaxaca.

3. We would like to make it clear that we are not suggesting that there are no cultural and historical commonalities within and between human social groups. We are saying only that such commonalities are socially constructed and what makes them understandable is the context of their expressions, which then leads back to difference and diversity. It is the assumption of pre-existing human nature or core human values that we reject; it is best to read social human commonalities in terms of plural realities rather than grand narratives. For example, there are no singular forms of heterosexuality or homosexuality; there are instead various social expressions of such behaviors (Lancaster 1997b).

4. Nancy Fraser has offered some interesting insights about these issues in terms of the politics of radical democracy. She argues forcefully that the "injustices of recognition are thoroughly imbricated with the injustices of distribution. They cannot be addressed in isolation from the latter" (Fraser 1997:174). She argues that cultural differences can be freely elaborated and democratically mediated only through struggles for social equality. That is, the creation of social spaces for identity politics requires politics of economic redistribution (Fraser 1997:187). She offers the rallying cry of "No recognition without redistribution" (Fraser 1997:187). That is what we suggest with the idea of the ordinariness of diversity.

5. In our view, the politics of representation and responsibility requires that we locate ourselves in the processes of social composition and action.

I am Michael Higgins, a fifty-three-year-old white, heterosexual male. I was born in Bangor, Maine, and about 1948 my father put the whole family (me, my mother, and two older brothers) in a van and started out for San Francisco, California. I grew up in the context of vaguely working-class realities in the San Francisco Bay Area. I say "vaguely working-class" because even though my parents were clearly working class in their occupations and lifestyles, as were their friends and mine, there was no working-class culture or consciousness expressed among ourselves. Through the advantages brought about by the general collective consumption of the 1950s and 1960s, I was able to attend public universities in order to obtain a doctorate in anthropology.

I was a full-blown participant in the 1960s. I was involved in civil rights struggles, the antiwar movement, feminism, and anticolonial issues. As successfully or unsuccessfully as others of this generation, I have attempted to integrate those ideas and the passions of those times into my everyday life, especially in terms of my personal relationships and the raising of my children.

As an anthropologist, I have been driven by a passion to understand the forces of inequality in the world of existing consumer capitalism. I was drawn to the urban poor of Oaxaca, for they seem to represent, in the Marxist sense, the group "in waiting" in terms of economic and social movements. I found out that the urban poor had more important things to deal with than waiting around to become historical agents for social transformation; they had to deal with their own everyday lives as best they could. I also began to learn that this marginality was a perception from outside, not one that the poor held about themselves. Later, working with Tanya Coen in Managua, Nicaragua, in an urban barrio that was predominantly poor, I learned how the folks in that barrio were attempting to undo this assumed marginalization through community-based revolutionary action. Also, from the failure of this revolution through the combined forces of domestic errors by the Sandinistas, international markets, and USA imperialism, I learned that even though local community action is the best site for resistance and revolution, it cannot be the only site for social transformations. I believe that in anthropology we need to understand the linkage between the local and the global in the context of people's everyday lives and how their lives intersected with the socially constructed realities of gender, sexuality, class, and ethnicity. These social dynamics are what has led me to the streets, bedrooms, and patios of urban Oaxaca. The issue for me is no longer attempting to understand the marginalized but seeing that we are all very ordinary in the diversity of the various hybrid cultures that make up postmodern existing consumer capitalism.

I am Tanya L. Coen, a thirty-seven-year-old female, the eldest of three offspring. My parents are natives of small-town Colorado, with rural backgrounds. I grew up in a white middle- to lower-middle-class household in Boulder, Colorado, which is a predominantly affluent, somewhat cosmopolitan, white city. I was influenced early on by my father, a successful superrealist painter and teacher of art. My mother devoted herself to her family, like many women of her generation. She ended her university education prematurely to support my father through school, working as a secretary, and later as a paralegal.

Throughout my public school upbringing and my undergraduate years I felt alienated academically because of a learning disability and the learning/ teaching Western model that merely disregarded students who were different. Somehow in my undergraduate post-Vietnam Reagan years, a budding politicization (in contrast to the conservatism espoused by my parents) grew into a deep interest and involvement in the Sandinista revolution.

Upon entering graduate studies in anthropology, I traveled to Nicaragua alone in 1986 and shortly after began fieldwork and solidarity work with Michael Higgins in Barrio William Díaz Romero in Managua, Nicaragua. This lasted off and on over the next five years until the fall of the Sandinistas. A deep respect and admiration for the intentions of the Sandinista model grew as I observed the tirelessness and dedication of those in Barrio William Díaz Romero who organized their community at the local level. I was greatly humbled by the Nicaraguan people's widespread graciousness toward the people of the United States—in light of our imperialist attacks on their small, valiant country. Also, Nicaraguans' lack of reliance on the label of "victim," given the endless hardships they endured, was impressive, to say the least. The contradictions leading to the fall of the Sandinista revolution did not diminish the accomplishments of those who struggled and still struggle, now out of the limelight, in the barrios where they live.

I began to know Oaxaca, Mexico, on my way to and from Managua during those yeras. But my more in-depth involvement began with a yearlong stay there in 1994–1995, where Michael and I began fieldwork. Being attracted to the diversity of Oaxaca was ordinary for Michael and me. However, this ordinary interest clearly seems to have fallen outside of the traditional venues of urban anthropology in Oaxaca. This was ironic to us, because clearly these subcultural groups were not marginal in any way to the panorama of actors that make up the culture and the city of Oaxaca. We thank those whose stories we tell here and feel privileged to be able to explore their insights and everyday lives in the streets, bedrooms, and patios of Oaxaca.

NOTES TO CHAPTER TWO

1. The ethnographic review of the city and state of Oaxaca comes from Bartolomé and Barabas 1986 and 1996, Butterworth 1962, de la Cruz 1983, Dennis 1976, El Guindi and Hernandez 1986, Greenberg 1988, Mahar 1992, Murphy 1979, Nahmad 1990, Stephen 1987, and Stepick 1974. For access to the most complete material on Oaxaca, see the Welte Library 1998.

2. This was one of the "*moda*" (something that's very "in") urban issues in the anthropology and urban studies of the 1960s. William Mangin was one of the first anthropologists to begin telling the stories of squatters, followed by many others (Mangin 1967). Urban squatters were seen as "*moda*" because of the debates at the time about the culture of poverty and the actions of radical political movements (Higgins 1974; Lewis 1970). Oscar Lewis's model of the culture of poverty was misread as a statement that the poor were so structured by the dynamics of their oppression that they were incapable of political action, which was countered by leftist rhetoric stating the hope that these emerging urban poor would be the new vanguard of political action. These squatters seemed to be the social actors who could, in some mysterious manner, represent this "third way" that everyone in these times was looking for. Squatters were active and creative social actors, building their own communities. In fact, some referred to these developments as unplanned urban planning (Turner 1968). Further, in terms of this political focus, squatters were not revolutionary per se but were locally focused on the immediate needs of their new communities' basic municipal services: water, electricity, roads, and schools (Hardoy and Satterthwaite 1987). After more than three decades of continuous urban growth throughout Latin America, however, squatters are no longer "*moda*" but are seen as one of the many urban groups contesting space within this rapidly changing social system, and it has developed that the particular social actors who made up these communities were no more conservative or radical than the overall population of humble people throughout Latin America (Hardoy and Morse 1988; Mahar 1992).

3. Sadly, we have to report that Doña María Elena de Sosa passed away in the fall of 1998. She was sitting at her table talking and eating with her daughters when she suffered a massive stroke. She went into a coma and died the next day. She was a wonderful woman who lived her life to the fullest. *Presente!*

4. Among the urban poor in Oaxaca, free union marriages are treated as a marriage, with each partner referring to the other as either wife or husband. This is true whether the "marriage" is the first or the second for the male involved.

5. We suggested to Victoria that in the telling of this story of her mother's history, there were details that Víctor still did not know. We suggested to Victoria that with the publication of this book, Víctor and many others were going to know the details of her mother's history. She indicated that she was aware of this fact.

NOTES TO CHAPTER THREE

1. During the years of this project the exchange rate has moved between 6 pesos to the U.S. dollar (1996) to the current rate of exchange (1999), which is 9.25 pesos to the U.S. dollar.

2. Below are some of our other personal reflections about interacting with the *chicas.*

I (MJH) found that in dealing with these *chicas* I had to remind myself who they were. When one just hung out with them, it seemed that one was in the presence of something that was neither male nor female but was clearly sexual. For me this seemed to move them into a third category—not male/not female (Herdt 1994).

Are they attractive in an erotic or sexual sense? Clearly so; otherwise they would have no clients. Did I find them so? I do not have a clear answer. Yes, they were attractive in a general sense, but I found them most attractive in their non-whore look, when they had on less makeup or were not dressed up in their night clothes, though that was when they thought they were least attractive. Were they sexually attractive to me? Again, it was not clear for me. Clearly, at times I found them to be quite sexy, but not in a way that was sexually attractive to me. Being at this point in my life still straight, I was intrigued as to how they composed the presentation of their sexuality in the activity itself. If you participate in such sexual activities, do you maintain a heterosexual illusion of male and female, or do you see yourself as involved in a homosexual act that is framed by the customs of heterosexuality?

To me they were most often their more or less normal selves when we would talk, drink, and joke in the fashion of *cuates* (friends). When they were drunk or in a party scene, some of them would get quite lewd and rude. They would often invite me to *chapiar* with them. This was the word they used for anal sex or sexual intercourse in general. They would slap the palms of their hands together loudly when they issued the invitation. I had two responses. First I would tell them that I would love to *chapiar* with them, but I was a passive male and since two passive males could not have sex with each other, I was sorry. They would ask Tanya if that was true, and she would say yes. That would confuse them for a moment, and then they would go back to their teasing. My second response was to tell them that I like the natural look or the schoolgirl look (two looks they would never do) and if they would just do that look then I would think about *chapiando* with them. That too would momentarily quiet the teasing.

As I reflected on how I related to the *chicas,* I realized that the most obvious factor was that I had never before really known either prostitutes or transvestites very well, and certainly this was my first encounter with the combination of the two. I think this gave me an opportunity to try not to read these experiences in either psychological terms or assumed political tendencies. What I was most struck by was how the transvestic component of their lives was composed through play. For them, their everyday lives are playgrounds for games of gender and sexuality.

Now, I (TLC) will present what my train of thought has been since we first started working with the *chicas.* I will use the word "transvestite" to refer to gay male transvestites (not straight men transvestites).

Why are men (particularly Latin men) attracted to male transvestite prostitutes? Do they prefer real women but want a more glamorous look over a more natural look and thus like the queens because they are more womanly than women?

Or perhaps they are just ordinary heterosexual men, as traditionally defined throughout Latin America, whose sexual repertoire involves having sex with both men and women.

Whatever may be the case, I like gay men. Why? Maybe it's because they aren't typically macho or threatening like many straight men. Since they are not really interested in me—sexually, that is—I don't have to worry about harassment from them. Or maybe I like them because I think they identify more with women than men, and I'm attracted to that because of women's historical subordination or thinking it's noble that gay male transvestites, like the *chicas,* would want to be women if they had a choice?

Here I want to return to the question we posed in this chapter about the kinds of images of women that the *chicas* like to compose. They certainly wouldn't emulate the image of women that some feminists/lesbians have adopted, an image free of the trappings of high heels, dressing for success, nylons, the right hair, and makeup. They are very critical of such a look, calling these women lazy. They have no sympathy or understanding of why a woman would choose to look this way, nor do they have any understanding of the actual issues related to subordination that women must deal with in their daily lives. They do reap the privileges of men, but they lack the privileges that straight men have.

They emulate an exaggerated image of women (more like a stripper, glamorous entertainer/movie star, or a high-class prostitute) when they are working. When they are attending a social function their appearance takes on more of a cheesy-upper-class, Hollywood-type image—a stereotypically "elitist" or Hollywood-type image. In both contexts, they assume variations of socially constructed, heterosexually defined images of women.

Whether it is a man or a woman who constructs that image, it takes a lot of work. No one is born or wakes up looking like that. A woman, like these men, really is transforming herself into a "drag queen" too, and is essentially unrecognizable when out of costume. And contrary to what the *chicas* think, we women do wake up and come out of the womb as women (or female); we are females, we are women even with body hair, without makeup and high heels.

But why am I drawn to drag queens? At some level, at different times in my life, I have been resistant to that socially constructed image in myself and in other women, finding it oppressive and nonliberating. So why would I be attracted to it in men? Maybe we are all secretly attracted to it—that fetishized/sexualized fake but seemingly real image that we have been bombarded with and sold throughout our lives. Or maybe it's because on a man it looks different. It isn't real; it's make-believe, theater, like a movie, like cartoons. It's escape or play. It allows me to identify with the image while not feeling like I'm identifying with it, not participating in my own oppression.

It is interesting how the *chicas,* not desiring to be transsexuals, have constructed their politics of pleasure as stereotypically female. By far the majority of the *chicas* perceive that the only use for their penis is for peeing. Only one (Vicky) said she actually has an orgasm or likes them. They describe sexual pleasure as emanating from all over their bodies rather than being primarily genitally located. They elevate kissing, hugging, and caressing over coming; in fact, that doesn't even enter the picture.

And, of course, as "gays" in Mexico, traditionally defined, they never penetrate and are always penetrated. This does not always mean they are totally passive (which I think they perceive women to be). Some are and some aren't, viewing themselves as taking a very active part in other ways, such as verbally, touching, kissing.

As Michael stated, the *chicas* do come across as a third gender, neither male or female. And maybe that's what they are. Maybe the gender of all of us is fluid and located somewhere on the continuum between what a culture defines as male and what a culture defines as female. In the end, the *chicas* have certainly been fun to know and hang with (even if we've had to wait for hours at times while they are getting ready), and they have challenged our thinking by the "breaking of their schemes."

3. Our emphasis on male sexuality derives from the fact that although we are friends with and know many lesbians living in Oaxaca, the lesbian scene is in no way as public as that of gay males, in terms of either political or social expressions. In Oaxaca there are no openly lesbian clubs or centers, nor are there any groups who openly express lesbian social positions or concerns. Such centers for lesbians do exist in Mexico City, and they do influence and inform the lesbians in Oaxaca, but not as yet in an open or public manner.

Further, even though this male sexual discourse of active/passive actors is a known reality, it is not voiced. In the numerous discussions that I (MJH) have had with males in Oaxaca during my thirty years of doing work there, I have never encountered a male who has talked about having sex with other men, though I have encountered negative slang terms applied to those thought to be gay. Also, in the past, I never asked any male directly about this. Though it is not vocalized, it is known by males that sex with another male is an option within their social context. We are not attempting to make a generalization here, only to express what we have encountered. For though the *hombre/hombre* is not stigmatized, it does not seem to be something that is talked about in casual conversations in Oaxaca. Since this was not something that we brought up until recently, it is not surprising that we did not encounter folks talking about it.

4. As often happens in fieldwork situations, we ran into some conflicts with Leslie and Tania that we never fully understood, but there was a period of time when our relationship with them was cool and distanced, and we hung with the others. However, upon our return in the summer of 1996 both Leslie and Tania were affectionate and super-cooperative in working on this project.

5. Leslie, this summer (1994), stated that her grandparents were Spanish immigrants who had lived in the Sierra Mixe and that was where her father was born. Her father left Oaxaca and moved to Chihuahua. So her return to Oaxaca was not a random selection but a move to a place where she had connections to some social networks. Also, though she says her relations with her family are good, she does not see them, and she wanted to send the video of the interview we did with them to her mother so she would know how well she was doing.

6. Her views would not translate into racist assumptions or behavior in the context of the racist discourse of the United States, but they are more akin to what Lancaster refers to as "colourism," which is a fluid system of status and prestige determined by perceived skin tones (Lancaster 1992). That is,

Leslie is a *güera* in her context, but in a more middle-class context she would find herself less *güera,* and in terms of the color codes of the United States, she would be perceived as nonwhite.

7. In the summer of 1998, Leslie and Adrián were beginning a trial separation and Leslie was also diagnosed as being HIV-positive.

NOTES TO CHAPTER FOUR

1. Bunster and Chaney's (1985) *Servants and Sellers: Working Women in Lima, Peru* discusses this pattern as well. For more information about maids in Oaxaca, see Howell 1996.

2. In theory, students are required to complete the sixth grade, but in practice many poor children in urban and rural areas do not finish grade school. In some cases, parents cannot afford to send their children to school because although primary school is "free," there are incidental costs such as supplies, transportation (if necessary), meals, and clothing.

3. All names used in this section, including the names of people and business establishments, are fictitious.

4. Currently, the formal discourses on AIDS in Oaxaca are about the prevention and recognition of the illness. The important and complex debates, the causes of AIDS and appropriate treatments, have not as yet been central to these public discourses. For more details on this debate, see Driskill 1998, Rofes 1996, Rotello 1997, Rudd and Taylor 1992, Schwartzberg 1996, and Waldby 1996.

5. In 1996 the Greeley Gay, Lesbian, Bisexual, and Transgendered Alliance at my (MJH) university (University of Northern Colorado) put on a drag queen show to raise funds to help Renacimiento with its projects.

NOTES TO CHAPTER FIVE

1. During the course of our work with Acceso Libre, the agency has also been involved with a project on people with disabilities in collaboration with the American Indian Rehabilitation Research and Training Center at the University of Northern Arizona. This project has been directed by Catherine Marshall and the folks at Acceso Libre. Last year with her help they received a Kellogg grant for more than $300,000. They have opened a new center and are now also developing programs for the blind and those with hearing problems.

2. We will put "able" in quotation marks to note its contested status, and we will translate *discapacitados* as "people with disabilities."

3. Monte Albán is the ancient Zapotec city that sits about three miles above the current city of Oaxaca; it is quite a ride in a car to this historical site, not to mention wheeling or running!

4. For a limited survey of multicultural research on people with disabilities, see Baine 1991, Conners and Donnellan 1993, Luborsky 1994, and Reid 1996.

5. This essay can be found in the Spanish version of Marshall et al., *Vecinos y Rehabilitación: Assessing the Needs of Indigenous People with Disabilities in Mexico.*

6. Germán and Gabriela had become *novios,* and her death was a great shock to him.

7. Translated by Josef N. Wachsmann.

8. Pedro and Patty had their second child at the end of the summer of 1997.

9. We are aware that these reflections upon sexuality and body forms are in terms of folks with problems of locomotion and body shapes. Folks with problems of hearing and sight might have different and equally interesting insights about these issues.

NOTES TO CHAPTER SIX

1. In the early 1980s I (MJH) wrote a long essay titled "The Fetishism of Heterosexuality." This was my attempt to link Marx's arguments on value forms to the logic of heterosexuality and to suggest that maybe this domain of sexuality was a cruel presentation of commodification as a lived experience. It was also my attempt to enter into the space of Marxist and feminist debates in anthropology. I was to learn that this forum was something of a closed shop, especially for someone coming out of the provinces. Friends of mine in New York got me invited to a critical feminist study group to present this essay. The essay was written in my casual style and, like this work, it treated other people's works in a summary fashion. Also, it was a very rough draft and it was full of exploratory ideas that I hoped to temper in this presentation. The members of the study group did not like the paper, thought it was way too rough and that I would be eaten alive by such heavies, and I was disinvited. The leader of the study group (a very prominent writer in New York City) thought that she was protecting me by withdrawing the invitation. I then went to the anthropology club at the New School of Social

Research and presented a version of the essay, framed in my ethnographic work in Oaxaca, and it was well received. Several years later, the important New York writer who had disinvited me was with a small delegation visiting Managua, Nicaragua, in relation to solidarity work with women in the Sandinista revolution. Tanya and I gave them a tour of the barrio we were working in and introduced them to various folks in Managua. At the end of the tour, the "famous" writer asked me if she did not know me from somewhere. I said yes, that she was the one who had disinvited me from their study group. I am telling this long story not just to impart academic gossip, but to explain why at least I am more comfortable conveying the stories we have presented than seeking theoretical victories.

2. Currently two grassroots movements are having national and international impact. We are speaking of the anti-smoking movement in the United States and the international movement to ban land mines. No doubt a critical analysis of either of these movements would reveal possible contradictions within their formations and political concerns, but the impact is real. The anti-smoking effort is interesting in that it was not assumed to have much impact—then in 1997 tobacco companies were seeking a settlement. Again the whys and hows of the situation are quite complex, but the example does illustrate that local action can be effective.

3. We find Jeffrey Weeks's argument on sexual values to be useful in addressing the issues we are discussing (Weeks 1995 and 1997). In his concerns about how to live within a social world of sexual diversity, Weeks suggests that we "radicalize" certain values of social action and interaction— the values of care, responsibility, respect, and knowledge. He defines care as an active concern for the life, hopes, dreams, and concerns of persons or people we love (Weeks 1997:54). Loving care implies a recognition of the autonomy of others through imaginative acts of concern that engender skills of responsibility (Weeks 1997:55). In alliance building, responsibility involves a "web of reciprocity" in which minor concession to one's worldview allows for a greater freedom for the expression of other values. Loving through responsibility means we accept that we are not isolated social actors but groups of ordinary folks who are interconnected through social respect (Weeks 1997:57). According to Weeks, respect involves "taking seriously the dignity of the other—both their autonomy as a person and their needs for you and others" (Weeks 1997:57), and affirming these values requires that we pursue in a fair and respectful manner accurate knowledge of the values of those with whom we seek to work and struggle (Weeks 1997:58). We suggest that

the values that Weeks has articulated for composing social spaces that will allow for more sexual tolerance would be useful guidelines for an ethnographic praxis that could be used for navigating the hegemonic terrains of postmodernity to move toward an *onda* of the ordinariness of diversity. This would involve various forms of political and social struggle, in which the diverse forms of personal agency could be united into an expression of historical agency for the construction of a material context for the affirmation of such values.

BIBLIOGRAPHY AND SUGGESTED READINGS

Abu-Lughod, Lila. 1993. *Writing Women's Worlds*. Berkeley: University of California Press.

AFECTO. 1997. *Prevención y atención del maltrato infatil*. Cartagena: Universidad de Cartagena.

Alonso, Jorge, ed. 1980. *Lucha urbana y acumulación de capital*. Mexico: Ediciones Casa Chata.

Anzaldúa, Gloria. 1987. *Borderlands/La Frontera*. San Francisco: Spinsters/Aunt Lute.

Arboleda G., Manuel. 1997. "On Some of Lancaster's Misrepresentations." *American Ethnologist* 24 (4): 931–939.

Arizpe, Lourdes. 1988. "La antropología mexicana en el marco latinoamericano: Viejos linderos, nuevos contextos." In *Teoría e investigación en la antropología social mexicana*, edited by Gonzalo Aguirre Beltrán, 315–338. Mexico: Instituto Nacional de Antropología e Historia.

Baine, David. 1991. "Methods of Instructing Students with Handicaps Integrated into Regular Classrooms in Developing Countries." *Psychology and Developing Societies* 3 (2): 57–169.

Bal, Mieke, and Inge Boer, eds. 1994. *The Point of Theory: Practices of Cultural Analysis*. New York: Continuum.

Balsamo, Anne. 1996. *Technologies of the Gendered Body*. Durham: Duke University Press.

Barabas, Alicia, and Miguel Bartolomé, eds. 1986. *Etnicidad y pluralismo cultural: La dinámica étnica en Oaxaca*. Consejo Nacional para Cultura y los Artes. Mexico: Instituto Nacional de Antropología e Historia.

Barahona, Vilma, Guadalupe Garzon-Aragon, and Guadalupe Musalem. 1986. *La problemática actual de la prostitución en Oaxaca.* Oaxaca: Universidad Autónoma "Benito Juárez" de Oaxaca.

Barbach, Lonnie, and Linda Levine. 1980. *Shared Intimacies: Women's Sexual Experiences.* New York: Bantam.

Barta, Roger. 1987. *La jaula de la melancolía: Identidad y metamorfosis del mexicano.* Mexico: Grijalbo.

Bartolomé, Miguel A. 1997. *Gente de costumbre y gente de razón: Las identidades étnicas en México.* Mexico: Instituto Nacional de Antropología e Historia.

Bartolomé, Miguel, and Alicia Barabas. 1986. "Los migrantes étnicos de Oaxaca." *Indígena* 13 (November–December): 23–25.

————. 1996. *La pluralidad en peligro.* Mexico: Instituto Nacional de Antropología e Historia and Instituto Nacional Indigenista.

Basilio M., Carlos. 1996. *Uruguay Homosexual.* Montevideo: Ediciones Trilce.

Bateson, Gregory. 1972. *Steps to an Ecology of Mind.* San Francisco: Chandler Publishing.

Battaglia, Debora. 1997. "Ambiguating Agency: The Case of Malinowski's Ghost." *American Anthropologist* 99 (3): 505–511.

Bauman, Zygmunt. 1973. *Culture as Praxis.* London: Routledge and Paul.

————. 1987. *Legislators and Interpreters.* New York: Cornell University Press.

Becker, Marjorie. 1994. "Torching La Purisima, Dancing at the Altar: The Construction of Revolutionary Hegemony in Michoacan, 1934–1940." In *Everyday Forms of State Formation: The Revolution and the Negotiation of Rule in Modern Mexico*, edited by Gilbert M. Joseph and Daniel Nugent, 230–263. Durham: Duke University Press.

Behar, Ruth. 1993. *Translated Woman.* Boston: Beacon.

Bell, Diane. 1983. *Daughters of Dreaming.* Melbourne: McPhee Gribble.

Beltran F., Alfredo. 1989. *La ideologia antiautoritaria del rock nacional.* Buenos Aires: Centro Editor de America Latina.

Benítez R., Antonio. 1992. *The Repeating Island: The Caribbean and the Postmodern Perspective.* Durham: Duke University Press.

Bonfil Batalla, Guillermo. 1988. "Los conceptos de diferencia y subordinación en el estudio de las cultures populares." In *Teoría e investigación en la antropología social mexicana*, edited by Gonzalo Aguirre Beltrán, 97–108. Mexico: Instituto Nacional de Antropología e Historia.

Boyd, Robert, and Joan Silk. 1997. *How Humans Evolved.* New York: Norton.

Brentlinger, John. 1995. *The Best of What We Were.* Amherst: University of Massachuetts Press.

Bunster, Xmena, and Elsa M. Chaney. 1985. *Servants and Sellers: Working Women in Lima, Peru.* New York: Praeger.

Butler, Judith. 1993. *Bodies That Matter*. New York: Routledge.

Butterworth, Douglas. 1962. "A Study of the Urbanization Process among Mixtec Migrants from Tilantongo in Mexico City." *América Indígena* 22:257–274.

Cabezas, Omar. 1988 (June 22). "No se debe mandar memo a las masas." *Barricada*. Managua.

Calderón, José Z. 1995. "Multi-Ethnic Coalition Building." *Critical Sociology* 21 (1): 100–111.

———. 1996. "Situational Identity of Suburban Mexican American Politicians in a Multiethnic Community." In *Chicanas and Chicanos in Contemporary Society*, 85–105. Boston: Allyn and Bacon.

Carrier, Joseph, and Roberto M. DeAnda, eds. 1995. *De los otros: Intimacy and Homosexuality among Mexican Men*. New York: Columbia University Press.

Castañeda, Jorge. 1993. *Utopia Unarmed*. New York: Knopf.

———. 1995. "La última sorpresa." *Proceso*, no. 952.

Chance, John. 1978. *Race and Class in Colonial Oaxaca*. Stanford: Stanford University Press.

———. 1989. *Conquest of the Sierra: Spaniards and Indians in Colonial Oaxaca*. Norman: University of Oklahoma Press.

Charlton, James I. 1998. *Nothing about Us without Us! Disability Oppression and Empowerment*. Berkeley: University of California Press.

Chomsky, Noam. 1987. *On Power and Ideology: The Managua Lectures*. Boston: Southend Press.

Clarke, Colin. 1992. "Components of Socio-Economic Change in Post-Revolutionary Oaxaca, Mexico." In *América Latina: La cuestión regional*, edited by Miguel Panadero Moya, Francisco Cebrián Abellán, and Carmen García Martínez, 147–170. Mexico: Colección Estudios.

———. 1996. "Opposition to PRI 'Hegemony in Oaxaca.'" In *Dismantling the Mexican State?*, edited by Rob Aitken, Nikki Craske, Gareth Jones, and David Stansfield, 267–290. London: Society for Latin American Studies.

Clifford, James. 1988. *The Predicament of Culture*. Cambridge: Harvard University Press.

Clinton, Hillary Rodham. 1996. *It Takes a Village*. New York: Simon and Schuster.

Cockcroft, James. 1996. *Latin America: History, Politics, and United States Policy*. 2d ed. Chicago: Nelson-Hall Publishers.

Coen, Tanya L., and Michael James Higgins. 1994. "Can There Be a Post-Modern/ Multicultural Revolutionary Consciousness?" *Journal of the High Plains Society for Applied Anthropology* 8 (Spring): 35–44.

Conners, J., and A. Donnellan. 1993. "Citizenship and Culture: The Role of Disabled People in Navajo Society." *Disability-Handicap and Society* 8 (3): 265–280.

Cornwall, Andrea. 1994. "Gendered Identities and Gender Ambiguity among

Transvestites in Salvador, Brazil." In *Dislocating Masculinity: Comparative Ethnographies*, edited by Andrea Cornwall and Nancy Lindisfarne. London: Routledge.

Cornwall, Andrea, and Nancy Lindisfarne. 1994. *Dislocating Masculinity: Comparative Ethnographies*. London: Routledge.

Dalton, Margarita. 1990. *Oaxaca, una historia compartida*. Oaxaca: Gobierno del Estado de Oaxaca.

De la Cruz, Victor. 1983. *En Torno a las Islas del Mar Oceano*. Juchitán, Oaxaca: H. Ayuntamiento Popular.

de Lauretis, Teresa. 1987. *Technologies of Gender*. London: Macmillan.

———, ed. 1991. Queer Theory: Lesbian and Gay Sexualities. Special issue of *Differences: A Journal of Feminist Studies* 3 (2).

Dennis, Philip. 1976. *Conflictos por tierras en el Valle de Oaxaca*. Mexico: Instituto Nacional Indigenista.

di Leonardo, Micaela, ed. 1992. *Gender at the Crossroads of Knowledge*. Berkeley: University of California Press.

Disken, Martin. 1983. *Trouble in Your Backyard: Central America and United States in the Eighties*. New York: Pantheon.

Driskill, Qwo-Li. 1998. "Living in the Decades of Death." Senior thesis, University of Northern Colorado.

Durrenberger, E. Paul, and Suzan Erem. 1997. "The Dance of Power: Ritual and Agency among Unionized American Health Care Workers." *American Anthropologist* 99 (3): 489–494.

El Guindi, Fadwa, and Abel Hernandez. 1986. *The Myth of Ritual: A Native's Ethnography of Zapotec Life-Crisis Rituals*. Tucson: University of Arizona Press.

Eller, Jack David. 1997. Anti-Anti-Multiculturalism. *American Anthropologist* 99 (2): 249–256.

Embry, Marcus. 1996. "Cholo Angels in Guadalajara: The Politics and Poetics of Anzaldúa's Borderlands/La Frontera." Queer Acts. Special issue of *Women and Performance: A Journal of Feminist Theory* 8 (2) (Issue 16): 87–110.

Escobar, Arturo. 1995. *Encountering Development: The Making and Unmaking of the Third World*. Princeton: Princeton Paperbacks.

Fanon, Frantz. 1963. *The Wretched of the Earth*. New York: Grove Press.

Finkler, Kaja. 1994. *Women in Pain: Gender and Morbidity in Mexico*. Philadelphia: University of Pennsylvania Press.

Foucault, Michel. 1978. *History of Sexuality*. Vol. 1. New York: Pantheon.

———. 1979. *Discipline and Punish*. New York: Vintage.

Franco, Jean. 1989. *Plotting Women: Gender and Representation in Mexico*. New York: Columbia University Press.

———. 1994. "What's Left Of Intelligentsia? The Uncertain Future of the Printed Word." *NACLA Report on the Americas* 28 (2): 16–22.

Fraser, Nancy. 1997. *Justice Interruptus: Critical Reflections on "Postsocialist" Condition*. New York: Routledge.

Fuentes, Carlos. 1995. "Feliz Año Nuevo." *Proceso*, no. 952, p. 18.

García Canclini, Nestor. 1988. La crisis teoría en la investigación sobre cultura popular. In *Teoría e investigación en la antropología social mexicana*, edited by Gonzalo Aguirre Beltrán. Mexico: Instituto Nacional de Antropología e Historia.

———. 1989. *Culturas híbridas: Estratégias para entar y salir de la modernidad*. Mexico: Era.

———. 1991. *Cultura y pospolítica: El debate sobre la modernidad en América Latina*. Mexico: Consejo Nacional para la Cultura y las Artes.

———. 1995. *Hybrid Cultures*. Minneapolis: University of Minnesota Press.

Gilroy, Paul. 1993. *The Black Atlantic*. Cambridge: Harvard University Press.

Gómez-Martínez, José Luis. 1990. "Consideraciones epistemológicas para una filosofía de la liberación." *Cuadernos Americanos*, nueva epoca 4: 16–27.

González, Ray. 1996. *Muy Macho*. New York: Anchor Books.

González Casanova, Pablo. 1986. *El poder al pueblo*. Mexico: Oceano.

Greenberg, David. 1988. *The Construction of Homosexuality*. Chicago: University of Chicago Press.

Greenberg, James B. 1989. *Blood Ties: Life and Violence in Rural Mexico*. Tucson: University of Arizona Press.

Gutmann, Matthew. 1996. *The Meanings of Macho*. Berkeley: University of California Press.

Haraway, Donna. 1991. *Simians, Cyborgs, and Women: The Reinvention of Nature*. New York: Routledge.

———. 1997. *Modest_Witness@Second_Millennium. FemaleMan_ Meets_ OncoMouse*. New York: Routledge.

Hardoy, Jorge, and Richard Morse. 1988. *Repensando la ciudad de América Latina*. Buenos Aires: Grupo Editor Latinoamericano.

Hardoy, Jorge, and David Satterthwaite. 1987. *La ciudad legal y la ciudad ilegal*. Buenos Aires: Grupo Editor Latinoamericano.

Harvey, David. 1989. *The Condition of Postmodernity*. London: Blackwell.

Hendriks, Aart, Rob Tielman, and Evert van der Veen, eds. 1993. *The Third Pink Book: A Global View of Lesbian and Gay Liberation and Oppression*. New York: Prometheus Books.

Herdt, Gilbert. 1994. *Third Sex, Third Gender*. New York: Zone Books.

Higgins, Michael James. 1974. *Somos gente humilde: Etnografía de una colonia urbana pobre de Oaxaca*. Mexico: Instituto Nacional Indigenista.

———. 1983. *Somos Tocayos: The Anthropology of Urbanism and Poverty*. Lanham: University Press of America.

————. 1986. "Quienes son los migrantes al teatro urbano del Valle de Oaxaca." In *Etnicidad y pluralismo cultural: La dinámica étnica en Oaxaca*, edited by Alicia Barabas and Miguel Bartolomé, 401–422. Mexico: Instituto Nacional de Antropología e Historia.

————. 1990. "Martyrs and Saints." In *Popular Religion in Mexico and Central America*, edited by James Dow and Linda Stephen, 187–206. SLAA Publication Series, vol. 10. Washington, D.C.: Society for Latin American Anthropology.

————. 1997. *Somos tocayos*. Oaxaca: Instituto Oaxaqueño de las Culturas.

Higgins, Michael J., and Tanya L. Coen. 1992. *Oigame! Oigame!: Struggle and Social Change in a Nicaraguan Urban Community*. Boulder: Westview Press.

hooks, bell. 1990. *Yearning: Race, Gender, and Cultural Politics*. Boston: South End Press.

Howell, Jayne. 1996. "Turning Out Good Ethnography, or Talking Out of Turn?" Paper read at the American Anthropological Association meeting, San Francisco.

Hunt, Linda, Mary Valenzuela, and Joseph A. Pugh. 1997. "¿Porque Me Toca? Mexican American Diabetes Patients' Causal Stories and Their Treatment Behaviors." *Social Science and Medicine*. In press.

Irigaray, Luce. 1985. *This Sex Which Is Not One*. Ithaca: Cornell University Press.

James, Joy. 1997. *Resisting State Violence*. Minneapolis: University of Minnesota Press.

James, Joy, and Ruth Farmer, eds. 1993. *Spirit, Space, and Survival: African American Women in (White) Academe*. New York: Routledge.

Jennaway, Megan. 1989. "Paradigms, Postmodern Epistemologies, and Paradox: The Place of Feminism in Anthropology." *Anthropological Forum* 6 (2): 167–189.

Joseph, Gilbert, and Daniel Nugent, eds. 1994. *Everyday Forms of State Formation: Revolution and the Negotiation of Rule in Modern Mexico*. Durham: Duke University Press.

Karim, Wazir Jahan. 1996. "Anthropology without Tears: How a 'Local' Sees the 'Local' and the 'Global.'" In *The Future of Anthropological Knowledge*, edited by Henrietta Moore, 158–176. London: Routledge.

King, Martin Luther. 1963. "I Have a Dream." Speech given at the March on Washington, August 28, 1963.

Klein, Fritz, and Timothy Wolf, eds. 1985. *Bisexualities: Theory and Research*. New York: Haworth Press.

Krauze, Enrique. 1997. *Mexico: Biography of Power*. New York: HarperCollins.

Kulick, Don. 1997. "The Gender of Brazilian Transgendered Prostitutes." *American Anthropologist* 99 (3): 574–585.

Laclau, Ernesto, and Chantal Mouffe. 1985. *Hegemony and Socialist Strategy.* London: Verso.

La Jornada. 1997a. "Encuesta nacional de alimentación y nutrición en el medio rural 1996." *Perfil de La Jornada,* July 22, 1997.

———. 1997b. "Letra: Salud, Sexualidad, SIDA." *La Jornada,* no. 13, August 7, 1997.

Lancaster, Roger. 1992. *Life Is Hard/La Vida Dura.* Berkeley: University of California Press.

———. 1997a. "Guto's Performance: Notes on the Transvestitism of Everyday Life." In *The Gender Sexuality Reader,* edited by Roger Lancaster and Micaela di Leonardo. New York: Routledge.

———. 1997b. "On Homosexualities in Latin America (and Other Places)." *American Ethnologist* 24 (4): 193–202.

Landi, Oscar. 1992. *Devorame otra vez: Que hizo la televisión con la gente. Que hace la gente con la televisión.* Buenos Aires: Planeta.

Leiner, Marvin. 1994. *Sexual Politics in Cuba: Machismo, Homosexuality, and AIDS.* Boulder: Westview Press.

LeVine, Sarah. 1993. *Dolor y Alegría: Women and Social Change in Urban Mexico.* Madison: University of Wisconsin Press.

Lewin, Pedro. 1998. "Fieldnotes on Trique Ethnography." Unpublished manuscript.

Lewis, Oscar. 1970. *Anthropological Essays.* New York: Random House.

Lowe, Donald M. 1995. *The Body in Late-Capitalist USA.* Durham: Duke University Press.

Luborsky, Mark. 1994. "The Cultural Diversity of Physical Disability: Erosion of Full Adult Personhood." *Journal of Aging Studies* 8 (3): 239–253.

Lumsden, Ian. 1991. *Homosexuality, Society, and the State in Mexico.* Toronto: Canadian Gay Archives.

———. 1996. *Machos, Maricones, and Gays: Cuba and Homosexuality.* Philadelphia: Temple University Press.

Luna Martínez, Jaime. 1994. "Discriminacion y democracia en un estado multietnico." Unpublished manuscript.

Mahar, Cheleen. 1975. "Integrative Aspects of Folk and Western Medicine among the Urban Poor of Oaxaca." *Anthropological Quarterly* 48 (1): 31–37.

———. 1986. "The Strategy of Urban Life: Reinventing Practice in a Disenchanted World." Ph.D. thesis, Massey University, New Zealand.

———. 1992. "An Exercise in Practice: Studying Migrants to Latin American Squatter Settlements." *Urban Anthropology and Studies of Cultural Systems and World Economic Development* 21 (3).

Mangin, William. 1967. "Latin American Squatter Settlements: A Problem and a Solution." *Latin American Research Review*, no. 3 (Summer): 65–98.

Marchand, Marianne H. 1995. "Latin American Women Speak on Development: Are We Listening Yet?" In *Feminism, Postmodernism, Development*, edited by Marianne H. Marchand and Jane Parpart, 56–72. London: Routledge.

Marchand, Marianne H., and Jane Parpart, eds. 1995. *Feminism, Postmodernism, Development*. London: Routledge.

Marcos, Sub-Comandante. 1995. *Correspondence*. New York: Monthly Review.

Mariateguí, José Carlos. 1979. *Obra politica*. Mexico: Ediciones Era.

Marley, Bob, the Wailers, and the I-Three. 1978. *Babylon by Bus*. London: Island Records.

Marshall, Catherine, George Gotto, Germán Pérez, Pedro Flores, and Gabriela García. 1996. *Vecinos y rehabilitación: Assessing the Needs of Indigenous People with Disabilities in Mexico*. Publication from the American Indian Rehabilitation Research and Training Center of the University of Northern Arizona.

Marx, Karl. 1967. *Capital*. Vol. 1. New York: International Publishers.

Mayoral Figueroa, Cesar. 1996. "Prostitución: Proyecto municipal de salud." Unpublished manuscript, Oaxaca.

McBeth, Sally. 1993. "Myths of Objectivity and the Collaborative Process in Life History Research." In *When They Write What We Read: The Politics of Ethnography*, edited by Caroline B. Bretell. Westport, Conn.: Bergin and Garvey.

McBeth, Sally, and Esther Burnett Horne. 1993. "I Know Who I Am": The Collaborative Life History of a Shoshone Indian Woman. In *Unrelated Kin: Race and Gender in Women's Personal Narratives*, edited by Gwendolyn Etter-Lewis and Michele Foster, 144–162. New York: Routledge.

———. 1998. *Essie's Stories: The Life of and Legacy of a Shoshone Teacher*. Lincoln: University of Nebraska Press.

McLaren, Peter. 1997. *Revolutionary Multiculturalism*. Boulder: Westview Press.

Melhuus, Marit, and Kristi Anne Stolen, eds. 1996. *Machos, Mistresses, Madonnas: Contesting the Power of Latin American Gender Imagery*. London: Verso.

Melucci, Alberto. 1989. Nomads of the Present. Philadelphia: Temple University Press.

Minh-Ha Trinh T. 1989. *Woman, Native, Other*. Bloomington: Indiana University Press.

Mohanty, Chandra, Anne Russo, and Lourdes Torres, eds. 1991. *Third World Women and the Politics of Feminism*. Bloomington: Indiana University Press.

Moore, Henrietta. 1996. *The Future of Anthropological Knowledge*. London: Routledge.

Moraga, Cherrie. 1993. *The Last Generation*. Boston: South End Press.

Muñoz, José, and Amanda Barret, eds. 1996. Queer Acts. Special issue of *Women and Performance: A Journal of Feminist Theory* 8 (2) (Issue 16): 87–110.

Murphy, Arthur D. 1979. "Urbanization, Development, and Household Strategies in Oaxaca." Ph.D. diss., Temple University.

Murphy, Arthur D., and Alex Stepick. 1991. *Social Inequality in Oaxaca.* Philadelphia: Temple University Press.

Musalem Merhy, Guadalupe. 1990. "Poplación y vida cotidiana. Los niños del portal: Estratégias de sobrevivencia en Oaxaca." *Oaxaca Población y Futuro* 1 (2): 4–7.

Nagle, Jill. 1997. *Whores and Other Feminists.* New York: Routledge.

Nahmad, Salomón. 1990. "Reflexiones sobre la identidad étnica de los Mixes." *Estudios Sociológicos* 8 (22): 34–46.

Nash, June. 1997. "The Fiesta of the Word: The Zapatista Uprising and Radical Democracy in Mexico." *American Anthropologist* 99 (2): 261–275.

Nicholson, Linda J., ed. 1990. *Feminism and Postmodernism.* London: Routledge.

Nicholson, Linda J., and Steven Seidman, eds. 1995. *Social Post-Modernism: Beyond Identity Politics.* Cambridge: Cambridge University Press.

Nieuwenhuys, Olga. 1996. "The Paradox of Child Labor and Anthropology." *Annual Review of Anthropology* 24:237–253. Palo Alto: Annual Reviews, Inc.

Norget, Kristin. 1996. "Beauty and the Feast: Aesthetics and the Performance of Meaning in the Day of the Dead in Oaxaca, Mexico." *Journal of Latin American Lore* 19 (Autumn): 53–64.

Oliveira, Orlandiana de, ed. 1989. *Trabajo, poder y sexualidad.* Mexico: El Colegio de Mexico.

Ortiz Nahón, Abraham J. 1998. *Estudio sobre los niños que trabajan en la calle en la Ciudad de Oaxaca.* Protocolo de Tésis en Planificación de Empresas y Desarrollo Regional. Oaxaca: Instituto Tecnológico de Oaxaca.

Phelan, Shane. 1994. *Getting Specific: Postmodern Lesbian Politics.* Minneapolis: University of Minnesota Press.

Pieterse, Jan Nederveen. 1995. "Globalization as Hybridization." In *Global Modernities*, edited by Mike Featherstone, Scott Lash, and Roland Robertson. London: Sage.

Plummer, Ken, ed. 1992. *Modern Homosexualities: Fragments of Lesbian and Gay Experience.* New York: Routledge.

Poniatowska, Elena. 1980. *Fuerte es el silencio.* Mexico: Biblioteca ERA.

———. 1993. "El otra gran arte." *Nexos* 1:183.

Prieur, Annick. 1996. "Domination and Desire: Male Homosexuality and the Construction of Masculinity in Mexico." In *Machos, Mistresses, Madonnas: Contesting the Power of Latin American Gender Imagery*, edited by Marit Melhuus and Kristi Anne Stolen, 83–107. London: Verso.

Rabasa, José. 1997. "Of Zapatismo: Reflections on the Folkloric and the Impossible in a Subaltern Insurrection." In *The Politics of Culture in the Shadow of Capital*, edited by Lisa Lowe and David Lloyd, 176–203. Durham: Duke University Press.

Radcliffe, Sarah, and Salle Westwood. 1993. *Viva: Women and Popular Protest in Latin America*. London: Routledge.

Rees, Martha, Arthur Murphy, Earl Morris, and Marcus Winter. 1991. "Migrants to and in Oaxaca City." *Urban Anthropology* 20 (2): 1530.

Reid, D. Kim. 1996. "Narrative Knowing: Basis for a Partnership on Language Diversity." *Learning Disability Quarterly* 19:138–151.

Reyes, Rafael G., and Arthur Murphy. 1996. "Comparación socioeconómica de seis colonias populares de la ciudad de Oaxaca." Paper read at the Welte Anthropology Congress Second Bianual Conferencia de Estudios Oaxaqueños, August 1996, Oaxaca, Mexico.

Richardson, Diane, ed. 1996. *Theorizing Heterosexuality*. London: Open University Press.

Rofes, Eric. 1996. *Reviving the Tribe: Regenerating Gay Men's Sexuality and Culture in the Ongoing Epidemic*. New York: Hawthorne Press.

Rosaldo, Renato. 1993. *Culture and Truth: The Remaking of Social Analysis*. Boston: Beacon.

Rotello, Gabriel. 1997. *Sexual Ecology: AIDS and the Destiny of Gay Men*. New York: Dutton.

Rowe, William, and Vivien Schelling. 1991. *Memory and Modernity: Popular Culture in Latin America*. London: Verso.

Rubin, Gayle. 1994. "Sexual Traffic: An Interview with J. Butler." differences: A Journal of Feminist Cultural Studies 6 (2+3).

Ruchwarger, Gary. 1987. *People in Power*. South Hadley, Mass.: Bergin and Garvey.

Rudd, Anne, and Diane Taylor. 1992. *Positive Women: Voices of Women Living with AIDS*. Toronto: Second Story.

Said, Edward W. 1978. *Orientalism*. London: Penguin.

Scheper-Hughes, Nancy. 1992. *Death without Weeping. The Violence of Everyday Life in Brazil*. Berkeley: University of California Press.

Schutte, Ofelia. 1993. *Cultural Identity and Social Liberation in Latin American Thought*. Albany: SUNY Press.

Schwartzberg, Steve. 1996. *A Crisis of Meaning: How Gay Men Are Making Sense of AIDS*. New York: Oxford University Press.

Selby, Henry, Arthur Murphy, and Stephen Lorenzen. 1990. *The Mexican Urban Household: Organizing for Self-Defense*. Austin: University of Texas Press.

Sen, Gita, and Caren Grown. 1987. *Development, Crisis, and Alternative Visions: Third World Women's Perspectives*. New York: Monthly Review Press.

Sheperd, Gill. 1987. "Rank, Gender, and Homosexuality: Mombasa as a Key to Understanding Sexual Options." In *The Cultural Construction of Sexuality*, edited by Pat Caplan, 1–36. London: Tavistock.

Singer, Linda. 1993. *Erotic Welfare: Sexual Theory and Politics in the Age of Epidemic*. New York: Routledge.

Spivak, G. C. 1988. *In Other Worlds: Essays in Cultural Politics*. New York: Routledge.

Springer, Claudia. 1996. *Electronic Eros*. Austin: University of Texas Press.

Stephen, Lynn. 1987. "Weaving Changes: Economic Development and Gender Roles in Zapotec Ritual and Production." Ph.D. diss., Brandeis University.

———. 1994. "Viva Zapata! Generation, Gender, and Historical Consciousness in the Reception of the Ejido Reform in Oaxaca." *Transformation of Rural Mexico*, 6. La Jolla Center for U.S.–Mexican Studies.

———. 1997. *Women and Social Movements in Latin America*. Austin: University of Texas Press.

Stepick, Alex. 1974. "The Rationality of the Urban Poor." Ph.D. diss., University of California at Irvine.

Taylor, Clark L. 1978. "El Ambiente: Male Homosexual Social Life in Mexico City." Ph.D. diss., University of California at Berkeley.

Turner, John. 1968. "Uncontrolled Urban Settlements: Problems and Policies." *International Social Development Review* 1: 107–130. New York: United Nations.

Valenzuela, José. 1988. *A la brava ese! Cholos, punks y chavos banda*. Tijuana: El Colegio de la Frontera Norte.

Varese, Stefano. 1988. "Multiethnicity and Hegemonic Construction." In *Ethnicities and Nations*, edited by Remo Guidilri, Francesco Pellizzi, and Stanley Tambiah, 55–77. Austin: University of Texas Press.

Viegener, Matias. 1993. "The Only Haircut That Makes Sense Anymore: Queer Subculture and Gay Resistance." In *Queer Looks*, edited by Martha Gever, John Greyson, and Pratibha Parmar, 116–134. London: Routledge.

Waldby, Catherine. 1996. *AIDS and the Body Politic: Biomedicine and Sexual Difference*. New York: Routledge.

Weeks, Jeffrey. 1995. *Invented Moralities: Sexual Values in an Age of Uncertainty*. New York: Columbia University Press.

———. 1997. "Sexual Values Revisited." In *New Sexual Agendas*, edited by Lynne Segal. New York: New York University Press.

Weitlaner, Roberto, and Walter A. Hoppe. 1969. "The Mazatec." *The Handbook of Middle American Indians*. Vol. 7, edited by Evon Z. Voyt. Austin: University of Texas Press.

Welte Institute for Oaxacan Studies. 1996. The Collection of Ethnographic Works on the Region of Oaxaca. Oaxaca, Mexico. www.welte.org.

Woodhouse, Annie. 1989. *Fantastic Women: Sex, Gender, and Transvestitism*. New Brunswick, N.J.: Rutgers University Press.

Yanagisako, Sylvia, and Carol Delaney, eds. 1995. *Naturalizing Power: Essays in Feminist Cultural Analysis*. New York: Routledge.

INDEX